Research in Networked Learning

Series Editors
Vivien Hodgson
David McConnell

More information about this series at http://www.springer.com/series/11810

Nina Bonderup Dohn • Susan Cranmer
Julie-Ann Sime • Maarten de Laat
Thomas Ryberg
Editors

Networked Learning

Reflections and Challenges

 Springer

Editors
Nina Bonderup Dohn
Department of Design and Communication
University of Southern Denmark
Kolding, Denmark

Susan Cranmer
Department of Educational Research
Lancaster University
Lancaster, UK

Julie-Ann Sime
Department of Educational Research
Lancaster University
Lancaster, UK

Maarten de Laat
Department of Learning
Teaching, and Curriculum
University of Wollongong
Wollongong, NSW, Australia

Thomas Ryberg
Department of Communication
and Psychology
Aalborg University
Aalborg, Denmark

Research in Networked Learning
ISBN 978-3-319-74856-6   ISBN 978-3-319-74857-3   (eBook)
https://doi.org/10.1007/978-3-319-74857-3

Library of Congress Control Number: 2018941103

Printed on acid-free paper

This Springer imprint is published by the registered company Springer International Publishing AG part of Springer Nature.
The registered company address is: Gewerbestrasse 11, 6330 Cham, Switzerland

Foreword

This is the sixth book in the Springer Series on *Research in Networked Learning* and it is based on selected papers from the tenth International Networked Learning Conference held in Lancaster in 2016. The series focuses on contemporary issues and concerns in networked learning theory, pedagogy and practice, and this book is another excellent contribution to the series.

The Networked Learning Conference itself was established in 1998, and some 20 years later we may ask the question – as indeed this book does – to what extent has the discourse of networked learning influenced educational practice? The success of the Conference and the associated Springer Book Series on *Research in Networked Learning* have undoubtedly led to networked learning making a significant contribution to thinking about the purpose of higher education in a digitally connected world. As the editors of this latest contribution to the book series point out, networked learning continues to position itself within current discussions and debates, and is now seen to be a distinct and important area of higher education research.

This latest addition to the book series helps us recognise that networked learning continues to contribute to our understanding of what learning mediated and supported by technology looks like in both formal and informal learning situations. The key values and characteristics of networked learning of learning community, connections, reflexivity, criticality, collaboration and relational dialogue persist as key areas of interest in many of the chapters. They are the source of inspiration for many networked learning researchers and practitioners, as well as being the focus for the examination of the practice of networked learning.

This latest book helps us characterise the field of networked learning today, and presents some challenges for future research and practice. Collectively, the chapters situate networked learning within contemporary ideas on learning and teaching, and within the broader field of higher education research and practice. This book provides an opportunity to reflect and look back at some important concerns that have occurred over the past 20 years, and to consider some of the potential future challenges. In the concluding chapter, the editors of this book take the opportunity to provide a critical analysis of the contents and identify significant emerging issues for future research and practice, including learning spaces; mobility; forms of openness; difference in student learning experience; social justice; and criticality.

In reading the chapters, it is clear to see that there is a healthy diversity of opinion on some of the details and perspectives of networked learning, which continue to be critically debated. However, it is equally evident that those values that underpinned networked learning in the early conferences endure and suffuse the fabric of this book. We recommend this book to all researchers and practitioners of networked learning and beyond.

Vivien Hodgson and David McConnell
Series Editors

Contents

About the Author

Alexander Fink is a Research Fellow in Youth Studies at the University of Minnesota, School of Social Work. His work – through participatory program evaluation, training, technical assistance, and university teaching – examines and supports the involvement of young people in the political, social, and cultural life of their communities. His current research focuses on the ways the helping professions' (including education) increasing collection, sharing, and use of (big) data often further marginalize and exclude young people from having a voice in their communal life. His research on higher education and networked learning with colleague and mentor Ilene Alexander seeks to counter these trends by exploring contexts for networked learning that promote deep, inclusive, and meaningful participation.

Apostolos Koutropoulos "AK" is the Program Manager for the online MA program in Applied Linguistics at the University of Massachusetts Boston. He is also a part-time Lecturer in the Instructional Design MEd program. Over the past few years, he has participated in many massive online open courses (MOOCs) and open learning opportunities, and has co-authored research papers on topics around open learning. AK is currently a doctoral candidate at Athabasca University and holds a BA in Computer Science, an MBA with a focus on Human Resources, an MS in Information Technology, an MEd in Instructional Design, and an MA in Applied Linguistics. His research interests include open education, social learning, educational technology, and languages.

Chris Jones is an Emeritus Professor at Liverpool John Moore's University (LJMU). His research focuses on the application of the metaphor of networks to the understanding of learning in higher education. Chris has led and participated in a number of UK and international research projects and was the principal investigator for a UK Research Council-funded project "The Net Generation encountering e-learning at university." He has published over 70 journal articles, book chapters, and refereed conference papers connected to his research. He is the author of *Networked Learning: An Educational Paradigm for the Age of Digital Networks*,

Springer, 2015. Chris has also edited two books on this subject – *Networked Learning: Perspectives and Issues* published by Springer in 2002 and *Analysing Networked Learning Practices in Higher Education and Continuing Professional Development* published by Sense Publishers, BV, in 2009.

Cristina Garduño Freeman is an academic in the fields of heritage, architecture, and digital media. Her research is focused on social value, participatory culture, and place attachment of World Heritage properties and Industrial Heritage. Currently, she is a Postdoctoral Research Fellow in the Australian Centre for Architectural History, Urban and Cultural Heritage (ACAHUCH) at The University of Melbourne. She has published in leading international journals and conferences and in 2014, received the International Visual Sociology Association Rieger Award for an Outstanding Doctoral Thesis. In 2017, she published her first research monograph titled *Participatory Culture and the Social Value of an Architectural Icon: Sydney Opera* House with Routledge. Prior to entering academia, she practiced professionally in architecture, landscape architecture and urban design, and in visual communication design.

Deirdre Hynes PhD, is a Senior Lecturer at Manchester Metropolitan University, Great Britain, in the field of Digital Media and Communications. Her research interests include football research, gender, and technological domestication and everyday life. She has edited two books on football and community and published several articles in media, technology, and anthropology journals.

Gale Parchoma is an Associate Professor of Educational Technology and Design (ETAD) in the Department of Curriculum Studies at the University of Saskatchewan, Saskatoon, Canada; an Adjunct Associate Professor in Educational Studies in the Learning Sciences at the Werklund School of Education, University of Calgary, Canada; an Associate Research Member in the Centre for Technology Enhanced Learning in the Department of Educational Research at Lancaster University in the UK; and the Program Coordinator for Canada's Collaboration for Online Higher Education Research. She has been a member of the Networked Learning Conference review committee since 2008.

Her research focuses on the intersections where people and technologies interact in the processes of teaching, learning, and working. Her research has particular interests including socio-material assemblages, distributed cognitions, and technological affordances. Her work has been published in peer-reviewed books, research journals, and presented at national and international conferences.

Ilene D. Alexander is a teaching consultant and Preparing Future Faculty instructor at the Center for Educational Innovation, and serves also as affiliate faculty in the College of Education and Human Development's Higher Education Graduate Program, and as an assistant faculty coordinator mentoring high school teachers of the "University Writing" course via the high school based College in the Schools program. She is a co-facilitator of four online faculty development seminars. Her research, presentation, and writing endeavors, as well as consulting and teaching practice focus on multicultural, inclusive, accessible learning and teaching as these intersect with learning science, diversity science, and networked learning. Ilene is co-editor of *Innovative Learning and Teaching: Experiments Across the Disciplines*, to be published during Fall 2018 as the first volume of the Centre's "Making a Difference" biennial monograph series; the second volume will focus on inclusion and accessibility in higher education teaching and learning.

Julie-Ann Sime is a Lecturer in Technology Enhanced Learning in the Department of Educational Research at Lancaster University, U.K. She is an experienced online educator who has been tutoring postgraduates in networked learning communities for over 25 years. She researches online and networked learning in professional development focusing on how new technologies (such as games, simulations, and virtual learning environments) can be designed and used to support online educators; how learners can develop an understanding of complex dynamic systems; and how to design for personalized learning experiences so that education is more inclusive. In 2016, she was on the steering committee of the tenth International Networked Learning Conference. With a wide range of experience of European industry/academia collaborative research projects (ETIOLE, A-TEAM, VirRad) and networks (Kaleidoscope, MONET, MONET2), she is currently researching into visual and video literacies of educators and the pedagogy of massive open online courses with funding from ERASMUS+ Strategic Partnership in Higher Education: https://www.viliproject.eu/

Kyungmee Lee is a Lecturer in the Department of Educational Research and co-Director of the Centre for Technology Enhanced Learning at Lancaster University. She earned her doctorate from the Ontario Institute for Studies in Education, University of Toronto, in 2015, where her work involved developing a *Double-Layered Community of Practice* model for online higher education. This model conceptualizes online learning as interlinked processes of participation and socialization in multiple communities across online and offline "layers" of learners' lives. It proposes pedagogical strategies to connect those two layers and support learners' simultaneous presence across the layers. Her current research program aims to develop more comprehensive understanding of learning in increasingly digitalized and internationalized educational contexts. Utilizing methodological strategies informed by Critical Discourse Analysis, her work examines and unpacks dominant discourses of online education that serve to obscure issues of accessibility and equality and that produce both practical and theoretical challenges in higher education.

Laura Czerniewicz The Director of the Centre for Innovation in Learning and Teaching (CILT) at the University of Cape Town in South Africa, Laura Czerniewicz is an Associate Professor in the Centre for Higher Education Development, committed to equity of access and success in higher education. Her research interests include the technologically mediated practices of students and academics, the nature of the changing higher education environment, and the geopolitics of knowledge, underpinned by a commitment to surfacing the expressions of inequality within and across contexts. She is the South African PI on a project on the Unbundled University: Researching emerging models in an unequal landscape (http://unbundleduni.com/) together with colleagues at Leeds University. Laura is involved with policy work, is a contributor to national and global conversations in varied formats, and serves on the advisory boards of a variety of international higher education educational and technology publications. Much of her work is available online at https://uct.aca-demia.edu/LauraCzerniewicz

Lucila Carvalho is a Senior Lecturer in e-learning and digital technologies in the Institute of Education, at Massey University (Auckland, New Zealand), where she teaches in the Master of Education and in the Bachelor of Arts programs. Lucila's research interests are in *design for learning* and *technology and new media*. Lucila has published in international journals and conference proceedings in the fields of education, sociology, systemic functional linguistics, and design and software engineering. Her most recent publications include *Place-Based Spaces for Networked Learning* (co-edited with Peter Goodyear and Maarten de Laat, Routledge, 2017) and *The Architecture of Productive Learning Networks* (co-edited with Peter Goodyear, Routledge, 2014).

Maarten de Laat is the Director of the Learning, Teaching & Curriculum division at the University of Wollongong. His expertise concentrates on social learning strategies, networked learning relationships, and technologies to facilitate teaching, learning, and innovation in agile learning environments.

Maarten's research addresses networks and social capital development, with a specific interest in informal learning, professional development, and knowledge creation through (online) social networks and communities and the impact technology, learning analytics, and social design has on the way these networks and communities work, learn, and innovate. He has published and presented his research on networked learning, professional development, and learning analytics extensively in international research journals, books, and conferences. He has given several invited keynotes at international conferences. He has been appointed a Visiting Professor at the University of South Australia in Adelaide. Finally, Maarten is co-chair of the International Networked Learning Conference (NLC).

Magdalena Bober was a Lecturer at Manchester Metropolitan University at the time of writing. Her research focused on media audiences and users, children and young people's use of digital media, digital research methods, and technology enhanced learning. She has published and presented her work in research journals, books, and conferences. She previously taught at Leeds University and was a researcher at the London School of Economics. Magdalena recently moved into market research, specializing in the education sector and international research.

Maria Cutajar holds a PhD in e-Research and Technology Enhanced Learning by Lancaster University. She is a Lecturer with the Faculty of Education of the

University of Malta currently teaching Computing at the post-secondary Junior College managed by the university. Her research interests focus on teaching and learning using networked technologies of information and communication. Through research practice, she also developed an interest in the theory and practice of phenomenography, qualitative research methods generally, and research processes. As an early career researcher, she investigated aspects of students' experiences of networked technologies for learning. Presently, she is also engaged looking into academics' experiences using networked technologies for teaching.

Nina Bonderup Dohn is an Associate Professor in Humanistic Information Science at the Department of Design and Communication, University of Southern Denmark. She holds an MA in Philosophy and Physics from Aarhus University, a PhD in Learning Theory from Aalborg University, and a Higher Doctorate Degree in Applied Philosophy from University of Southern Denmark. She is a member of the Steering Committee of the International Networked Learning Conference. She has been a Visiting Scholar at the Centre for Research on Computer Supported Learning and Cognition, University of Sydney (2013–2014) and at the Department of Philosophy, University of California, Berkeley (2009–2010 and 2000–2001). She currently holds a research grant from the Danish Council for Independent Research on the project *Designing for situated knowledge in a world of change*. Her main research areas integrate epistemology, learning sciences, web communication, and technology-mediated learning with a focus on the role of tacit knowledge. She has published extensively in Danish and English on philosophical and pedagogical issues within knowledge theory, web 2.0, ICT-mediated learning, and teaching and learning in higher education. Nina's webpage is found here: http://www.sdu.dk/staff/nina

Sue Cranmer is a Lecturer in the Centre for Technology Enhanced Learning, Department of Educational Research, Lancaster University, UK. She teaches on the Doctoral Program in E-Research and Technology Enhanced Learning. Her main research interests are in digital technologies, social justice, and in/equality. Sue's innovative research on disabled children's uses of digital technologies is becoming increasingly recognized and she is currently working on a monograph entitled *Disabled Children and Digital Technologies: Everyday Practices in Childhood* for Bloomsbury Academic. Sue has led a number of research projects including "Expert Perspectives on Creativity and Innovation in European Schools" for the Institute of Prospective Technological Studies (IPTS) in Spain, and a major work package designing pedagogical scenarios for engaging classrooms as part of the EU-funded iTEC project (http://fcl.eun.org/itec). Other projects have included research into digital inclusion, digital pedagogy, inclusive pedagogical design, digital literacy, digital innovation, and universal design. Sue has been widely published in leading journals in the field including *Technology, Pedagogy and Education, Learning, Media and Technology"* and *Studies in Higher Education*. In 2010, she co-authored *"Primary Schools and ICT: Learning from Pupil Perspectives"* (Continuum) with Neil Selwyn and John Potter.

Suzan Koseoglu is an Academic Developer in Technology Enhanced Learning at Goldsmiths, University of London. She holds a PhD in Learning Technologies, Curriculum, and Instruction from the University of Minnesota. Suzan's area of expertise is online learning with an emphasis on open and networked scholarship and socio-cultural aspects of learning in further and higher education contexts. Before joining Goldsmiths, Suzan has worked as an online instructor in the Learning Technologies program area at the University of Minnesota, teaching undergraduate and graduate level classes on technology and ethics, youth's use of social media, and online learning communities.

Thomas Ryberg is a Professor of Digital Learning in the Department of Communication and Psychology at Aalborg University (AAU), Denmark. He is part of the research center: "E-Learning Lab – Center for User Driven Innovation, Learning and Design" (http://www.ell.aau.dk). His primary research interests are within the fields of Networked Learning, Problem Based Learning (PBL), Computer Supported Collaborative Learning (CSCL), and Technology Enhanced Learning (TEL). In particular, he is interested in Problem Based Learning, and how new media and technologies transform our ways of thinking about and designing for Networked and Hybrid Learning. He is co-chair of the International Networked Learning Conference (http://networkedlearningconference.org.uk/) and editor of *Journal of Problem Based Learning in Higher Education* (JPBLHE). He has participated in European and international research projects and networks (EQUEL, Kaleidoscope, COMBLE, PlaceMe, EATrain2), and in development projects in South East Asia and Latin America (VISCA, VO@NET, ELAC). Currently, he is engaged in the EU-funded knowledge alliance: Innovative Open Data Education and Training based on PBL and Learning Analytics.

Chapter 1
Celebrating the Tenth Networked Learning Conference: Looking Back and Moving Forward

Maarten de Laat and Thomas Ryberg

Abstract The chapters in this book are based on a selection of papers from the Networked Learning Conference 2016 which was the 10th anniversary conference in the series. In acknowledgement of the anniversary, the authors of this Introduction look back and reflect on past networked learning conferences with the aim to describe some general trends and developments in networked learning research as they emerge and fade out over the years. In order to do so the authors use the proceedings of each networked learning conference (from 1998 till 2016) as a compiled dataset. This dataset forms a text corpus that has been analysed with Voyant tools (Sinclair and Rockwell 2016) specifically designed for analysing digital texts. Voyant tools are used to generate a set of word clouds (Cirrus) in order to visualise networked learning research-related terms that feature most frequently in each set of proceedings and conduct a trends analysis of these terms to generate a visual representation of the frequencies of these terms across the proceedings over the years. The outcomes have been thematically organised around the following topics: learning theory (e.g. cognitivism, constructivism, social learning, actor network theory), learning environments and social media (e.g. LMS, MOOC, Virtual Worlds, Twitter, Facebook), technologies (e.g. phone, laptop, tablet), methodology (e.g. quantitative, qualitative) and related research in the domain of e-learning (e-learning, CSCL, TEL). The findings are placed in their historical context to understand how research presented in the domain of networked learning has developed over the years and influenced our work. Towards the end of the Introduction, the two main sections of the book are presented. The overview discussion of individual chapters is deferred to the Conclusion chapter.

M. de Laat (✉)
Learning, Teaching & Curriculum, University of Wollongong, Wollongong, NSW, Australia
e-mail: mdelaat@uow.edu.au

T. Ryberg
Department of Communication and Psychology, Aalborg University, Aalborg, Denmark
e-mail: ryberg@hum.aau.dk

© Springer International Publishing AG, part of Springer Nature 2018
N. Bonderup Dohn et al. (eds.), *Networked Learning*, Research in Networked Learning, https://doi.org/10.1007/978-3-319-74857-3_1

Fig. 1.1 Tag cloud of 10 year Networked Learning

To celebrate the tenth anniversary of the biennial Networked Learning Conference, the conference chairs Maarten de Laat and Thomas Ryberg presented an overview of emerging and trending themes that have been featured at the conference series over the years. The selection of topics and trends was based on semantic analysis drawing on a dataset that comprised the full conference proceedings published from 1998 to 2016, see Fig. 1.1. The statistical material underpinning the presented graphs was created using the text- and data-mining tool Voyant Tools.[1] Voyant Tools is an open-source web-based text reading and analysis environment where all PDF versions of the conference proceedings were uploaded and processed. Voyant Tools can – amongst other things – be used to count, for example, how many times particular words or phrases occur in a body of text. In the analysis presented in this chapter, each conference proceeding featured as a data point creating a timeline presentation showing the development or decline of networked learning research trends over the years.

In this introduction, we have expanded the trend analysis initially presented at the Networked Learning Conference held in 2016 in Lancaster and discuss the findings we see from analysing the textual material. We will reflect on the limitations of

---

[1] https://voyant-tools.org/

our approach, the value and biases of statistical treatment of word occurrences, and what we can meaningfully draw from such analyses. For example, our analysis suffers from an inability to meaningfully explore the concept of 'networked learning' itself as it occurs so often in the proceedings (e.g. in headers and footers) that it is rendered meaningless. Similarly, it proved difficult to generate sociographs to map social interaction or author networks based on paper publications around the identified topics.

In this chapter we present our findings grouped into a number of themes, representing the areas in which networked learning has had most traction. We start with theoretical perspectives that have been used to understand and frame networked learning practices. We then reflect on the dominant research methods that have been used, followed by various modes of delivery or designing for networked learning, and we wrap it up with a presentation of the technological devices that have dominated networked learning research over the years. Within each of these themes, we discuss in more depth how we have approached the analysis and our rationale for the words chosen after we provide an analysis and reflection and ponder what the findings might suggest in terms of moving forward.

As an initial caveat, we should say that we do not ourselves consider our analysis an authoritarian analysis or solid, sturdy anchoring point from which we can say that we have attained a 'god's eye' overview of the past and future of networked learning. We see the analysis as a first attempt to provide a preliminary analysis of trends in a manner that we do not think has previously been attempted within networked learning. In the spirit of recognising the limitations and preliminary nature of this analysis and approach, we lay our material open for others to explore as open datasets, so that other researchers – within or outside the networked learning community – can consult and work with the data to debate, dismiss, or enrich the findings of our analysis. Thus, we see the analysis as a first preliminary attempt to understand the field of networked learning through the lenses and techniques of data-mining and textual analysis of corpora.

The Field of Networked Learning

Networked learning is learning in which information and communications technology (ICT) is used to promote connections: between one learner and other learners, between learners and tutors; between a learning community and its learning resources. (Goodyear et al. 2004, p. 1)

The quote above is the often-used definition for networked learning as proposed initially by Goodyear et al. (2004). It stresses the importance of both human and digitally mediated interactions through the notion of 'connections' and underlines that interactions with technologies and resources in isolation are not sufficient to constitute networked learning.

At the first Networked Learning Conference in 1998, the aim was to bring networked learning research and praxis together, and there was a strong focus on

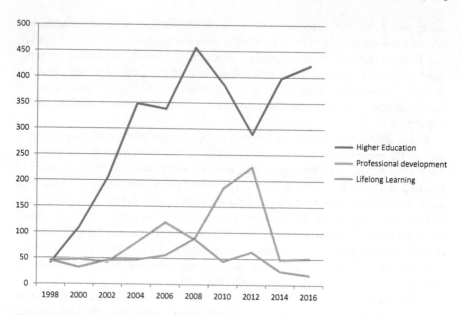

Fig. 1.2 Focus of networked learning research

lifelong learning, professional development and implications for educational theory and the current paradigm shift from traditional learning to distributed and distance learning (Banks et al. 1998) – in fact the proceedings were titled 'Networked Lifelong Learning'. This early broad orientation of networked learning is visible in Fig. 1.2, but over the years, it has become clear that a lot of the research has been driven by exploring particularly the potential of networked learning for higher education.

In Fig. 1.2, one can see how frequently the words 'higher education', 'professional development' and 'lifelong learning' have been used in the networked learning conference papers over the years. From this, it becomes quite clear that the predominant focus has developed to become the area of higher education. The attention to lifelong learning and professional development has always been present with a pronounced peak in 2012 for 'professional development' when the conference was hosted in Maastricht in the Netherlands. The interest in lifelong learning seems to be gradually fading, which perhaps is part of a wider trend, as the same pattern holds true if one looks up 'lifelong learning' in Google Trends (from 2004 to 2017, there is a decline in interest from index 100 to approximately 30).

From the beginning of the conference series, there was a very broad understanding of networked learning, and the *space of possibilities for networked learning was seen as vast*[2] (Jones et al. 2001). This is still true today, as illustrated in Goodyear et al. (2016a) where a number of cases from different domains are presented. But it is also clear that the conference series bends strongly towards higher education and professional development, over, for example, primary or secondary education or

---

[2] http://csalt.lancs.ac.uk/jisc/definition.htm

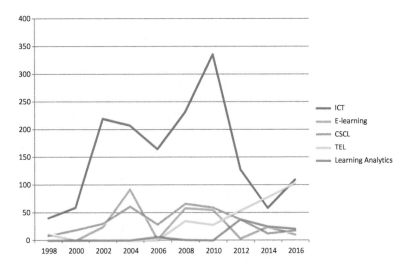

Fig. 1.3 Related areas of research

informal learning (these were all terms we searched for, but they returned only a few results). This, of course, is hardly surprising as the conference has always been understood and promoted as a conference addressing higher education, professional development and lifelong learning (but has always been open to incorporating papers lying outside of this scope). While we were not surprised that higher education features prominently over the years, we were a bit surprised to see the comparatively smaller uptake in 'professional development'. This, as we believe it, will increasingly become an area of political interest and one where the field of networked learning has a lot to contribute to in terms of critical, dialogical and collaborative perspectives over a more individualised trajectory of microdegrees.

With the domain of inquiry being firmly settled within higher education and to some extent professional development, we were also interested in looking further into what constitutes the field of networked learning more broadly. We have therefore made searches into particular neighbouring research fields such as technology-enhanced learning (TEL), computer-supported collaborative learning (CSCL), learning analytics and knowledge (LAK) and more broadly information and communication technology (ICT) and e-learning. The results can be seen in Fig. 1.3.

What is immediately notable from Fig. 1.3 is the gradual rise of interest in the term ICT with a steep decline in 2012 and 2014. This, most likely, does not suggest that the interest in ICTs has waned, but probably that the term ICT is gradually and more broadly being replaced by other terms, e.g. digital technologies. Again a Google Trends search for ICT does seem to confirm that this term is losing traction over the years from 2004 till now.

Quite interestingly, the term 'e-learning' seems to live a bumpy life, peaking at some conferences (2004, 2008 and 2010) and being almost non-existing at other times (2000, 2006, 2012). There is no immediate good explanation for this, other than the term 'e-learning' in general is a broader (and less precise) term than net-worked learning, which would therefore often be the term chosen at NL conferences over e-learning.

We further queried into specific fields of research, such as TEL, CSCL and learning analytics. In general, as we shall return to in the concluding chapter, the area of learning analytics seems little explored within the networked learning community, which does not seem to reflect a wider trend within educational technology. The term had a small surge in 2012 and has been explored further – though to a lesser degree – in 2014 and 2016. Comparing to Google Trends, this is markedly different from the broader interest, as since 2012 the interest in learning analytics has risen (from index 11 in 2012 to nearing a 100 in 2017). In contrast the use of the term TEL has risen since 2008 in the NL conferences, and it seems that this is generally a term that has become increasingly popular amongst national governments, the EU and other funders (which has also provoked criticism of the term (e.g. Bayne 2015; Hayes 2016)). Finally, we queried into the term CSCL, which has gathered a rela-tively stable amount of interest within networked learning over time, though with a slight decline in the recent years. As argued by Jones et al. (2015), there are strong overlaps between CSCL and networked learning, as well as some areas where they follow different paths:

> Networked learning has a close relationship with computer-supported collaborative learn-ing (CSCL), in that both fields have a keen interest in collaborative orchestrations of learn-ing. However, CSCL tends to focus on smaller groups, including dyads, whereas networked learning extends to medium- to large-scale groupings. Also CSCL has a strong connection with formal learning in education, whereas networked learning has been picked up in a wider context, for example, lifelong learning, professional development, and organizational learning. (Jones et al. 2015, p. 2)

CSCL when compared to networked learning has a stronger anchorage in educa-tion more generally including a strong presence in primary and secondary schools, whereas networked learning, as illustrated in Fig. 1.2, extends further into profes-sional development and lifelong learning, although this to a lesser degree than we had actually expected (see Fig. 1.2).

Theoretical Perspectives: Theory and Focus of NL Research

Within the area of networked learning, it seems particularly worthwhile to under-stand what theoretical perspectives are underpinning ideas of networked learning. As several authors have explored, networked learning is not a unison theoretical perspective but rather is a theoretical perspective that is composed by or under-pinned by a range of other theoretical outlooks (Hodgson et al. 2014; Jones 2015; Jones et al. 2015; Ryberg et al. 2016).

In analysing these trends, it is important to understand that the mention in a paper of a theoretical perspective does not necessarily translate to a positive stance towards or preference for that theory. Just as much as citation counts in isolation do not show that an author or perspective is agreed upon, popular, or found worthwhile. For example, one might find – within the networked learning literature – quite a few references to Prensky (2001), but the majority of those might be critical to or debate the notions of 'digital natives' proposed initially by Prensky (e.g. Bennett et al. 2008; Kennedy et al. 2008). Likewise, people might mention activity theory, but disagree with or dismiss it. Therefore, what follows from the trends analysis cannot, in isolation, be taken to mean that authors subscribe to the theory. Establishing just an approximation of positivity or negativity towards the theory mentioned would require a substantially more complex and detailed data-mining technique looking, for example, for adjacent words in sentences that could unearth positive or negative stances. This goes far beyond our capabilities and intentions, so we should remind the reader that the trend mapping merely signals attention/awareness. However, that a theory merits attention and is on the radar of the community is also an important measure of its impact on a community; whether for good or bad, it does show that it is or has been a topic of interest.

We should also mention that different words may often be used for the same theory. For example, some differ between social constructivism and constructivism, whereas others take it for the same. Likewise, the term social constructionism is a term that has also featured in the conference over the years and one that should not be confused with constructionism. Another term that is frequently used in this context is social constructivism. Both terms follow a similar curve over the years (see Fig. 1.4). Although these terms have a slight different meaning, they have also been used in substitution of one another.

Actor-network theory might be spelled in a number of ways, with or without hyphens, and might more recently be phrased as a sociomaterial perspective (or perhaps socio-material or social material), and, for example, activity theory could also be referred to as socio-cultural, sociocultural, or cultural historical perspective. These ambiguities or even little differences in spellings (dash or no dash) make it difficult to assess the occurrence of a theoretical perspective.

In the following, we discuss the selection of the overall concepts we have chosen to include. The main concepts we have explored are cognitivism, constructivism, communities of practice, social learning, actor-network theory and activity theory.

While, from an experiential point of view, we did not expect there would be strong mentions of 'cognitivism', we included this perspective nevertheless, as it is often positioned as an overarching learning theoretical perspective together with behaviourism and constructivism (Jones 2015). As networked learning is more often associated with relational, social and non-dualists views of learning, we expected that cognitivism, understood as particularly associated with cognitive science/psychology, or cognitive theory would be a more fringe perspective within networked learning. This is not to say that a cognitive perspective is strange to networked learning; indeed Peter Goodyear (e.g. 2002) has explored this topic extensively, and in Chap. 2 by Gale Parchoma in this volume, she explores the notion of distributed cognition. However, the work grounded in cognitive science/cognitive psychology seems less pronounced in networked learning as Jones puts it:

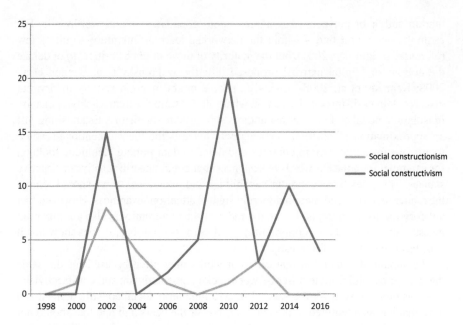

Fig. 1.4 Social constructivism and social constructionism

For networked learning the influence of cognitivism has been limited but there are some elements that have a continuing relevance. Firstly there is a concern with the thinking and intentions of learners. Networked learning still has an interest in what happens in the brain and an interest in what can be called the mind (Carvalho and Goodyear 2014; Goodyear and Ellis 2010). (Jones 2015, p. 52)

The notion of constructivism was included as it is often positioned as an overarching learning theoretical perspective along with, for example, behaviourism and cognitivism. It is a term that has broad meanings, but usually refers to the idea that knowledge is constructed by the learners, rather than being transmitted to the learner by, for example, a teacher:

The central ideas of constructivism are that knowledge is created by people, either as individuals or as part of groups, through experiencing the world and reflecting upon those experiences. In this view knowledge is constructed by the knower and as a consequence it does not exist externally and independently of the knower(s) and knowledge cannot simply be transmitted and received. (Jones 2015, p. 52–53)

Under the hood of constructivism, however, a number of different theories are often subsumed, for example, Piaget and Vygotsky, as well as ideas such as radical constructivism and constructionism. So, constructivism is a rather broad term that can cover quite a spectrum of different meanings. Finally, we have added three theoretical frameworks that we know/assumed from experience might be widely adopted (activity theory, actor-network theory and community of practice), as well as the broader term 'social learning'.

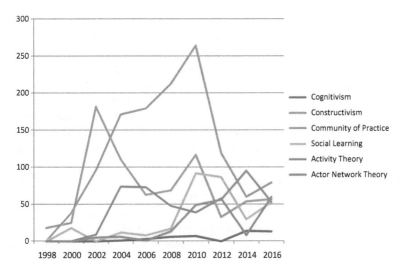

Fig. 1.5 Theoretical perspectives within networked learning

Looking at the graph (Fig. 1.5), we see that the broad label of 'constructivism' has generally featured quite extensively throughout the years, with a steep rise around 2002, but seems to have gradually lost popularity in the recent years (from 2010 until now). Similarly, the notion of community of practice has been extensively popular and rising for every conference peaking at 2010, where after the term seems to decrease in popularity quite significantly from 2010 and onwards. Similarly, it seems that the notion of social learning follows a similar pattern to that of 'communities of practice'. This could be explained by the fact that since 2004 Wenger began more intensively to refer to communities of practice (CoPs) as a 'social theory of learning'. This term was mentioned in Wenger (1998), but became more widespread with the publication of the research agenda 'learning for a small planet' (Wenger 2004). The decline in the number of mentions of CoPs from 2010 and onwards could indicate that the popularity of the theory maybe has started to 'wear out', but it is also interesting, as there have been a number of discussions (and critiques) of the notion of community. For one thing, the notion of 'community' (not necessarily community of practice) has been critiqued to ignore the darker sides of hierarchy, oppression or 'the tyranny of participation' (Fox 2005; Roberts 2006; Ferreday and Hodgson, 2008), and also there have been discussions of communities versus networks and what the ideas of community might overlook (e.g. the strength of weak ties (Granovetter 1973)) (Wenger et al. 2011; De Laat et al. 2014; Vrieling et al. 2016). Thus, the notion of community has always played the role of both an ideal and a contentious, problematic notion within networked learning, and this double role might also be an explanation of why it has held such a strong role as a topic of discussion. It is also well worth noting that the interest in 'communities' within networked learning preceded the popularity of communities of practice as a distinct concept. The interest in community-oriented and community-collaborative forms of learning has always been strong within networked learning; in fact it is probably because the notion of communities of practice resonates well with the foundational ideas of networked learning that is has become so pervasive.

For the other theories, we have highlighted that the trends are less pronounced. This might have to do with the semantic difficulties of capturing those frameworks, whereas 'Communities of Practice' is a more easily encapsulated concept, activity theory and actor-network-theory could equally be referred to by many other names as stated earlier. However, from the graphs, it seems that activity theory was more popular from 2004 to 2006 and then has gradually diminished to have a bit of a renaissance in 2016. In relation to this, it is interesting to see the interest in actor-network theory gradually gaining traction from particular 2008 to peak in 2014. In 2014 it seems to have displaced activity theory – experiencing a surge in 2014 – where actor-network theory is peaking and an inverse relationship in 2016 where there is an almost equal amount of interest. We should, however, as previously written be careful in granting too much explanatory power to the graphs or deduce larger trends.

It does seem fair, though, to state that networked learning seems overwhelmingly underpinned by theories that take a broader social, cultural and relational view of learning, rather than, for instance, a more specific cognitive or neural perspective. Again, this is not entirely surprising and is also well established in the networked learning literature – particularly this has also been argued in the book series that summarises general trends in the area of networked learning.

Methods

Apart from querying into the theoretical underpinnings, we found that it would be relevant and interesting to look further into methods and methodologies adopted within networked learning. We initially queried into the broad distinction between 'qualitative' and 'quantitative' and incorporated also the more recently popularised idea of 'mixed method' (see Fig. 1.6).

Figure 1.6 clearly illustrates that networked learning is a field leaning more towards qualitative methods than quantitative. From our experience with the conference and reading through many papers, this did not come as a surprise to us, though it is a bit surprising to see that between 2002 and 2008, there – apparently – was more quantitative work present, but that its volume seems to have diminished somewhat since then. Interestingly, mixed methods, which seems to have become a very popular approach within many areas of research, had in the past few years an early start in the networked learning community and seems to live a quiet, but stable live outside the spotlight of hundreds of mentions. However, we should again be careful attributing too much explanatory power to the graphs; even one paper discussing quantitative vs. qualitative and mentioning these concepts often could contribute heavily to a peak.

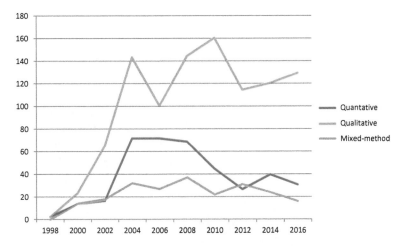

Fig. 1.6 Overarching research orientations within networked learning

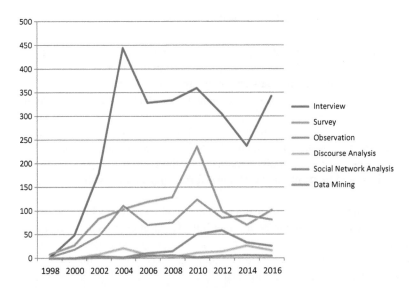

Fig. 1.7 Data collection methods used in networked learning

Adding more detail to the very broad query into methods, we decided to be more specific and query the terms such as interview, survey, observation, discourse analysis, social network analysis and data mining (Fig. 1.7) as well as phenomenography, ethnography, design-based research and grounded theory (Fig. 1.8).

Figure 1.7 more or less confirms the overall impression of networked learning leaning more towards the qualitative side. Interviews are by far the most mentioned method, followed by survey and observation (noting that observation could also occur as a regular word not affiliated with the method observation, just as one can

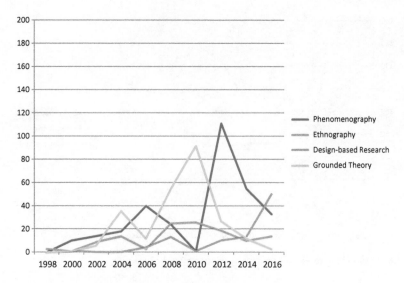

Fig. 1.8 Qualitative methodologies in networked learning

make a survey of the literature). Somewhat surprisingly discourse analysis is quite rare. We had expected this would be a more prominent method, as often authors have analysed forum interactions or policy texts from a critical perspective. In this vein, it could be interesting in a future analysis to identify the types of qualitative textual analysis networked learning researchers engage in.

From Fig. 1.7, we can further see that from 2004 social network analysis is beginning to take a place as a method that is adopted within networked learning research, whereas data mining remains a method rarely adopted or mentioned (though it should be mentioned that some forms of social network analysis rely on data mining).

In Fig. 1.8, which can be seen as an extension of the previous Fig. 1.6, we can see how qualitatively oriented methodologies hold a central place in networked learning research (although many forms of phenomenography and early grounded theory also entail quantitative aspects). Ethnography, often associated with observation and interviews, holds a stable – yet modest – place, whereas both grounded theory and phenomenography are more common. This most probably has to do with the nature of networked learning, as much networked learning occurs online making it more amenable to textual analysis of interviews, forum transcripts and so forth than perhaps sustained observations in the 'field' (though online ethnography or multisited ethnography is a blooming field within online educational research more broadly speaking). From the graphs, one can see that both phenomenography and grounded theory have been gaining traction over the years (though mentions of grounded theory seem to be waning), and a peculiar observation is that there seems to be a strange inverted relationship between phenomenography and grounded theory. For example, in 2010 mentions of grounded theory peak, whereas phenomenography is absent and the inverse for 2012 where phenomenography peaks and the mentions of grounded theory plummet (and a somewhat similar pattern on a smaller scale can be seen in 2004 and 2006). Finally, we can see how the concept of design-based research seems to be on the rise since 2004 – a methodology that also seems to be gaining more attention within educational research at large.

In summary, it is notable that networked learning research leans broadly towards qualitative research, yet also including surveys, social network analysis and phenomenography and grounded theory, which in some interpretations include aspects of quantitative methods. Equally it is worth noting that approaches such as data mining seem to be completely absent from networked learning research, which in many ways is not surprising but perhaps worth reflecting on whether there is a need to pay more attention to such fields and methods, as much attention now seems to be directed towards 'big data', 'analytics', 'algorithms' and so forth.

Networked Learning Delivery Modes

In this section on networked learning delivery modes, we look into three different dimensions moving from the more general modes of delivery (e.g. online, f2f) to more specific technological learning environments and social media infrastructures.

In Fig. 1.9, we have queried into different overarching modes of delivery, i.e. f2f, distance, online, blended, hybrid and open. It should be noted that several of these are difficult to assess, as words such as online, distance and open could equally refer to ordinary usage of the words, rather than delivery modes per se.

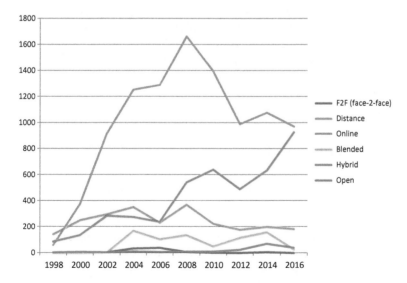

Fig. 1.9 Delivery modes for networked learning

From Fig. 1.9 it seems that there is little work referring to f2f (face-2-face) work, which is perhaps not surprising, considering that networked learning traditionally has been strongly associated with various forms of 'online' or 'distance' learning – two concepts that also feature more prominently in the graphs. However, a caveat here could be the potentially many ways of expressing face-to-face in terms of variations of spelling or expressing 'physical' formats in education. Having said that, it is noteworthy that there are quite a few occurrences of blended learning, which can entail a mixture of online and face-to-face, and the same for 'hybrid' (though both of these terms have many meanings).

In the past few conferences, it has become apparent that there is now a greater interest in delivery modes that are not only online, such as blended/hybrid or understanding how students and teachers use educational technologies as part of on-campus teaching. Here it is particularly worth noting how 'place' and 'mobility' have entered as particular fields of interest (Carvalho et al. 2016; Gourlay and Oliver 2017; Gallagher et al. 2016) in contrast to students sitting at home participating in online conferences via a desktop computer (Goodyear et al. 2016b):

> At the risk of over-simplifying, one might say that people involved in networked learning were generally assumed to be experiencing remote interaction with others: while sitting down, using a desktop computer or terminal; [...] Twenty years later, changes in technology, media habits and expectations mean that this sedentary, exotic, keyboard-tethered image of networked learning is no longer tenable. Mobile, personal, voice-enabled multifunctional devices such as laptops, tablets and smartphones have made it possible to participate in networked learning 24/7 from almost any location, including in workplaces, the home, the bus and the street. (Goodyear, Carvalho & Dohn, pp. 97–98)

We return to these issues in the final discussion in this book as these changes also have an impact on how we can understand the notions of 'network' in networked learning.

A final remark in relation to Fig. 1.9 is the increasing interest in the notion of 'open' which is now nearing occurrences of the even more generic term 'online'. This could for one thing be associated with massive open online courses (MOOCs), but more widely probably also reflects an interest in 'open' as 'open educational resources' and increasing interest in moving courses beyond the confines of a singular university module or course.

Learning Environments

In terms of learning environments (see Fig. 1.10), we have queried it into four quite broad categories: learning management system/virtual learning environment (LMS/VLE), MOOCs, Virtual Worlds and Clouds. Apart from LMS/VLE, there are few occurrences of any of these words prior to 2008, which might not be very surprising in terms of concepts as MOOCs and Cloud are terms that have only surfaced or become more widely popular around 2008–2010. Virtual Worlds (second life) seems to have been represented in the networked learning field only very marginally

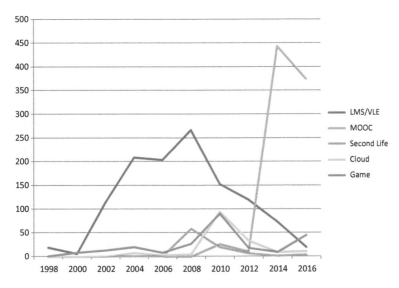

Fig. 1.10 Learning environments featuring networked learning research

and with few occurrences over the years – it really shows no clear trend that was taken up in this research community. To the contrary, the terms LMS/VLEs (i.e. Blackboard, Firstclass, WebCT, Moodle, Fronter) began an upwards trend after 2000, to peak around 2008, and then start to decline somewhat rapidly in the years following.

Most noticeably is obviously the appearance of MOOCs that seem to follow a wider cultural trend of becoming excessively popular after 2012 following the rise of platforms such as Coursera, EdX and the whole MOOC craze taking off at that time – but it should be noted that the earlier MOOCs (e.g. developed by Siemens and Downes) also received some attention in the Networked Learning Conference around 2010. It is, however, quite striking with this explosive interest in MOOCs happening between 2012 and 2014 showing a steep rise in mentions from around 25 to 450 (a graph that we could perhaps dub the 'Nessie graph' as it looks a bit like the 'Loch Ness Monster' rearing its head). Whether MOOCs become a 'Loch Ness Monster' lurking in the deep waters of higher education remains to be seen. On the one hand, MOOCs have been subject to criticism; on the other hand, MOOCs are globally seen as a pathway for higher education institutes to offer courses online to attract students in the global higher education marketplace. The interest in MOOCs reflects of course the wider cultural and political interest in the MOOC phenomenon. However, since the networked learning community often praises itself for its critical and distanced stance to 'boosterism' and technological determinism (Jones 2015), it would be interesting to dive deeper into an analysis of how the MOOC phenomenon was addressed in the papers from the 2014 to 2016 conferences.

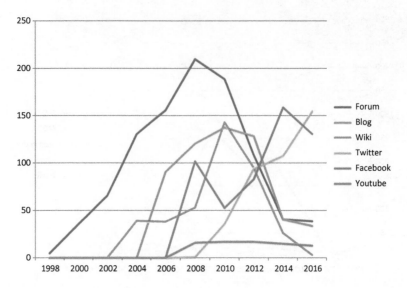

Fig. 1.11 Tools and social media use within networked learning

To understand what might be the more concrete technologies that are adopted for learning, we queried into some more generic types of tools (forum, blog, wiki), as well as particular services (Facebook, Twitter and YouTube).

From this graph (Fig. 1.11), we can see that 'forums' were of increasing interest from 1998 until around 2008 where the use of the term 'forum' starts to decline. The interests in forums are hardly surprising for a field particularly interested in dialogue and collaboration as 'forums' were one of the dominant 'technologies' to support asynchronous dialogue at the time. This is also reflected in a steeply growing interest in blogs and wikis that were often portrayed as some of the paradigmatic 'web 2.0 technologies' (Dohn 2009) within education; and it also follows the general interest in web 2.0 that started to take off around 2004–2005. What is interesting to see is how these terms also seem to be wearing off and be replaced by an interest in social networking sites and services such as Twitter and Facebook and, to a much lesser degree, Youtube. In relation to YouTube, it is somewhat puzzling that a platform, which is so pervasive in the broader cultural landscape, seems to hold such a little space within networked learning.

Technological Infrastructure

Regarding the use of technological devices and infrastructure by learners, we were interested in querying into broad categories such as 'computer', 'mobile', 'laptop', 'phone' and 'tablet' to see if there were any trends that might be interesting (see Fig. 1.12). In relation to this and which is perhaps not surprising is that the term

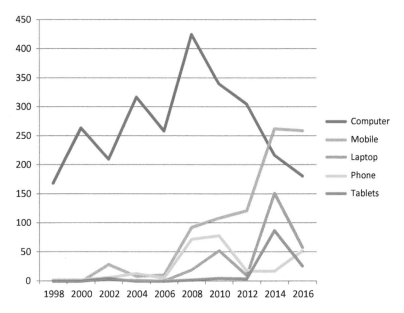

Fig. 1.12 Technological devices used for networked learning

'computer' is slowly declining, whereas terms such as phone, tablets and laptop were on the rise, but most noticeably the word 'mobile' shows a clear upward trend since 2006 and exceeding 'computer' around 2014. This change follows the more general trend where over time we have become more specific about the type of computer technologies we are using.

Rounding Off

Celebrating the tenth anniversary of networked learning conferences covering a period of almost 20 years of research in the area is a great opportunity to reflect and look back. Some clear patterns have emerged, and although not always that surprising it provides a good summary of what happened over the years and where the focus of attention has been. What seems evident is that the field of networked learning is strongly linked to research within higher education, but equally professional development and lifelong learning are areas of interest. However, it is worth mentioning that there have certainly been numerous papers addressing also other contexts, e.g. informal learning, upper secondary schools and museums. We believe that the field should always be open and inviting to papers and thoughts that do not necessarily emanate from studies in a higher education context provided they contribute to advancing and developing our understanding of networked learning.

From a theoretical perspective, it seems clear that networked learning is strongly associated with theories that emphasise social, relational and cultural aspects of learning, be they ANT, activity theory, communities of practice, socio-material, social constructionist, or constructivist perspectives. It is a field interested in community-oriented and community-collaborative forms of learning, but equally social learning in more loosely tied, diverse, complex networks increasingly exploring movements across online and 'physical' places. Methodologically, it leans strongly towards qualitative methods, but with noticeable interest in quantitative methods as well or methodologies involving aspects of quantification (social network analysis, grounded theory). It is a field that – being interested in digital technologies – also reroutes its interest or object of study as the technological landscapes and trends change. For example, following the wider political and cultural interest in MOOCs, but also we see how there seems to be shift in focus from the LMS/VLE towards social media, such as Twitter and Facebook, or from institutional technologies to technologies and services that reside outside the technological infrastructures of higher education institutions.

In relation to this, it is also interesting to note that we might be experiencing a growing interest in forms of learning that are social in a different way than suggested by collaborative learning, communities, or communities of practice.

The next 'wave' in educational technology and networked learning research might involve a growing interest in the importance of being networked in the sense of personal, social networks in a global learning landscape, where the core is not necessarily learning communities and group learning, but rather a greater attention to the degrees of freedom and choice that social networks and learning relationships provide – as well as the challenges of such personalised, social networks to central networked learning values such as community and collaboration. In this light, social theories of learning, social network analysis and actor network theory may be used to understand the socio-material relationships that shape our learning and where (if it all still relevant) this learning takes place. Through their connectivity and use of mobile devices, learners become even more aware that they are learning all the time and that they through their contributions are not only consumers of knowledge but indeed creators of knowledge. Using Twitter, Facebook and other social media, a lot of our learning takes place in the 'wild' and therefore increasingly outside of traditional educational institutions. In this regard, phenomena such as MOOCs – or more importantly – being able to connect with learners on a global scale, can be seen as truly disruptive and something that will fuel future discussions within the networked learning research community. However, it is also clear that this 'global wild' is not necessarily a 'democratic' utopian realisation of the 'global village' but equally a 'wild' that is heavily guided by commercial platforms driven mainly by the desire for profit. In this 'wild', it will be increasingly important for the networked learning research community to critically ask what should be the role of dialogue, community and collaboration and how we can sustain and promote central values such as widening access to education and supporting democratic processes, diversity and inclusion. These are questions that were foundational in the establishment of the networked learning research community and are equally valid – if not more important – in the years to come.

References

Banks, S., Graebner, C., & McConnell, D. (Eds.). (1998). *Networked lifelong learning: innovative approaches to education and training through the internet.* Proceedings of the International Conference, University of Sheffield, April 1998. DACE, University of Sheffield.

Bayne, S. (2015). What's the matter with "technology-enhanced learning"? *Learning, Media and Technology, 40*(1), 5–20. https://doi.org/10.1080/17439884.2014.915851.

Bennett, S., Maton, K., & Kervin, L. (2008). The 'digital natives' debate: A critical review of the evidence. *British Journal of Educational Technology, 39*(5), 775–786.

Carvalho, L., & Goodyear, P. (2014). *The architecture of productive learning networks.* Sydney: Routledge.

Carvalho, L., Goodyear, P., & de Laat, M. (2016). Place, space and networked learning. In L. Carvalho, P. Goodyear, & M. de Laat (Eds.), *Place-based spaces for networked learning* (pp. 1–10). Sydney: Routledge.

De Laat, M., Schreurs, B., & Nijland, F. (2014). Communities of practice and value creation in networks. In R. F. Poell, T. Rocco, & G. Roth (Eds.), *The Routledge companion to human resource development* (pp. 249–257). New York: Routledge.

Dohn, N. B. (2009). Web 2.0-mediated competence – implicit educational demands on learners. *Electronic Journal of e-Learning, 7*(2), 111–118.

Hayes, S. (2016). Learning from a deceptively spacious policy discourse. In T. Ryberg, C. Sinclair, S. Bayne, & M. de Laat (Eds.), *Research, boundaries, and policy in networked learning* (pp. 23–40). Springer. https://doi.org/10.1007/978-3-319-31130-2_2.

Ferreday, D., & Hodgson, V. (2008, May). The tyranny of participation and collaboration in networked learning. *In Proceedings of the 6th International Conference on Networked Learning* (pp. 640–647).

Jones, C., Asensio, M., Goodyear, G., Hodgson, V., & Steeples, C. (2001). *Final report on the field studies. Networked learning in higher education project (JISC/CALT).* Lancaster: CSALT (The Centre for Studies in Advanced Learning Technologies), Lancaster University.

Jones, C. (2015). *Networked learning – an educational paradigm for the age of digital networks.* Berlin: Springer.

Fox, S. (2005). An actor-network critique of community in higher education: Implications for networked learning. *Studies in Higher Education, 30*(1), 95–110.

Gallagher, M. S., Lamb, J., & Bayne, S. (2016). The sonic spaces of online, distance learners. Place-based spaces for networked learning. In L. Carvalho, P. Goodyear, & M. de Laat (Eds.), *Place-based spaces for networked learning* (pp. 87–99). Sydney: Routledge.

Goodyear, P. (2002). Psychological foundations for networked learning. In *Networked learning: Perspectives and issues* (pp. 49–75). London: Springer.

Goodyear, P., Banks, S., Hodgson, V., & McConnell, D. (Eds.). (2004). *Advances in research on networked learning.* Dordrecht: Kluwer Academic Publishers.

Goodyear, P., Carvalho, L., & De Laat, M. (Eds.). (2016a). *Place-based spaces for networked learning.* London: Routledge.

Goodyear, P., & Ellis, R. (2010). Expanding conceptions of study, context and educational design. *Rethinking learning for a digital age: How learners are shaping their own experiences,* 100–113.

Goodyear, P., Carvalho, L., & Dohn, N. B. (2016b). Artefacts and activities in the analysis of learning networks. In T. Ryberg, C. Sinclair, S. Bayne, & M. de Laat (Eds.), *Research, boundaries, and policy in networked learning* (pp. 93–110). Springer. https://doi.org/10.1007/978-3-319-31130-2_6.

Gourlay, L., & Oliver, M. (2017). Students' physical and digital sites of study: Making, marking and breaking boundaries. In L. Carvalho, P. Goodyear, & M. de Laat (Eds.), *Place-based spaces for networked learning* (pp. 73–89). Sydney: Routledge.

Granovetter, M. S. (1973). The strength of weak ties. *American Journal of Sociology, 78*(6), 1360–1380.

Hodgson, V., de Laat, M., McConnell, D., & Ryberg, T. (Eds.). (2014). *The design, experience and practice of networked learning*. New York: Springer.

Kennedy, G. E., Judd, T. S., Churchward, A., Gray, K., & Krause, K. L. (2008). First year students' experiences with technology: Are they really digital natives? *Australasian Journal of Educational Technology, 24*(1), 108–122.

Prensky, M. (2001). Digital natives, digital immigrants part 1. *On the horizon, 9*(5), 1–6.

Roberts, J. (2006). Limits to communities of practice. *Journal of Management Studies, 43*(3), 623–639.

Ryberg, T., Sinclair, C., Bayne, S., & de Laat, M. (Eds.). (2016). *Research, boundaries, and policy in networked learning*. London: Springer.

Vrieling, E., Van den Beemt, A., & De Laat, M. F. (2016). What's in a name: Dimensions of social learning in teacher groups. *Teachers and Teaching: Theory and Practice, 22*(3), 273–292.

Wenger, E. (1998). *Communities of practice – learning, meaning, and identity*. New York: Cambridge University Press.

Wenger, E. (2004). Learning for a small planet – a research agenda. Retrieved from http://learninghistories.net/documents/learning%20for%20a%20small%20planet.pdf

Wenger, E., Trayner, B., & De Laat, M. (2011). *Promoting and assessing value creation in communities and networks: A conceptual framework*. Heerlen: Ruud de Moor Centrum.

Part I
Situating Networked Learning: Looking Back – Moving Forward

Chapter 2
Traces of Cognition as a Distributed Phenomenon in Networked Learning

Gale Parchoma

Abstract In this chapter, I begin with historical and ongoing debates about the nature of cognition in relation to critical and humanistic traditions underpinning networked learning theory and practice. In this context, knowledge is not perceived a transmissible property that can be moved across a network from one person to another; rather, knowledge is viewed as emergent. I go on to trace points in the past decade where networked learning understandings of cognition have come to include sociomaterial perspectives that acknowledge the agencies of both human and non-human actors in knowledge emergence. In the following section on the conceptualizations of the human mind, I critically examine five contemporary perspectives: neuropsychological, environmentalist, phenomenological, situated sociocultural account, and mentalist. From a relational view, each of these perspectives can accommodate the proposition of cognition as a distributed phenomenon without becoming caught in the dualism of abstract mind and concrete material social practice. I conclude the chapter with positing distributed cognition as a unifying theoretical concept underpinning the political, ontological, and epistemological aspects of networked learning.

Introduction

Over the past ten conferences and three earlier books in this series, networked learning theorist-practitioners have set their work apart from the broader comparable fields of educational technology, learning sciences, computer-supported collaborative learning, and technology-enhanced learning via articulating a political-ethical stance and associated interests in "radical emancipatory and humanistic educational theories and approaches" (McConnell et al. 2012, p. 15). The practice of networked learning is marked by engagement with critical, democratic, and experiential pedagogies, underpinned by sociocultural perspectives on designing and facilitating

G. Parchoma (✉)
Curriculum Studies: Educational Technology and Design, University of Saskatchewan, Saskatoon, SK, Canada
e-mail: gale.parchoma@usask.ca

© Springer International Publishing AG, part of Springer Nature 2018
N. Bonderup Dohn et al. (eds.), *Networked Learning*, Research in Networked Learning, https://doi.org/10.1007/978-3-319-74857-3_2

technologically mediated opportunities for knowledge construction. From its out-set, networked learning theory and practice have aligned with the critical and humanistic traditions of the likes of Freire (1970), Dewey (1916), and Mead (1967), including the belief in the importance of focusing on making sense from one's own personal experiences and view of the world—or indeed one's own practice (Hodgson et al. 2012, p. 292).

The tenets of networked learning have remained quite consistent over time and primarily continue to focus on enabling technologically mediated connections "between one learner and other learners, between learners and tutors, and between a learning community and its resources" (Goodyear et al. 2004, p. 1). Embedded in the philosophical and pedagogical principles of networked learning are the notions that connectivity and dialogue are key to the learning process, but knowledge is *not a transmissible property* that can be moved across a network from one person to another. Rather, knowledge is *emergent*: a socioculturally influenced outcome of sense-making of experiences through relational dialogue and/or collaborative inter-actions (Hodgson et al. 2012). Knowledge emerges from learning processes rather than being a stable entity that is predetermined by powerful experts. This difference has long placed networked learning theory at odds with cognitivist notions of knowledge as either a transmissible entity or an attribute possessed by an individual that can be indirectly observed through performances of tasks or skills (Driscoll 2005).

Originating with Fox's (2001, 2005) contributions to highlighting the need to symmetrically analyse human and technological actors in networked learning assemblages, sociomaterialist perspectives expanded the remit of the networked learning community. Extending the work of Waltz (2006), Thompson (2012) argued that teaching and learning practices that involve Web 2.0 technologies are tangled sociomaterial alliances, wherein digital objects have the capacity to influence human interactions with them. Hannon's (2014) critique of the processes involved in adopting institutional-level learning technologies focused attention on how "organisational practices are entangled and inseparable from materials" (p. 68). While these move away from conceptualizing agency, influence, and alliance as uniquely human capabilities could have resulted in a schism within the networked learning community—a departure from the community's humanist beginnings—the maintenance of a critical, relational perspective and political-ethical imperative lim-ited this possibility. Space opened to theorize the materials—the technologies we use (Oliver 2013)—within our understanding of teaching and learning practices and in relation to broader societal trends and concerns (Jones 2015). As this sociomate-rial space opened, networked learning discourses became even more distinct from cognitivist discourses that situate agency as an outcome of cognitive change [the development of new actionable knowledge] within the constraints of an individual's brain (Damasio 2012), mind (Bereiter 1991; Driscoll 2005), or consciousness (Ohlsson 2011). Rather, networked learning theorists have in the past worked and continue to work towards transcending "the dualism between abstract mind and concrete material social practice" (Hodgson et al. 2014, p. 3). This boundary-crossing work acknowledges the value of considering differing perspectives on how design and teaching practices can attempt to inscribe or at least influence connections and relationships among learners, tutors, and materials. Learners' emergent activities, which in formal learning networks are guided by designed tasks, explicit goals, and tutor facilitation (Goodyear et al. 2016), become temporal, embodied, socioculturally situated sites for cognition.

Jones (2015) contended that learning was "too slippery and complex as a term" for there to be one grand theory of learning but went on to argue that networked learning tends to focus on "a broadly social approach" that includes accounts of individual experiences in relation to the social and material contexts in which they learn (p. 67). This relational approach sheds light upon and can bridge ontological debates about the sites of learning between what Alexander and Booth (2008) have described as individualistic and social orientations. Conole (2010) argued that the individualist orientation is rooted a world view where learning occurs *in here* [within an individual mind] and the social orientation that is rooted in a view where learning occurs *out there* [in relation to a socio-technological context]. A relational stance provides boundary-crossing opportunities in that it accommodates space for critically examining relationships among conceptualizations of the human mind and body, material and social environments, and learning and cognition.

Decoding Cognition Through Varied Conceptualizations of the Human Mind

Neuropsychological conceptualizations of the human mind define cognition as a series of brain-based processes, embedded in neural connections that dynamically change over time in response to sensory information from the environment and result in both changes in the architecture of the brain and "a range of phenomenon that underpin learning and change" (Markauskaite and Goodyear 2017, p. 129). Ohlsson (2011) rejects the neuropsychological conceptualization of cognition on the basis that "a description of human cognition at the level of individual brain cells" is "impractical" because of "its overwhelming complexity" (p. 26). Markauskaite and Goodyear reject the notion of cognition as a result physiological processes "created by a modular mind" (p. 135) and position neuropsychological understandings of cognitions as emerging from interactions across brain systems. By positioning neuropsychological cognitions as emergent and entangled in physiological interactions, Markauskaite and Goodyear open space for considering an act of cognition as inclusive of coordination, not only coordination within an individual's brain-based activities but also coordinations that implicate others, events, and material and social environments. This broader set of coordinations allow for room for considering emergent cognitions as being distributed.

Environmentalist conceptualizations of human behaviour shift our attention towards finding evidence of cognitions in relationships between the body and the environment (Ohlsson 2011; Markauskaite and Goodyear 2017). Behaviouralist explanations of the mind ask us to perceive cause-effect chains of environmental stimuli and embodied responses (Skinner 1938), which in an educational context account for learning as a "direct reaction to the task set before a learner" (Vygotsky 1978, p. 39). Thus, behaviouralist accounts of the capacities of the mind to learn *black-box* cognitions (Fenwick and Richards 2010) by making them unknowable processes that are temporally situated between stimuli and responses. Gibson's (1979) more complex, ecological understanding of relationships between perception and action are captured in the concept of an affordance. Gibson argued that an affordance "is equally a fact of the environment and a fact of behaviour. It is both physical and psychical, yet, neither. An affordance points both ways, to the environment and to the observer" (Gibson 1979, p. 129). While Oliver (2005) argued that this *neither/nor, but both* conceptualization of an affordance could not account for Gibson's "essentialist position" of a direct linkage between perception and action rendered the term, affordance, as "speculative rather than analytic" (p. 403), so of little or no utility for research. However, Suthers (2006), Bonderup Dohn (2009), Parchoma (2014), and Jones (2015) have argued that the strength of Gibsonian affordances is their capacity to describe relationships between perception and action as arising from interactions. From an ecological perspective, cognitions are situated within emergent distributed interactions.

Phenomenological conceptualizations of the human mind are no more than "descriptions of subjective experience[s]" (Ohlsson 2011, p. 25); however, these descriptions are useful in that they provide insights into cognitive processes through individuals' conscious interpretations of their experiences through articulations and actions. Markauskaite and Goodyear (2017) contend that this dependency on consciousness to understand cognition is limited because consciousness alone cannot account for all of human thought, behaviour, and emotion because we experience more than we can express. Therefore, from a phenomenological perspective, evidence of an individual's cognitions can only be indirectly accessed through his or her discursive and actionable reifications of experiences of the world and the associated affects of the experienced world on an individual (Marton and Pang 2008). Marton and Pang assert that experiences of the world and associated affects of the experienced world on an individual are paired perspectives that shed light on a single phenomenon. Interrelationships between experiences and affects align well with Markauskaite and Goodyear's notion of phenomenological cognitions as instances of dynamic couplings that bring together pieces of knowledge and additional resources into interactions that can lead to learning. Where a phenomenological definition of cognition may not be able to account for all aspects of an individual's experiences and their associated affects on thoughts or actions that can result in learning, a phenomenological definition of cognition aligns well with the intent of networked learning to highlight "the importance of focusing on making sense from one's own personal experiences and view of the world" (Hodgson et al. 2012, p. 292) as a central tenet of practice. Because the sense-making process occurs within interactions among pieces of knowledge and additional resources, cognition needs to be distributed.

Situated sociocultural accounts of the human behaviour focus on searching for patterns or processes (Markauskaite and Goodyear 2017) that emerge from individuals' interactions with the "social environment or the surrounding culture" (Ohlsson 2011, p. 27). These linkages between learning and culture reach back into the early twentieth century, where two psychologists, Wilhelm Wundt and Hugo Münsterberg, argued that an individual human mind was inseparable from its cultural linguistic context. Wundt claimed "individual consciousness is wholly incapable of giving us a history of the development of human thought, for it is conditioned by an earlier history concerning which it cannot of itself give us any knowledge" (Wundt 1921, p. 3). Comparably, Münsterberg (1914) focused attention on interrelationships across cognitions within the individual mind, sensory functions of the human body, and sociomaterial artefacts and the institutions within which humans engage. He posited that the notion of an individual mind was an "artificially isolated fragment" in the larger picture of the "social mind" (pp. 265–267), claiming:

> There is a "synapsis" between any two brain neurons, and the same "synapsis" between any two social neurons. But in all communication and intercourse the individual transmits by his motor apparatus, his muscles, and the next receives by his sensory apparatus, his sense organs.... The brain cells cause the contraction of the muscles in the arms or fingers, and these contracted muscles awake new sensations in the brain cells. The interplay of the mental states demands this constant reference to the products outside of the brain. (pp. 267–268)

Münsterberg went on to argue that books, newspaper articles, and personal letters act as intermediators of human communications and understandings of chronicled events and ideas. These artefacts of previous human cognitions play an active role in influencing contemporary individual cognitions, public discourses, as well as future ideas and social actions.

> Every objectified expression becomes a social short cut. As any psychophysical explanation of the individual mental life must give attention to those unconscious brain processes, the explanation of the social mind necessarily involves the objectified records of experience and suggestions, which intermediate between individuals. They are an organic part of the psychophysical mechanism of the social group. (Münsterberg 1914, p. 268)

Münsterberg's (1914) conceptualized cognition as a distributed phenomenon not only embodied and socioculturally situated but also interconnected with practices. His explanation of social institutions (e.g., administrative, legal, educational, religious, economic, and technical) is based on a relational view, where social groups cooperate to construct institutions. Any change in the social practices within these institutions has consequences for both individuals and the social group. Across Münsterberg's argument, he shifts foci on phenomena of analysis from the physical workings of the individual brain; to the embodied nature of understanding; to the notion of social neurons; to roles of artefacts of human communications, actions, and decisions in the development of the social mind; and finally to institutional practices. However, his thesis that each of these phenomena is inherently interconnected and consequential suggests an early socio-psychological endeavour to overcome the dualism of abstract mind and sociomaterial practice that aligns with current networked learning conceptualizations of distributed cognition. See, for example, Dohn's (2014) explication of distributed cognition where:

> Knowledge is characterised as tacit, situated, context-dependent, embodied doing, grounded in immediate recognition of and response pairing to the situation's gestalt. Thinking and communicating are phenomena of this doing and as such take their meaning in part from the situation in which they arise. (p. 36)

While Münsterberg's (1914) perspective on cognition differed in many respects from Vygotsky's *Mind in Society* (1978), parallels can be drawn. There is an alignment between Vygotsky's notion of distributed cognition as a "unity of perception, speech, and action" (p. 26), within activities mediated by tools and others in the social and physical environment and Münsterberg's conceptualization of distributed cognition as physically, socially, and artefact-mediated. For example, just as Münsterberg observed labourers as they engaged in learning manual tasks for the influences of "colors of the surroundings", the "character of the signals, by the position during work, by the filling of the pauses, by pleasant or unpleasant distractions, by continuity or interruption" (p. 425), Vygotsky observed children's approaches in solving "practical tasks" by "applying as tools those objects that lie near at hand" and also "searching for and preparing such stimuli as can be useful in the solution of the task, and planning future actions" (p. 26). Both Münsterberg and Vygotsky theorized learning as embodied, social, situated, and materially mediated, in ways that align well with Bonderup Dohn's (2014) notion of "embodied doing" (p. 36) and Cole and Engeström's (1993) cultural-historical conceptualization of "cognition as distributed phenomenon" (p. 1).

In a similar vein, Dewey (1910) attributed designed objects and tools with the capacity to support reflective thought and plan systematic actions. For example, Dewey argued, "We deliberately erect monuments and memorials, lest we forget", and we "deliberately institute, in the advance of the happening of the various contingencies and emergencies of life, devices for detecting their approach and registering their nature" (1910, p. 15) in order to minimize negative impacts. He defined learning as "of, by, and for" experience (p. 249) and forwarded the premise that we live in a world of persons and things that are linked to or are artefacts of previous human experiences; therefore, a new experience cannot be "treated as if it were something which goes on exclusively in an individual's mind and body" (1938, p. 34). The influences of our physical and social surroundings "contribute to experiences that are more worthwhile" (p. 35). Therefore, Dewey argued that teachers should approach learners with an intimate acquaintance with the "conditions of the local community, physical, historical, economic, occupational, etc." (p. 36) and approach teaching and learning as a collaborative, democratic, activity-based, and sociomaterial set of practices. As the Deweyian accounts of experiences traverse individual thoughts, actions, and social and material environments, cognition is equally distributed.

Finally, from a mentalist perspective, the human mind is conceptualized as a system (Markauskaite and Goodyear 2017) that "cannot be reduced to conscious experience, the brain, the material environment or sociocultural factors" (Ohlsson

2011, p. 28). Rather, the mind is made up of mental representations and operates as central control mechanism capable of abstraction, goal setting, and imagination. Within Ohlsson's account of mentalism, cognitions become system-bound functions and processes that enable thoughts, decision-making, and action. However, as Barsalou et al. (2007) have argued, cognition cannot be fully understood as limited to a collection of processes operating within a closed system because cognitive processes must coordinate with other internal (embodied) and external (sociocultural and environmental) systems. Knowledge construction is embedded in and distributed across interacting real-time processes that not only occur in the individual mind but also extend beyond it. Cognitions are therefore distributed among interacting individual, sociocultural, and environmental systems.

Ohlsson (2011) and Markauskaite and Goodyear (2017) agreed that neuropsychological, environmentalist, phenomenological, situated sociocultural, mentalist perspectives differ on the nature of the human mind and behaviour that results in potentially contrasting accounts of the phenomenon of cognition. Where Ohlsson's argument concludes with favouring the mentalist perspective, Markauskaite and Goodyear (2017) contend that a thorough understanding of the human mind requires encompassing all five perspectives, perceiving them as complementary insights into the complexities of knowledge construction and action. From a relational view, each of the five perspectives can also accommodate the proposition of cognition as a distributed phenomenon without becoming caught in the dualism of abstract mind and concrete material social practice.

Problematizing Computational Cognitivist Influences on E-Learning in Relation to Networked Learning Scholarship

While networked learning scholarship includes some individualistic orientations to understanding cognition, it has clearly rejected the notions of the isolated individual mind (Ryberg et al. 2012) and instructivist approaches to design and teaching (Jones, 2015). However, the broader field of e-learning, computational cognitivist models of learning have contributed to isolated individualist projects, such as personal learning environments (Hodgson et al. 2012), and instructivist (highly structured, sequenced, and prescriptive) approaches to the design of learning resources.

Computational cognitivist models of learning that evoke the metaphor of a computer as a representation mind and explain cognitive processes as "information processing … composed of the basic elements: sensory receptors, perception, short-term and long-term memory" (Tennyson and Rasch 1988, p. 369) have for decades portrayed the individual mind as isolated and mechanistic. Over that time computationally oriented theorists have claimed a clearer understanding of cognitive processes can lead to "instructional strategies that can directly improve" learning (Tennyson and Rasch, p. 370). For example, Clark and Paivio (1991) hypothesized that within the structure of the brain there are separate verbal and information subsystems. Mayer and Anderson's multiple representation principle (Mayer and Anderson 1992) posited that technology-enhanced learning designs can be made more effective through simultaneous presentations of audio and visual representations of information to ensure efficient short-term memory processing and long-term memory storage. However, the split-attention effect (Mayer and Moreno 1998) can tax short-term memory; therefore, "using the audio system for verbal information and the visual system for imagery is a more efficient division of labour" (p. 4).

Time allocations for specific tasks within instructional settings (managing the display and order of declarative, procedural, and conceptual information, linking coding and decoding tasks, etc.) influence the effectiveness and efficiency of the "cognitive system" (Tennyson and Rasch 1988, p. 373). An instance of a time concern that can be "managed" via design is that "cognitive load may be increased if technology skills and specific subject content area concepts are learned concurrently" (van Merrienboer et al. 2003, p. 95); therefore, learning tasks need to be purposefully sequenced (Morrision and Anglin 2005). An underpinning assumption of the computational cognitivist design project has been to specify design procedures and skills, control variables, inscribe foci of attention, and structure all tasks with precision in order to ensure effective learning becomes joint properties of well-designed resources and prescribed use.

In response to international e-learning initiatives to standardize distribution of reusable digital learning resources, Koper and Olivier (2004) critiqued the emphasis on IEEE and LOM specifications and argued that these "solutions" were based on the metaphor of learning as knowledge transmission from expert to novice via technology. Koper and Olivier noted a disregard of contextual considerations and theory-based pedagogical practices. Conole (2006) forwarded this inquiry by rejecting the notion of focusing the "design of learning at the resource level" (p. 3) and refocusing learning design scholarship and practice on the activities in which learners are asked to engage. Conole highlighted six networked learning design foci: (1) learning contexts; (2) teaching and learning approaches; (3) tasks to be undertaken; (4) technological tools and digital resources; (5) expectations for interactions among all involved, including negotiated roles; and, importantly, (6) the influence of assessment practices on sustainability of networked learning communities. This shift in focus from the e-learning research focus on resource level to the networked learning focus on the activity level was examined further in Zenios and Goodyear's (2008) discussion of researching epistemic activities in networked knowledge construction. Zenios and Goodyear put forwards the argument that inquiries into collaborative learning can benefit from acknowledgement that learning is:

> By no means and individual process separated from the context of the lived experience of participation in the world. The relations between members of the community are brought into perspective as they are interconnected with the practices of the community. (p. 608)

Conole's (2006) rejection of the proposition that learning opportunities can be designed at the resource level and her refocusing design scholarship on future learners' potential experiences of the tasks they are asked to undertake, expectations for interactions, provision of suitable technological tools and materials to support emergent activities and knowledge, and the influence of assessment practices on sustainability provide clear distinctions between the central concerns of learning design and instructional design principles, such as Gagné's (1965, 1992) *nine events of instruction* or Merrill's *first principles of instruction* (2002), derived from the Piagetian notion of cognitions as predictable events that occur within an individual's mind as a result of successfully completing expertly designed tasks with predetermined learning outcomes. Conole's focus on centrality of negotiation and collaboration across a sociomaterial network leave traces of conceptualizing cognition as a distributed phenomenon.

Tracing Distributed Cognition in Networked Learning Design and Facilitation

Dirckinck-Holmfeld et al. (2012) made a call for closer examinations of how networked learning environments can be designed and shaped in different ways, depending on the underlying values of and views of human cognition, learning, formation, the technology, and pedagogy. At one extreme, they can be designed as constellations of technologies, where the individuals are free to form and control their learning processes by connecting to others for inspiration and resources and used across various levels of aggregation in the group, the network and the collective, while at the other extreme, networked learning environments can be designed as platforms for greater levels of mutual engagements and dedication, critical reflection, emancipatory formation, and empowerments (p. 300).

This focus on theoretically informed and ethically enacted learning designs is again emphasized by Hodgson et al. (2014), who remind us of the centrality of the "critical and humanistic traditions" (p. 2). Keeping these traditions at the fore requires designers and facilitators to be empathetic, to value imagined future learners and current learners as persons (Gourlay and Oliver 2016), and to see difference as an opportunity for learning rather than a quality in need of accommodation (Reynolds et al. 2004). Hodgson et al. (2014) highlight the inevitable messiness and unpredictability of designing networked learning tasks and facilitating emergent activities and the resultant needed to deal with tensions between the expected and the unexpected.

Goodyear et al. (2014) questioned "whether it is actually possible to design for someone else's learning" (p. 139). In part, they respond to their own question, in their framework for learning design, which makes a distinction between designable tasks and emergent activities. They argued that the physical setting for networked learning includes places, material and digital tools and artefacts, designed tasks, and associated divisions of labour. These physical architectures need to provide human-to-human, things-to-human, and things-to-things connections to allow activities to emerge. While these architectures may support the development of relational affordances, however well-designed they are, they will also have constraints.

Orlikowski (2000) posited the notion that designs are situated within sociotechnical systems and that people who use sociotechnical systems can and do use technologies as they were designed; they also can and do circumvent inscribed ways of using the technologies—either ignoring certain properties of the technology, working around them, or inventing new ones that may go beyond or even contradict designers' expectations and inscriptions (p. 407).

Goodyear et al. (2014) referred to these unanticipated, sometimes purposeful, creative emergent activities and sometimes distractive, unhelpful emergent activities as slippages: movements away from designers' expectations of pathways that lead to constructing and accomplishing shared goals. These sociomaterial pathways are equally implicated in the "subjective mind and physical body in activity in the world" (Goodyear et al. p. 141), where humans and materials are mutually constitutive and where "significance is the ever-changing result of the dynamic co-constitution of the entities" (p. 142). Goodyear, Carvalo, and Dohn's explication of significance (meaning-making) as a co-constitutive emergence of cognitions from interactions among designed tasks as pathways that can lead to reciprocal, collaborative meaning-making activities evokes and challenges Ingold's (2011) account of individual *wayfaring*.

Wayfaring is Ingold's metaphor for an individual's choices to follow an existing pathway, diverge from it, and/or forge a new pathway that leads towards a personal goal, and as a result of each choice, both pathways and the surrounding environment are changed. Ingold's notion of wayfaring presents us with the proposition that individual choices to comply with a designed pathway, find an alternative route, or create new a pathway explain how "lives are lived, skills developed, observations made and understandings grown" (2011, p. 12). Where Ingold's description of agency as individualistic instances of conforming to, diverging from designed pathways to learning, and/or creating new pathways that simultaneously change both the learner and the environment, Goodyear et al. (2014) conceptualization of distributed agency as a collaborative endeavour to at once find significance through emergent activities in a networked learning assemblage and, in the process, change the assemblage through dialogue and contribution of additional material resources transforms Ingold's solitary form of wayfaring into a community journey. In networked learning, wayfaring is working with distributed cognitions.

Tracing Distributed Cognition in Networked Learning Communities

For two decades, delegates of networked learning conferences have been differentiating networked learning praxis from broader e-learning research via shared interests in participatory pedagogies, collaborative assessment practices, and a relational view of virtual learning communities. McConnell (1998) emphasized "collaboration as the major form of social relationship within a learning context" and the role of technologies as "networking people and resources" into "learning communities" whose members share "resources, knowledge, expertise, and responsibility through reciprocal collaborative learning" (p. v.ii). This situated sociocultural perspective emphasizes the role of intersubjectivity in knowledge construction and clearly distributes opportunities for collaborative knowledge construction across a sociotechnical teaching and learning assemblage intended to sustain community. In this foundational model for networked learning, technologies were primarily viewed as tools for distributing resources and enabling connections (Jones 2000). However, the Networked Learning 2002 manifesto clearly positioned community as inclusive of "models of learning that are based on participation and not ones that are based on transmission" (Beaty et al. 2002, p. 6). The manifesto included expectations that "teachers and learners collaborate in the assessment process" and that learners contribute to "the development of learning resources" (Beaty et al. pp. 5–6). Learning resources were conceptualized as "both human and material" (Beaty et al. p. 8). Making connections with human and material resources for the purpose of collaboratively constructing meaning can be seen as a trace of distributed cognition in the early years of theorizing networked learning.

While shared valuing of a critical, democratic, digitally connected learning community has been pivotal in distinguishing networked learning from broader research in the field, participation and collaboration discourses have also been interrogated. Reynolds et al. (2004) critiqued three approaches to online design and assessment practices. In instrumentalist approaches to interactive learning designs, "the idea of 'community' is used as a *motivational* device", and there are "fairly normative values about how groups *should* work which are conveyed and reinforced by the reward process" (para, 4). In emancipatory approaches, technologies are perceived as "means by which hierarchical power differentials can be levelled out amongst networked individuals", but pedagogies remain primarily tutor led and/or facilitated (para, 5). In communitarian approaches, democratic principles are valued for their own sake; design and assessment decisions tend to include learner perspectives, but the darker sides of community—"coercion, conformity, marginalisation of minority interests" (para. 6)—tend to be ignored. Thus, Reynolds, Sclater, and Tickner posited a cosmopolitan approach to design and assessment in networked learning communities that values subcommunities and where there is emphasis on learning *from* difference. The process of learning from difference has been described as a *third space* (Bhabha 2004), "a space for the coexistence of distinct narratives" (Ikas and Wagner 2009, p. 2), where there is room to negotiate shared meanings and work towards respectfully reconciling differing positionalities without evoking power relationships or including a requirement of consensus. Communications in the third space are made up of intersubjectivities developed from distributed cognitions.

Ryberg et al. (2012) call for setting aside "the phenomenon of the individual mind" (p. 47), in favour of conceptualizing learning as a collaborative endeavour that contributes to community formations that focus on social engagement, shared cognitive responsibility, and interactional connections that lead to critical reflections on experiences, provides admittance to a distributed conceptualization of cognition in networked learning. Working from a sociomaterial perspective on practices and learning, Fenwick (2012) emphasized the agencies of technologies in distributing capacities across networks. Oliver (2012) posited the notion of technology as practice and highlighted the efficacy of acknowledging its "socially constructed character" (p. 441). He suggested that technology be understood in a "relational way—as something in flux, its meaning determined in important ways by the contexts and manner of its use" (p. 442), in order to gain insights into "how people undertake and coordinate sociomaterial practices" (p. 443). This positioning of teaching and learning as sociomaterial practice highlights interactions among human and material agencies, distributes sites of learning, surfaces issues of power, and reiterates the need for awareness of underlying values enacted in the design in technological environments. As agential contributors to human capacities to connect, to engage in, and in turn, be changed by emergent social practices, technologies become not quite so silent partners of a networked learning community. They co-constitute community activity through what they permit and what they prohibit. Their influences become entangled in the community's cognitions.

Conclusion

Underlying democratic values and sociomaterial, relational views of learning experiences set networked learning apart from broader educational technology scholarship. A key characteristic of this difference has long been the rejection of the notion of the individual, isolated mind as a distinct system that produces and contains the sum of a person's cognitions. The epistemology of networked learning focuses on moving beyond dualist notions of abstract mind and concrete social practice. The ontology of networked learning is based upon a view of the world where learning and teaching are sociomaterial assemblages that are held together by commitments to criticality, reciprocity, ongoing negotiation, respect for difference, and fostering emergent knowledge. Within this political, epistemological, ontological context, cognitions are distributed across coordinations, introspections, discourses, materials, communities, institutions, intentions, and practices. Cognitions in networked learning are *neither in here nor out there: they are both*.

References

Alexander, S., & Booth, S. (2008). Methodologies for researching the learning in networked learning: Introduction. Retrieved from: http://www.networkedlearningconference.org.uk/past/nlc2008/abstracts/PDFs/AlexanderIntro_443-444.pdf

Barsalou, L. W., Breazeal, C., & Smith, L. (2007). Cognition as coordinated non-cognition. *Cognitive Processing, 8*(2), 79–91.

Beaty, L., Hodgson, V., Mann, S., & McConnell, D. (2002). Understanding the implications of networked learning for higher education. Retrieved from: http://csalt.lancs.ac.uk/esrc/manifesto.pdf

Bereiter, C. (1991). Implications of connectionism for thinking about rules. *Educational Researcher, 20*(3), 10–16.

Bhabha, H. K. (2004). *The location of culture*. London: Routledge.

Bonderup Dohn, N. (2009). Affordances revisited: Articulating a Merleau-Pontian view. *International Journal of Computer Supported Collaborative Learning, 4*(2), 151–170.

Bonderup Dohn, N. (2014). Implications for networked learning of the 'practice' side of social practice theories: A tacit-knowledge perspective. In V. Hodgson, M. de Latt, D. McConnell, & T. Ryberg (Eds.), *The design, experience and practice of networked learning* (pp. 29–50). New York: Springer.

Clark, J. M., & Paivio, A. (1991). Dual coding theory and education. *Educational Psychology and Instruction, 3*, 149–170.

Cole, M., & Engestrom, Y. (1993). A cultural-historical approach to distributed cognition. In G. Salomon (Ed.), *Distributed cognitions: Psychological and educational considerations* (pp. 1–46). New York: Cambridge University Press.

Conole, G. (2006). The role of 'mediating forms of representation' in learning design. Retrieved from http://www.networkedlearningconference.org.uk/past/nlc2006/abstracts/pdfs/P32%20 Conole.pdf

Conole, G. (2010). *Theory and methodology in networked learning*. London: The Open University.

Damasio, A. R. (2012). *Self comes to mind: Constructing the conscious brain*. New York: Vintage Books.

Dewey, J. (1910). *How we think*. Boston: D. C. Heath & Co..

Dewey, J. (1916). *Democracy and Education*. New York: Macmillan.

Dewey, J. (1938). *Education and experience*. West Lafayette: Kappa Delta Pi.

Dirckinck-Holmfeld, L., Hodgson, V., & McConnell, D. (2012). The theory, practice and pedagogy of networked learning. In L. Dirckinck-Holmfeld, V. Hodgson, & D. McConnell (Eds.), *Exploring the theory, pedagogy and practice of networked learning* (pp. 290–304). New York: Springer.

Driscoll, M. P. (2005). *Psychology of learning for instruction* (3rd ed.). Boston: Allyn and Bacon.

Fenwick, T. (2012). *Learning sustainability*. Paper presented at the Eighth International Conference on Networked Learning Maastricht, The Netherlands. http://www.lancaster.ac.uk/fss/organisations/netlc/past/nlc2012/abstracts/pdf/Fenwick_Slides.pdf

Fenwick, T., & Edwards, R. (2010). *Actor-network theory in education*. London: Routledge.

Fox, S. (2001). Studying networked learning: Some implications from socially situated learning theory and actor-network theory. In C. Steeples & C. Jones (Eds.), *Networked learning: Perspectives and issues* (pp. 77–92). London: Springer.

Fox, S. (2005). An actor-network critique of community in higher education: Implications for networked learning. *Studies in Higher Education, 30*(1), 95–110.

Freire, P. (1970). *Pedagogy of the Oppressed*. New York: Continuum.

Gagné, R. M. (1965). *The conditions of learning and theory of instruction* (1st ed.). New York: Holt, Rinehart & Winston.

Gagné, R., Briggs, L., & Wager, W. (1992). *Principles of instructional design* (4th ed.). Fort Worth: HBJ College Publishers.

Gibson, J. J. (1979). *The ecological approach to visual perception of experimental psychology*. Hillsdale: Lawrence Erlbaum.

Goodyear, P., Banks, S., Hodgson, V., & McConnell, D. (2004). Research on networked learning: An overview. In P. Goodyear, S. Banks, V. Hodgson, & D. McConnell (Eds.), *Advances in research on networked learning*. Dordrecht: Kluwer.

Goodyear, P., Carvalho, L., & Bonderup Dohn, N. (2014). *Design for networked learning: Framing relations between participants' activities and the physical setting*. Paper presented at the Ninth International Conference on Networked Learning Edinburgh, UK.

Goodyear, P., Carvalho, L., & Bonderup Dohn, N. (2016). Artefacts and activities in the analysis of learning networks. In T. Ryberg, C. Sinclair, S. Bayne, & M. de Latt (Eds.), *Research, boundaries and policy in networked learning* (pp. 93–110). New York: Springer.

Gourlay, L., & Oliver, M. (2016). It is not all about the learner: Reframing students' digital literacy as sociomaterial practice. In T. Ryberg, C. Sinclair, S. Bayne, & M. de Latt (Eds.), *Research, boundaries and policy in networked learning* (pp. 93–110). New York: Springer.

Hannon, J. (2014). Making the right connections: Implementing objects of practices in a network for learning. In V. Hodgson, M. de Latt, D. McConnell, & T. Ryberg (Eds.), *The design, experience and practice of networked learning* (pp. 67–86). New York: Springer.

Hodgson, V., McConnell, D., & Dirckinck-Holmfeld, L. (2012). The theory, practice and pedagogy of networked learning. In L. Dirckinck-Holmfeld, V. Hodgson, & D. McConnell (Eds.), *Exploring the theory, pedagogy, and practice of networked learning* (pp. 291–306). New York: Springer.

Hodgson, V., de Latt, M., McConnell, D., & Ryberg, T. (2014). Researching design, experience and practice of networked learning: An overview. In V. Hodgson, M. de Latt, D. McConnell, & T. Ryberg (Eds.), *The design, experience and practice of networked learning* (pp. 1–28). New York: Springer.

Ikas, K., & Wagner, G. (2009). Introduction. In K. Ikas & G. Wagner (Eds.), *Communicating in the third space* (pp. 1–10). New York: Taylor & Francis.

Ingold, T. (2011). Prologue: Anthropology comes to life. In *Being alive: Essays on movement, knowledge and description* (pp. 3–14). Abington: Routledge.

Jones, C. (2000). Understanding students' experiences of collaborative networked learning. Retrieved from http://www.networkedlearningconference.org.uk/past/nlc2000/Proceedings/Jones_152-158.pdf

Jones, C. (2015). *Networked learning: An educational paradigm for the age of digital networks*. Cham Heidelburg: Springer.

Koper, R., & Olivier, B. (2004). Representing the learning design of units of learning. *Educational Technology & Society, 7*(3), 97–111.

Markauskaite, L., & Goodyear, P. (2017). *Epistemic fluency and professional education: Innovation, knowledgeable action, and actionable knowledge*. Dordreacht: Springer Science + Business Media.

Marton, F., & Pang, M. F. (2008). The idea of phenomenography and the pedagogy of conceptual change. In S. Vosinadou (Ed.), *International handbook of research on conceptual change* (pp. 533–599). New York: Routledge.

Mayer, R. E., & Anderson, R. B. (1992). The instructive animation: Helping students build connections between words and pictures in multimedia learning. *Journal of Educational Psychology, 84*, 444–452.

Mayer, R. E., & Moreno, R. (1998). A split-attention effect in multimedia learning: Evidence for dual processing systems in working memory. *Journal of Educational Psychology, 90*, 312–320.

McConnell, D. (1998). Developing networked learning professionals: A critical perspective. Retrieved from http://www.networkedlearningconference.org.uk/past/nlc1998/Proceedings/Keynote1.pdf

McConnell, D., Hodgson, V., & Dirckinck-Holmfeld, L. (2012). Networked learning: A brief history and new trends. In L. Dirckinck-Holmfeld, V. Hodgson, & D. McConnell (Eds.), *Exploring the theory, pedagogy, and practice of networked learning* (pp. 3–26). New York: Springer.

Mead, G. H. (1967). Mind, self and society: From the standpoint of a social behaviorist. Chicago: University of Chicago Press.

Merrill, M. D. (2002). First principles of instruction. *Educational Technology Research and Development, 50*(3), 43–59.

Morrision, G. R., & Anglin, G. J. (2005). Research on cognitive load theory. *Application to e-learning Educational Technology Research and Development, 53*(3), 94–104.

Münsterberg, H. (1914). *Psychology, general and applied*. New York: Appleton.

Ohlsson, S. (2011). *Deep learning: How the mind overrides experience*. Cambridge: Cambridge University Press.

Oliver, M. (2005). The Problem with Affordance. *E-Learning and Digital Media, 2*(4), 402–413.

Oliver, M. (2012). Learning with technology as coordinated sociomaterial practice: Digital literacies as a site of praxiological study. Retrieved from: http://www.lancaster.ac.uk/fss/organisations/netlc/past/nlc2012/abstracts/pdf/oliver.pdf

Oliver, M. (2013). Learning technology: Theorizing the tools we study. *British Journal of Educational Technology, 44*(1), 31–43.

Orlikowski, W. J. (2000). Using technology and constituting structures: A practice lens for studying technology in organizations. *Organization Science, 11*(4), 404–428.

Parchoma, G. (2014). The contested ontology of affordances: Implications for researching technological affordances. *Computers in Human Behavior, 37*, 360–368.

Reynolds, M., Sclater, M., & Tickner, S. (2004). A critique of participative discourses adopted in networked learning. Retrieved from: http://www.networkedlearningconference.org.uk/past/nlc2004/proceedings/symposia/symposium10/reynolds_et_al.htm

Ryberg, T., Buus, L., & Georgsen, M. (2012). Differences in understanding of networked learning theory: Connectivity or collaboration? In L. Dirckinck-Holmfeld, V. Hodgson, & D. McConnell (Eds.), *Exploring the theory, pedagogy, and practice of networked learning* (pp. 43–58). New York: Springer.

Skinner, B. F. (1938). *The behaviour of organisms: An experimental analysis*. New York: Appleton-Century.

Suthers, D. D. (2006). Technology affordances for intersubjective meaning making: A research agenda for CSCL. *International Journal of Computer-Supported Collaborative Learning, 1*(3), 315–337.

Tennyson, R. D., & Rasch, M. (1988). Linking cognitive learning theory to instructional prescriptions. *Instructional Science, 17*(4), 369–385.

Thompson, T. L. (2012). Who's taming who? Tensions between people and technologies in cyberspace communities. In L. Dirckinck-Holmfeld, V. Hodgson, & D. McConnell (Eds.), *Exploring the theory, pedagogy, and practice of networked learning* (pp. 157–172). New York: Springer.

van Merrienboer, J. J. G., Kirschner, P., & Kester, L. (2003). Taking a load off a leaner's mind: Instructional design for complex learning. *Educational Psychologist, 38*, 5–13.

Vygotsky, L. S. (1978). *Mind in society*. Cambridge: Harvard University Press.

Waltz, S. B. (2006). Nonhumans unbound: Actor-network theory and the reconsideration of "things" in educational foundations. *Educational Foundations, 20*(3/4), 51–68.

Wundt, W. (1921). *Elements of folk psychology*. London: Allen & Unwin.

Zenios, M., & Goodyear, P. (2008). Where is the learning in networked knowledge construction. Retrieved from http://www.networkedlearningconference.org.uk/past/nlc2008/abstracts/PDFs/Zenios_607-615.pdf

Chapter 3
Experience and Networked Learning

Chris Jones

Abstract This chapter reviews the way experience has been understood, and the research agendas associated with that understanding, in networked learning. In the contemporary context the student 'experience' is part of common speech and often associated with a consumerist discourse, especially in the UK and USA. The widespread use of digital and networked technologies in education has also given rise to a decentring of the subject and an identification of actors in network settings as hybrids of humans and machines (including software and code in this category) or including machines and objects as actors within a network. With a decentred subject does it still make sense to understand learning in terms of the subject's personal experience anymore?

This chapter explores these debates in the context of current educational discourse and in relation to prior research and theory in networked learning. Experience has a long history associated with phenomenological research and the related but distinct approach of phenomenography. It is related to central issues for education and learning, in particular the place of the 'individual' cognising subject. Experience can be thought of as either the essential distinguishing component of the individual human subject, or experience can be understood as the subjective component of one kind of element in a wider assemblage of humans and machines. In the later understanding of experience in assemblages human experience does not separate the human actor from other actors in a network and they are understood symmetrically.

It is a long-standing position that the human sciences have a different relationship to their objects of study than natural sciences because the human sciences can have access to interior accounts from the 'objects' they observe and because human subjects can behave in ways that are not predicable, replicable, and which depend on an active construction of experience in the world. For networked learning the position and role of the human subject is a central concern and human-human interaction has always been considered essential. This chapter reasserts the need for a proper understanding of experience and explores the place of the human subject in the developing research agendas found in networked learning.

C. Jones (✉)
School of Education, Liverpool Jon Moores University, Liverpool, UK
e-mail: c.r.jones@ljmu.ac.uk

© Springer International Publishing AG, part of Springer Nature 2018   39
N. Bonderup Dohn et al. (eds.), *Networked Learning*, Research in Networked
Learning, https://doi.org/10.1007/978-3-319-74857-3_3

The question addressed in this chapter is: In what ways can networked learning think about and incorporate the idea of experience with regard to decentred persons in the entanglements forming assemblages?

Introduction

The student experience has become an accepted 'buzzword' in higher education, a fashionable term that has largely lost its original technical meaning. In many education systems across the world, universities and other higher education providers are using standard national and approved institutional surveys as a form of student feedback intended to measure the student experience (Shah et al. 2016). In an earlier paper, Shah and Richardson defined student experience as:

> [...] the learning experience of students in an institution which enriches their learning irrespective of the mode of education delivery. The experience subsumes their transition to university from school or work, engagement with staff, teaching methods, curriculum content and learning resources, assessments, technology used in learning, peers, campus life, and the value-add of their qualification after graduation. (Shah and Richardson 2016, p. 353)

It can be seen from this definition that the apparently simple 'student experience', even when carefully defined, contains several potentially discrete elements. This is not how it is widely used, especially in the more heavily marketised education systems of the USA and UK in which students are regularly referred to as 'customers' and the student experience is measured in terms of 'satisfaction'. This is not always the same in other European countries (e.g. Germany in which the states have abolished fees) although a degree of marketisation can be found in many national HE systems (Altbach 2015).

The marketisation of education and the adoption of neo-liberal forms of accountability via quasi-market mechanisms necessitate the development of processes to surface information allowing students to act as customers in choosing between institutional providers and providing evidence for government on which they can base systems of reward and punishment. This is illustrated in the introduction to a report by Universities UK which states:

> Students need information so that that they can make informed choices about where to study. Universities need information to review and innovate in their teaching and learning practices. Government and the public want to be assured that the sector delivers value to students, wider society and the economy. (Universities UK 2016, p. 2)

Universities routinely sell a vision of a lifestyle as much as they promote university as providing an education or as the strapline to my own university website put it in 2015: 'just studying for a degree' (Fig. 3.1). Universities sell themselves as a commodified service, something worth paying for, using images of smiling happy young people. Perhaps this is not surprising in England given that a typical student (on a 3-year course outside of London) might expect to graduate with around £35,000–£40,000 (42,000–48,000 euros at late 2016 exchange rates) of debt in stu-

Fig. 3.1 The student experience: LJMU website (2015). (video link: https://youtu.be/ApsOmWnjBoO)

dent loans (Bournsell 2015). This does not include interest charges which currently stand at 5.5% per annum. It is reasonable to argue that currently the experience of debt is one of the most defining aspects of the overall student experience in the UK and USA. However, the partially glossed account of student life captured as 'the student experience' ignores some of the related and negative effects of marketisation. In the English system, drop out of students, previously relatively rare, has recently increased (Havergal 2016), and there is also increasing evidence of poor mental health amongst the student population (Gani 2016). Student experiences of a university are varied and not always positive, but it is not in the interests of organisations selling a service to identify this varied set of experiences.

The student experience is part of the competition that is encouraged by league tables ranking universities in national and international hierarchies (Sabri 2011). The student experience expressed in these tables has become part of the news cycle with 'success' in surveys and league tables being widely reported. There are now several international league tables that reflect national ambitions as well as the ambitions of specific institutions. This process gives rise to a peculiar kind of policy agenda in which universities are measured against each other with only the top 10, 50 or 100 places being deemed relevant (Hazelkorn 2015). An average performance and being an average institution which offers an average experience is now judged to be unacceptable – even though this is statistically irrational. Every university has an aim to be amongst the best and provides an excellent student experience. Institutions have formal mechanisms to monitor their league table performances and adjust their institutional policies to optimise their chances of improving their rankings. This competition between institutions is part of a process of the internationalisation and commodification of learning which valorises 'the' individual student experience and undermines the conception of education and learning as a benefit for all society (Altbach 2015).

It is in this context that this chapter wishes to review and reinstate an older scholarly concern with the student experience, understood as a means of gaining insight into how the processes of networked learning are understood by those who participate in them. This longstanding interest has been associated with phenomenographic research in networked learning, using both qualitative and quantitative methods (e.g. see Booth 2008; Cutajar and Zenios 2012; Goodyear et al. 2005; Jones and Asensio 2001). There has also been a tradition that is more closely identified with phenomenology and a strong notion of what experience and student experience might entail (Dohn 2006, 2014; Creanor et al. 2006). Another strong influence has been a socio-cultural understanding of learning (Engeström 2009; Hodgson et al. 2012; Lave and Wenger 1991; Wenger 1998), and more recently there has been a shift towards a more sociomaterial understanding of learning, informed by post-humanism and actor-network theory (ANT) (Bayne 2016; Fenwick and Edwards 2010; Thompson 2012). For clarity and convenience, I have organised the consideration of experience into three parts with the headings, individual, social and assemblage. The chapter ends with a discussion which aims to explore the locus of experience and whether it makes sense to understand learning in terms of a subject's personal experience when the subject is decentred in an assemblage.

Individual Experience

Networked learning has an approach to learning which prioritises the connections between different elements, and this attitude to learning is complimented by the relational approach found in phenomenography (Ellis and Goodyear 2010). Ference Marton described phenomenography as:

> [...] the empirical study of the differing ways in which people experience, perceive, apprehend, understand, or conceptualize various phenomena in, and aspects of, the world around them. (Marton 1994, p. 4424)

The aim of phenomenographic research is to describe qualitatively different ways of experiencing phenomena (Marton and Booth 1997). Phenomenography's non-dualist approach has generated an extensive literature concerning the learner experience (e.g. Marton et al. 1997; Ramsden 2002). In phenomenographic terms there is no objective 'world out there' nor a subjective world 'in here' experience is constituted in the relationship between the internal and external, but crucially it is is constituted internally (Marton and Booth 1997). Experience in phenomenographic terms is the internal relationship constituted between persons and phenomena. This approach facilitates a second-order research perspective and a focus on the learner's experiences of learning as opposed to learning itself (Marton et al. 1993). The outcome of phenomenographic research is expressed in qualitative descriptions of the variations found in experiences of learning, and this tradition is strongly associated with the idea of 'deep' and 'surface' learning (Haggis 2009) and the broader approaches to learning tradition (Ashwin and McLean 2005).

Early work in networked learning informed by phenomenography attempted to include the lived experience of students in the discussions about technologies in education. A 2-year JISC-funded project concerning students' experiences of networked learning (1999–2000) had a key role in formalising and stabilising the developing field of networked learning in continental Europe and the UK (Goodyear and Carvalho 2014). That project had as its main aim:

> To help the UK HE sector come to a better understanding of the potential and problems of networked learning, particularly by attending to the student experience and to learning and teaching issues. (Goodyear 2000, p. 3)

At that time there was a clear link drawn between networked learning and the student experience based on a relational view of learning and the phenomenographic tradition (see Jones and Asensio 2001).

Phenomenography allows for both a psychological (individual) and a social reading. For example, Ellis and Goodyear emphasising the internal nature of experience argue that learning remains an individual process and that what goes on 'between a person's ears' is important for the learning process (Ellis and Goodyear 2010: 6). They also argue for an ecological framework that locates student difficulties in a mismatch with their environment rather than as individual characteristics which are persistent, context free failings. More recently, Markauskaite and Goodyear (2017) discuss four accounts of learning, including the phenomenological approach based on experience in the context of professional knowledge work. They state that they broadly agree with a 'mentalist' model rather than either a phenomenological or sociocultural model, which is one that suggests 'stable schemas, models or frameworks that represent structures, causal and logical relationships and processes in the social and material world' (ibid, p. 131). However, they take a distinctly relational approach to mind and mental operations by opening up the mind to noncognitive processes such as perception, action and emotion. Phenomenography and the mentalist model, as identified by Markauskaite and Goodyear (2017), stand in contrast to specifically social and situated views of learning by locating themselves in a more individualist tradition. The phenomenographic and mentalist approaches understood in this way stand out as distinctly relational and monist (as opposed to dualist) approaches that emphasise context dependence, rather than essential characteristics or styles. Monism in this context refers to the refusal to allow for two distinct forms, one internal and one external, and an insistence on the constitution of experience in a relationship between a phenomenon and a person. For this reason a monist perspective is often described as relational:

> [...] there are some particular advantages to be gained from avoiding dualism entirely and seeing the phenomena concerned as relational – neither objective nor subjective, or perhaps both at once. One escapes the question of how to bridge between the perceptions of the mind and the events of the "outside world". (Goodyear et al. 2014, p. 141)

The location of the person-in-context opens phenomenography and mentalist approaches to a social reading, in which personal characteristics are provisional and they can be altered by external interventions such as design, the use of technologies, social settings and environments.

Phenomenography has a limited and disputed relationship with phenomenology (Hasselgren and Beach 1997) and in networked learning phenomenology has only had a limited development (Creanor et al. 2006; Dohn 2006; Oberg and Bell 2012).

More broadly, issues concerning networked learning practices, such as the use of MOOCs, have also been analysed using phenomenological approaches (Adams 2014). Phenomenological approaches are relational in a similar way to phenomenography and vary according to the stress placed on the emphasis on the internal nature of experience or conversely on the nature of the phenomenon experienced. They also differ in the way that they discuss the location of experience in relation to knowledge. Dohn (2006), for example, draws on Merleau Ponty to emphasise the bodily nature of experience and also to suggest a distinction between two senses of experience referred to in German as (a) Erfahrung, which relates to cultural learning and being experienced in some way, and (b) an experience of a phenomena in the here and now and referenced by the word Erlebnis.

The phenomenographic tradition has also provided a bridge between academic research and the recent policy initiatives and practice associated with marketisation. The quantitative branch of phenomenographic research developed a number of instruments (e.g. the Approaches to Studying Inventory (ASI) and the Approaches and Study Skills Inventory for Students (ASSIST)), which went on to inform the development of national survey instruments deployed as part of public policy initiatives (Entwistle and Ramsden 1983; Haggis 2003; Sabri 2011). More broadly, an understanding of learning in terms of approaches, conceptions and outcomes has become an orthodox policy perspective in the UK and Australia, and it has informed the training of teachers in higher education, national student surveys and government policies. The incorporation of approaches to learning research into educational policy has led to context-specific elements of learning being fixed and generalised so that the relational aspect of the original approach has often been lost (Haggis 2003; Sabri 2011).

The key ideas that phenomenography, phenomenology and the mentalist approach have brought to networked learning are:

- A relational view of learning (non-dualist)
- An understanding that learning was context dependent
- A focus on how plans and actions were understood by participants

This clear focus on the relational nature of learning seems to have a natural connection with those theories of learning that emphasised the social context of learning which was another aspect of research strongly represented in networked learning. The connection arises through a common relational conception of learning and experience in which experience and learning arise from the person-in-context.

Social Experience

A key idea of constructivism is that knowledge is created by people, either as individuals or as part of groups, through experiencing the world and reflecting upon those experiences. Because knowledge is constructed by the knower from experience in the world, it has a relational character and it does not exist externally and independently. Consequently knowledge cannot simply be transmitted and received. Constructivism can take individual or social forms, but the most significant influence on networked learning has been through ideas related to social constructivism and a broadly social view of learning. The divisions that arose between an individual/acquisition metaphor and a social/participation metaphor of learning were captured in a seminal article by Sfard (1998) in which she argued that neither view was sufficient alone. Sfard argued that:

> All our concepts and beliefs have their roots in a limited number of fundamental ideas that cross disciplinary boundaries and are carried from one domain to another by the language we use. One glance at the current discourse on learning should be enough to realize that nowadays educational research is caught between two metaphors that, in this article, will be called the acquisition metaphor and the participation metaphor. (Sfard 1998, p. 5)

Networked learning clearly sat at one end of this spectrum with a clear emphasis on participation (e.g. see Hodgson et al. 2012), but following Sfard networked learning has never completely abandoned the alternative metaphor of acquisition. For example, Markauskaite and Goodyear (2017) argue that:

> Over the last three decades (or more), an unhelpful Caresian divide has persisted between understanding and doing, mind and body, representation and interaction, cognitive and sociocultural, symbolic and situated and material and conceptual. (p. 151)

This view retains a conception of mind and the possibility of acquisition alongside a rejection of traditional boundaries such as social and cognitive.

Networked learning has particularly drawn on social theories of learning including the idea of legitimate peripheral participation and communities of practice (Lave and Wenger 1991; Wenger 1998) and activity theory (especially cultural-historical activity theory; Engeström 2009). Dewey has been a less explicit influence on networked learning, but his views have been influential because of their emphasis on participation, action and experience (Dewey 1916, 1980; Hodgson et al. 2012). Elkjaer set out Dewey's use of experience which she argued was distinct but easily confused with more recent accounts:

> Experience is both the process of experiencing and the result of the process. It is in experience, in transaction, that difficulties arise, and it is with experience that problems are resolved by inquiry. Inquiry (or critical and reflective thinking) is an experimental method by which new experience may be had not only through action but also by using ideas and concepts, hypotheses and theories as "tools to think with" in an instrumental way. (Elkjaer 2009, p. 75)

This distinction is reminiscent of the comment by Dohn (2006), which was noted earlier, on how the German language differentiates between Erfahrung (from the root fahren that implies something which occurs over time and is encultured) and Erlebnis (an inner lived experience). The word experience in the English language conflates these two different senses of experience, but building on a social view of learning and informed by Dewey's ideas, networked learning conceives of experience (in both senses) as a key aspect of the process of learning and in addition as a resource for researchers attempting to understand the ways networked learning is enacted through practice.

Lave contrasted her views with many of those associated with the term constructivism and the separation of the individual and cognitive in opposition to an external world. She also rejected the radical constructivist relativism in which the world is only subjectively or intersubjectively constructed.

Learning, it seems to me, is neither wholly subjective nor fully encompassed in social interaction, and it is not constituted separately from the social world (with its own structures and
meanings) of which it is part. This recommends a decentered view of the locus and meaning
of learning, in which learning is recognized as a social phenomenon constituted in the
experienced, lived-in world.... (Lave 1991, p. 64)

It is this notion of learning as a social and cultural phenomenon constituted in the
experienced, lived-in world that has been so influential in networked learning.

Whereas constructivism often makes a distinction between the individual's cognitive experiences and the environment in which the experience takes place, sociocultural approaches take a more phenomenological (in the sense of person-in-context)
and monist approach to experience, understanding experience as being experience
in the world (De Laat and Lally 2004). The emphasis in sociocultural approaches is
placed on learning constituted in joint activity, a process of participation in cultural
practice(s), mutual exchange and dialogue. Subjective experience is understood as
one aspect of social practice, of activity in the world, inseparable from the nonsub-
jective elements that may be experienced as external. The subject retains a key position in activity systems because it is the source of intentional action. The material
context also plays a role in sociocultural approaches, and technologies are viewed
as mediating 'tools' and cultural artefacts. In this approach the emphasis remains on
the cultural, social and organisational processes through which learning takes place
and in which technologies and artefacts are deployed. Phenomenological and sociocultural approaches both see technologies and tools as mediators of human experience, and they have a fundamentally asymmetrical understanding of these
relationships (Kaptelinin and Nardi 2006). In sociocultural theory humans and
machines are distinct in character and cannot be treated as being alike.

Sociocultural approaches have provided these key ideas in networked learning:

- Learning as a social and cultural activity
- Technology as a mediating aspect of human experience
- Intentionality and object orientation as key components of activity and
  experience

The sociocultural approach has some key differences with other approaches that
have become popular in networked learning, particularly actor-network theory
(ANT) and post-humanism which tend to have a symmetrical understanding of the
relationships between humans and technology in which heterogeneous networks of
humans and machines are treated as various nodes in a network or as entanglements
in an assemblage with humans and machines treated in the same way (Bayne 2015,
2016; Bayne and Ross 2013; Fenwick and Edwards 2010; Fenwick et al. 2011).

Assemblages and Experience

Both ANT and post-humanism have distinct positions with regard to the place of
technologies in relation to humans and of particular relevance to networked learning.
Both are concerned with how we think about an educational process in which the

human subject is not central, and they incline towards a decentred view of education and learning which are seen as emergent processes taking place in assemblages of humans and non-humans. Post-humanism is a distinct and ambitious project which is concerned with 'what comes after philosophical humanism' (Bayne 2016, p. 83). In the context of this chapter, the important feature of post-humanism is its critical stance in relation to how the human subject needs to be rethought in education. Post-humanism moves away from a notion of education as a process of 'leading out' some aspect of an essential humanity and refocuses on how the knower and the known are co-constituted in relations between the material (including bodily and technological) and linguistic and dialogic expressions of intention and understanding.

Although related to social theories of learning, ANT has its own distinctive position, but this has been merged by some authors with other social theories of learning and post-humanism and universalised as sociomaterialism (Fenwick and Edwards 2010; Fenwick et al. 2011). Fox had previously drawn attention to the potential of ANT in relation to networked learning (Fox 2000 2002, 2005, 2009), but sociomaterialism has only recently become a mainstream concern in networked learning. The use of the blanket term sociomaterialism has been justified by the claim that all of the foundational theories for this approach (ANT, activity theory, post-humanism and complexity theory) conceptualise knowledge and capacities as being *emergent* from the webs of interconnections between heterogeneous entities, both human and non-human. ANT and more broadly sociomaterialist approaches offer the prospect of being able to integrate the material technologies and media found in networked learning into a framework that encompasses people and machines in a symmetrical way.

> In an effort to bring Web technologies to critical enquiry, they are treated as key participants in this study. The participant list, therefore, included postings; avatars; tool bars; emoticons; archives; community member profiles; viruses; hyperlinks; the delete button; passwords and the technology that delivers postings, such as e-mail, discussion forum or RSS feed. Human actants include "newbies", "wannabies", colleagues, "big names", celebrities, competitors, posers, lurkers, employment recruiters, clients, friends, strangers and online paparazzi. (Thompson 2012)

In this example technologies are introduced as component parts of lists that include both human and non-human participants that form assemblages – entanglements of actors in a symmetrical relationship. These assemblages are dynamic and components act upon each other to bring forth emergent properties that cannot be reduced to either context or individual cognition (Fenwick and Edwards 2011).

Learning understood from an ANT perspective is a network effect; it is neither understood as an essential cognitive process nor as a personal or social achievement (Fenwick and Edwards 2011).

> [...] no agent or knowledge has an essential existence outside a given network: nothing is given in the order of things, but performs itself into existence. (Fenwick and Edwards 2011, p. 5)

Unlike other sociocultural accounts, sociomaterialism rests on a particular and peculiar kind of materialism (Harman 2009; Latour 2005). The 'relational materiality' found in sociomaterialism understands matter not as discrete reified objects but as the effects of dynamic indeterminate processes. Sociomaterialism questions accepted categories such as individual and organisation and many accepted binaries such as subject/object and knower/known. ANT clarifies how assemblages and entanglements are formed and how they hold together in associations that produce effects (Fenwick and Edwards 2011). Agency becomes an outcome of a network, a network effect and not an inherent (essential) property of any particular kind of agent, either human or machine. Humans, non-humans and hybrid combinations of the two are all capable of exerting force, and through their mutual interactions, they co-constitute the effect of the assemblage.

Kaptelinin and Nardi (2006) capture different kinds of agency and different kinds of agent that arise in computing and computer networks. They distinguish between action when thought of as simply having an effect and action which involves an intention. This distinction clearly separates their approach from ANT, despite the inclusion of activity theory as a contributing source to sociomaterialism. Kaptelinin and Nardi argue that despite the fact that different kinds of agents can exhibit similar agencies, humans and machines are distinct because of the object orientation and intention found in human activity. In this Kaptelinin and Nardi draw on the earlier work of Pickering who argued:

> We [humans] construct goals that refer to presently non-existent future states and then seek to bring them about. I can see no reason to suppose that DNA double helices or televisions organise their existence thus… (Pickering 1993, p. 566)

A problem I see with this formulation is that it relies on a clear distinction between people and machines, one which is often blurred in assemblages of both people and machines. It is conceivable that complex human-machine networks may allow for the emergence of intentions which are neither the sole property of a single human nor of humans more generally. Assemblages can give rise to human-machine configurations that do have their 'own' needs, objects and most importantly intentions (Jones 2015). Subjective experience still resides in component parts [black boxes] of these assemblages, and experience as a process and experience as an outcome both remain of interest for learning and for researchers of networked learning systems. Persons and the human form remain relatively stable entities over a lifetime that educators are still keen to develop.

Sociomaterial approaches have provided these key ideas in networked learning.

- Learning as an emergent property of complex systems, a network effect
- Technologies and the material as co-constructors with humans of complex assemblages
- Human agents and their accounts as outcomes of an emergent co-constitutive process with the material

This approach has implications for the ways in which we conduct our research and the status we grant our data sources (Bayne 2016). The interview no longer strives to reveal an essence rather it becomes a temporal and material encounter in which the account is a coming together of the persons and the material in an entanglement at a particular point in time and space. This approach also has significant consequences for new forms of quantitative research often referred to as 'big data' and for learning analytics in education (Knox 2014). Sociomaterial approaches do not sit easily with approaches that suggest data 'reveals' patterns and describes reality. Rather they focus on how the complex systems of data production and representation co-constitute the very systems they purport to describe, and in this process, they often embed, replicate or reinforce pre-existing attitudes and prejudices (Williamson 2016b).

The Contemporary Experience of Being a Student

This chapter argues that while the role of the subject and intentionality remains an important and distinguishing feature of human actors in human-machine assemblages, the significance of the experience of intentional actors is displaced in these configurations. Complex systems have an emergent character in which no single actor has a determining role (Clayton and Davies 2006). There are those that go on from this feature of emergence to suggest that outcomes in complex assemblages are consequences of an uncontrolled process, blind in the way that the evolutionary process takes place with no overall designer (Dennett 1995). I want to suggest otherwise and argue that in sociomaterial assemblages, the conscious human element retains an important and at times decisive role, through (a) design and (b) intentional actions by socially located people, but one that needs to be seen as distinctly different from a reductive methodological individualism. In particular, intentions are often enacted via organised entities in which the individual human actor is constrained by their social role and entangled in interactions with a variety of material forces which enable and constrain them. Within networks some nodes are more influential than others, and over time patterns of entanglement in assemblages can produce effects that are persistent and instantiate power relations. While there may not be any single controller/point of control in such systems, there are regulatory controls and some nodes in the network which have considerable influence and a significant shaping role.

The role for experience and intentional action that I argue for is especially relevant to education and networked learning in particular. The process described by ANT using the terms 'punctualisation' and 'black boxing' leads to forms of relative stability.

> [...] the process of punctualization thus converts an entire network into a single point or node in another network. (Callon 1991, p. 153)

This stability is a central concern in relation to a learner imbricated in a sociomaterial culture because the aim of education is to set up persistent patterns of practice and stable forms of awareness that prepare students for their futures, a supremely intentional activity. Human actors are formed in educational processes via their experiences. They become fashioned into stable forms but they remain malleable, in the memorable construction ascribed to the Jesuits – 'Give me a child until they are seven and I'll give you the man (sic)'. The human actor is constantly changing, but there remains a stubborn stability, a recognisable continuity over time in persons and personalities, across a range of contexts and through a myriad of experiences. This is a similar point to that made by Markauskaite and Goodyear (2017, p. 131) and reported earlier when discussing their adaptation of a mentalist approach. However, the approach taken here is an inverse process. Whereas Markauskaite and Goodyear are opening out from a mentalist model to the conditions beyond the individual, I am suggesting *opening into* the individual from the assemblage in which the person is enmeshed. This stability within persons is not passive; it rests on persistent intentional activity and active co-construction in various networks. Networked learning is interested in these interactive processes that co-constructively shape persons and which provide characteristics that can be mobilised over a long period, if not a complete lifetime. Networked learning is also concerned with the culture of learning, both in the means which are used to shape persons and enrol people in their own shaping and in the outcomes of that shaping. Learning in networked learning has a social and cultural form. In contemporary conditions when experience is standardised and homogenised into 'the' student experience, it leads to a cultural and educational outcome which reduce learning, and the learner, to measurable outputs that can be tabulated, ranked and processed by hidden codes and algorithms (Williamson 2016a). In contrast, networked learning is interested in enabling diverse human experiences and a variety of often immeasurable outcomes.

An example of the way experience can play out in an assemblage of humans and machines comes from the use of a 'teacher bot' reported by Bayne (2015). The 'teacher bot' was developed by a team at the University of Edinburgh to provide a level of co-teaching within the massive open online course (MOOC) on 'E-learning and digital cultures'. It was part of an experimental course design which emphasised the development of critical understanding and explored a critical approach to educational automation. A developer built an automated teacher presence for the course Twitter feed which 'coded in' something of the teacher function so that it became less a question of a living teacher presence and more an assemblage of code, algorithm and teacher-student agency. In this research, Student 4 recorded their experiences in this way:

> [...] the teacher bot led me on a merry chase looking up quotes and obscure academic references, which had the interesting side effect of "ambush teaching" me. I will happily admit, that I do not feel like I have been to a class. I do not feel like I have been taught, either. I do, however, think I have learned something. I've certainly been prompted to think.... (Bayne 2015: 463)

The questions this kind of approach inclines me to think about are: Who/what prompted this thinking, and who/what is the author of this experience? Within this assemblage the course was designed, the teacher bot developed and the student actively engaged. At all these points there are access points to the experiences of humans that can be used to inform future iterations of activity. Furthermore, all the human activities display a future-oriented intention. This is a classic point about intentionality and human agency and therefore the distinction between human and natural sciences, which has been often stated, and as noted earlier, it was made strongly in relation to strict symmetry by Pickering (1993). Although there are assemblages of humans and machines, there is additional access to the human actor in ways that the logs of machines or the presence of things do not provide, and these humans are acting with a future objective informing their activities.

Conclusions

The question addressed in this chapter was: In what ways can networked learning think about and incorporate the idea of experience with regard to decentred persons in the entanglements forming assemblages? To even begin to consider this significant question, networked learning researchers and practitioners need to clearly separate themselves from the popularised use of 'the' student experience found in student surveys, league tables and the commercialised discourse which surrounds the introduction of market mechanisms into higher education. Networked learning is interested in the many varieties of student experiences not an essentialised and singular student experience. This non-essentialist approach also has to deal with a second question concerning the symmetry or the nonsymmetrical relations between human and non-human actors in the assemblages that arise in networked learning. The position argued for in this chapter is that human actors have a specific place, even though it is one in which they may have been decentred, one that is not symmetrical with non-human actors.

This chapter reviewed the ways experience has been approached in networked learning and noted the ways in which this is distinct from the public discourse in which student experience is reified and homogenised into 'the' student experience as a gradable, numerical outcome. Networked learning is interested in experience because it provides an additional account from actors. These accounts are relevant for learning because they provide an insight into how human actors respond in and to the interactions they encounter in educational assemblages and the world more generally. The accounts also provide claims made by subjects about their intentions, setting out what they assert are their future-oriented rationales for action. They are a source of evidence, information and inspiration that can be drawn on for design and understanding. Networked learning has been interested in experience as a source of knowledge about how human actors interpret the world they are interacting with and how they planfully engage in these interactions.

This outlook remains broadly sociomaterialist in that it continues to conceptualise knowledge and capacities as being emergent from the webs of interconnections between heterogeneous entities, both human and non-human.

However, it differs from the strong readings found in ANT and post-humanism in that the author argues that all actors cannot be treated as completely symmetrical for research purposes because of the particular access that we have to accounts of experience from human actors. These accounts are a resource, but they also illustrate another aspect of human agency in that they illuminate how a human actor can for no apparently good reason do other than that which is expected, a form of existential choice or freedom. Accounts are a resource that separates human actors from non-human actors including complex machines and the non-human parts of assemblages they are entangled in. Moreover, the human actor, whether alone or when acting as an agent of an organisation, is engaged in intentional and object-oriented activity. The designer of a course or a technology anticipates the future and engages in the shaping of the entanglements that result from their designs. It is of course the case that the designer is not a pure individual, acting alone, and design emerges from interactions involving the designer (intentional actor) in context, an interaction between embodied person(s) and things both artefacts and technologies. Other non-human actors do not (at least currently and in the immediately foreseeable future) envisage the future with the intention of managing and manipulating it, and this provides an a priori separation of human actors from them. It is possible for human actors to envisage that non-human actors and assemblages could exhibit intentions and goal-oriented activities, even existential choice, but in these cases, evidence must be shown that this is the case and the activity engaged in is not simply a form of delegated agency.

In summary, this chapter argues that networked learning research needs to retain a focus on human experience and to develop an empirical and theoretical understanding of how the decentred human experience in human-machine assemblages can help in the design and development of successful learning networks.

References

Adams, C., Yin, Y., Vargas Madriz, L. F., & Scott Mullen, C. (2014). A phenomenology of learning large: The tutorial sphere of xMOOC video lectures. *Distance Education, 35*(2), 202–216. https://doi.org/10.1080/01587919.2014.917701.

Altbach, P. (2015). Knowledge and education as international commodities. *International Higher Education, 28*, 2–5.

Ashwin, P., & McLean, M. (2005). Towards a reconciliation of phenomenographic and critical pedagogy perspectives in higher education through a focus on academic engagement. In C. Rust (Ed.), *Improving student learning: Diversity and inclusivity* (pp. 377–389). Oxford: Oxford Centre for Staff and Learning Development.

Bayne, S. (2016). Posthumanism and research in digital education. In C. Haythornthwaite, R. Andrews, J. Fransman, & E. M. Meyers (Eds.), *The SAGE handbook of E-learning research* (2nd ed., pp. 82–99). London: Sage.

Bayne, S. (2015). Teacherbot: Interventions in automated teaching. *Teaching in Higher Education, 20*(4), 455–467.

Bayne, S., & Ross, J. (2013). Posthuman literacy in heterotopic space: A pedagogic proposal. In R. Goodfellow & M. Lea (Eds.), *Literacy in the digital university: Critical perspectives on learning, scholarship, and technology* (pp. 95–110). London: Routledge.

Booth, S. (2008). Researching learning in networked learning-Phenomenography and variation theory as empirical and theoretical approaches. In V. Hodgson, C. Jones, T. Kargidis, D. McConnell, S. Retalis, D. Stamatis, & M. Zenios (Eds.), *Proceedings of the sixth international conference on networked learning, Halkidiki, Greece* (pp. 450–455). Lancaster: Lancaster University. Online HTTP http://networkedlearningconference.org.uk.

Bournsell, P. (2015). Student finance. Online HTTP http://university.which.co.uk/advice/student-finance/how-much-debt-will-i-actually-get-into-by-going-to-university

Callon, M. (1991). Techno-economic networks and irreversibility. In J. Law (Ed.), *A sociology of monsters: Essays on power, technology and domination* (pp. 132–161). London: Routledge.

Clayton, P., & Davies, P. (Eds.). (2006). *The re-emergence of emergence: The emergentist hypothesis from science to religion.* Oxford: Oxford University Press.

Creanor, L., Gowan, D., Howells, C., & Trinder, K. (2006). The Learner's voice: A focus on the e-learner experience. In S. Banks, V. Hodgson, C. Jones, B. Kemp, D. McConnell, & C. Smith (Eds.), *Proceedings of the fifth international conference on networked learning, 10–12 April 2006.* Lancaster: Lancaster University. Online HTTP http://networkedlearningconference.org.uk.

Cutajar, M, & Zenios, M. (2012). Variations in students' experience of networked learning in a post-compulsory pre-university context. In V. Hodgson, C. Jones, M. de Laat, D. McConnell, T. Ryberg, & P. Sloep (Eds.), *Proceedings of the 8th International Conference on Networked Learning*, 2-4th April 2012, Maastricht, NL (pp. 41–49). Online HTTP http://networkedlearningconference.org.uk

De Laat, M., & Lally, V. (2004). Complexity theory and praxis: Researching collaborative learning and tutoring processes in a networked learning community. In P. Goodyear, S. Banks, V. Hodgson, & D. McConnell (Eds.), *Advances in research on networked learning* (pp. 11–42). Dordrecht: Kluwer Academic Publishers.

Dennett, D. C. (1995). *Darwin's dangerous idea: Evolution and the meanings of life.* London: Allen Lane.

Dewey, J. (1916/1980). Democracy and education: An introduction to the philosophy of education. In J. A. Boydston (Ed.), *Middle works 9.* Carbondale: Southern Illinois University Press.

Dohn, N. B. (2014). Implications for networked learning of the 'practice' side of social practice theories – a tacit-knowledge perspective. In V. E. Hodgson, M. De Laat, D. McConnell, & T. Ryberg (Eds.), *The design, experience and practice of networked learning* (pp. 29–49). Heidleberg/London: Springer.

Dohn, N. B. (2006). Affordances- a Merleau-Pontian account. In S. Banks, V. Hodgson, C. Jones, B. Kemp, D. McConnell, & C. Smith (Eds.), *Proceedings of the fifth international conference on networked learning 2006.* Lancaster: Lancaster University. Online HTTP http://networkedlearningconference.org.uk.

Elkjaer, B. (2009). Pragmatism: A learning theory for the future. In K. Illeris (Ed.), *Contemporary theories of learning: Learning theorists... in their own words* (pp. 74–89). London: Routledge.

Ellis, R., & Goodyear, P. (2010). *Students experiences of e-learning in higher education: The ecology of sustainable innovation.* New York: Routledge.

Engeström, Y. (2009). Expansive learning: Toward an activity-theoretical reconceptualization. In K. Illeris (Ed.), *Contemporary theories of learning: Learning theorists... in their own words* (pp. 59–73). London: Routledge.

Entwistle, N. J., & Ramsden, P. (1983). *Understanding student learning.* London: Croom Helm.

Fenwick, T., Edwards, R., & Sawchuk, P. (2011). *Emerging approaches to educational research: Tracing the Sociomaterial.* London: Routledge.

Fenwick, T., & Edwards, R. (2010). *Actor network theory in education.* London: Routledge.

Fenwick, T., & Edwards, R. (2011). Introduction: Reclaiming and renewing actor network theory for educational research. *Educational Philosophy and Theory, 43*(S1), 1–14.

Fox, S. (2000). Communities Of Practice, Foucault And Actor-Network Theory. *Journal of Management Studies, 37*(6), 853–868.

Fox, S. (2002). Studying networked learning: Some implications from socially situated learning theory and actornetwork theory. In C. Steeples & C. Jones (Eds.), Networked learning: Perspectives and issues, 77–91. London: Springer.

Fox, S. (2005). An actor-network critique of community in higher education: implications for networked learning. *Studies in Higher Education, 30*(1), 95–110.

Fox, S. (2009). Contexts of teaching and learning: an actor-network view of the classroom. In Biesta, G. Edwards, R. and Thorpe, M. (eds.) Rethinking Contexts for Learning and Teaching, 31–43. London: Routledge.

Gani, A. (2016). Tuition fees 'have led to surge in students seeking counselling'. The Guardian 13 March 2016. Online HTTP: https://www.theguardian.com/education/2016/mar/13/tuition-fees-have-led-to-surge-in-students-seeking-counselling

Goodyear, P. (2000). Final Report, Volume 1: Networked Learning in Higher Education Project (JCALT). Online HTTP http://csalt.lancs.ac.uk/jisc/

Goodyear, P., & Carvalho, L. (2014). Introduction: Networked learning and learning networks. In L. Carvalho & Goodyear (Eds.), *The architecture of productive learning networks* (pp. 3–22). London/New York: Routledge.

Goodyear, P., Carvalho, L., & Dohn, N. (2014). Design for networked learning: framing relations between participants' activities and the physical setting. In Bayne S, Jones C, de Laat M,

Ryberg T & Sinclair C (Eds.), *Proceedings of the 9th International Conference on Networked Learning 2014* (pp. 137–144). Online HTTP http://networkedlearningconference.org.uk

Goodyear, P., Jones, C., Asensio, M., Hodgson, V., & Steeples, C. (2005). Networked learning in higher education: students' expectations and experiences. *Higher Education, 50*(3), 473–508.

Haggis, T. (2009). What have we been thinking of? A critical overview of 40 years of student learning research in higher education. *Studies in Higher Education, 34*(4), 377–390.

Haggis, T. (2003). Constructing images of ourselves? A critical investigation into 'approaches to learning' research in higher education. *British Educational Research Journal, 29*(1), 89–104.

Harman, G. (2009). *Prince of networks: Bruno Latour and metaphysics*. Melbourne: Re.press. Online HTTP http://re-press.org/books/prince-of-networks-bruno-latour-and-metaphysics/.

Hasselgren, B., & Beach, D. (1997). Phenomenography-a "good-for-nothing brother" of phenomenology? Outline of an analysis. *Higher Education Research & Development, 16*(2), 191–202.

Havergal, C. (2016). Rise in UK university dropout rate 'disappointing'. Time Higher Education 23 March 2016. Online HTTP: https://www.timeshighereducation.com/news/rise-uk-university-dropout-rate-disappointing

Hazelkorn, E. (2015). *Rankings and the reshaping of higher education: The battle for world-class excellence* (2nd ed.). Basingstoke: Palgrave-Macmillan.

Hodgson, V., McConnell, D., & Dirckinck-Holmfeld, L. (2012). The theory, practice and pedagogy of networked learning. In L. Dirckinck Holmfeld, V. Hodgson, & D. McConnell (Eds.), *Exploring the theory, pedagogy and practice of networked learning* (pp. 291–305). New York: Springer.

Jones, C. (2015). *Networked learning: An educational paradigm for the age of digital networks*. Heidelberg/London: Springer.

Jones, C., & Asensio, M. (2001). Experiences of assessment: Using phenomenography for evaluation. *Journal of Computer Assisted Learning (JCAL), 17*(3), 314–321.

Kaptelinin, V., & Nardi, B. A. (2006). *Acting with technology: Activity theory and interaction design*. Cambridge: MIT Press.

Knox, J. K. (2014). Active algorithms: Sociomaterial spaces in the E-learning and digital cultures MOOC. *Campus Virtuales, 3*(1), 42–55. Online HTTP: http://uajournals.com/ojs/index.php/campusvirtuales/article/view/49.

Latour, B. (2005). *Reassembling the social. An introduction to actor-network theory*. London: Routledge.

Lave, J. (1991). Situating learning in communities of practice. In L. Resnick, J. Levine, & S. Teasley (Eds.), *Perspectives on socially shared cognition* (pp. 63–82). Washington, DC: APA.

Lave, J., & Wenger, E. (1991). *Situated learning: Legitimate peripheral participation*. Cambridge: Cambridge University Press.

Markauskaite, L., & Goodyear, P. (2017). *Epistemic fluency and professional education: Innovation, knowledgeable action, and actionable knowledge*. Dordrecht: Springer.

Marton, F. (1994). Phenomenography. In T. Husen & T. N. Postlethwaite (Eds.), *The international encyclopedia of education* (2nd ed., pp. 4424–4429). Oxford: Pergamon.

Marton, F., & Booth, S. (1997). *Learning and awareness*. Mahwah: Lawrence Erlbaum Associates.

Marton, F., Dall'Alba, G., & Beaty, E. (1993). Conceptions of learning. *International Journal of Educational Research, 19*, 277–300.

Marton, F., Hounsell, D., & Entwistle, N. (1997). *The experience of learning: Implications for teaching and studying in higher education*. Edinburgh: Scottish Academic Press.

Oberg, H., & Bell, A. (2012). Exploring phenomenology for researching lived experience in Technology Enhanced Learning. In V. Hodgson, C. Jones, M. de Laat, D. McConnell, T. Ryberg, & P. Sloep (Eds.), *Proceedings of the 8th International Conference on Networked Learning*, 2-4th April 2012, Maastricht, NL (pp 203–210). Online HTTP http://networkedlearningconference.org.uk

Pickering, A. (1993). The mangle of practice: Agency and emergence in the sociology of science. *The American Journal of Sociology, 99*(3), 559–589.

Ramsden, P. (2002). *Learning to teach in higher education* (2nd ed.). London: Routledge.

Sabri, D. (2011). What's wrong with 'the student experience'? *Discourse: Studies in the Cultural Politics of Education, 32*(5), 657–667.

Sfard, A. (1998). On two metaphors for learning and the dangers of choosing just one. *Educational Researcher, 27*(2), 4–13.

Shah, M., Cheng, M., & Fitzgerald, R. (2016). Closing the loop on student feedback: The case of Australian and Scottish universities. *Higher Education.* https://doi.org/10.1007/s10734-016-0032-x. Online 27 July 2016.

Shah, M., & Richardson, J. T. E. (2016). Is the enhancement of student experience a strategic priority in Australian universities? *Higher Education Research & Development, 35*(2), 352–364. https://doi.org/10.1080/07294360.2015.1087385.

Thompson, T. L. (2012). Who's taming who? Tensions between people and technologies in cyberspace communities. In L. Dirckinck-Holmfeld, V. Hodgson, & D. McConnell (Eds.), *Exploring the theory, pedagogy and practice of networked learning* (pp. 157–172). New York: Springer.

Universities UK. (2016). *Student experience: Measuring expectations and outcomes.* London: Universities UK.

Wenger, E. (1998). *Communities of practice: Learning, meaning, and identity.* Cambridge: Cambridge University Press.

Williamson, B. (2016a). Digital education governance: An introduction. *European Educational Research Journal 2016, 15*(1), 3–13.

Williamson, B. (2016b). Digital methodologies of education governance: Pearson plc and the remediation of methods. *European Educational Research Journal, 15*(1), 35–53.

Chapter 4
Discursive Effects of a Paradigm Shift Rhetoric in Online Higher Education: Implications on Networked Learning Research and Practice

Kyungmee Lee

Abstract The aim of this chapter is to critically examine some discursive effects of the 'paradigm shift' rhetoric that is commonly used in the advocacy of online higher education. The chapter will unpack how that particular rhetoric—which permeates *generalist* discourse about online higher education—impacts upon actual distance education practices in *specific* higher education settings, such as 'open universities', where distance education is the core institutional function and where the historical development of practice has been separated from that of 'mainstream' higher education. The chapter focuses on the transition *from* the earlier form of distance education, which was largely associated with and led by dedicated distance universities, *to* the current form of online higher education, which operates and is discussed more and more frequently in mainstream higher education contexts, such as traditional campus-based universities. The particular 'paradigm shift' rhetoric that emerged during that transition will be discussed, and its discursive effects on distance education practices in open universities will be analysed. The main argument is that the rhetoric, as a widespread academic discourse, has generated and continues to perpetuate a 'gap' between learning theories and instructional practices in the open university settings—where current distance education practices have arisen from a unique course of historical development but which are now subjected to 'paradigm shift' rhetoric being imposed from outside. The implications for networked learning research and practice will be discussed, and several suggestions will be made, whereby the networked learning community might develop a more balanced and critical discourse about online higher education.

K. Lee (✉)
Educational Research, Lancaster University, Lancaster, UK
e-mail: k.lee23@lancaster.ac.uk

Short Introduction

The aim of this chapter is to critically examine some discursive effects of the 'paradigm shift' rhetoric[1] that is commonly used in the advocacy of online higher education (e.g. Harasim 2000; Nachmias 2002). The chapter will unpack how that particular rhetoric—which permeates *generalist* discourse about online higher education—impacts upon actual distance education practices in *specific* higher education settings, such as 'open universities', where distance education is the core institutional function and where the historical development of practice has been separated from that of 'mainstream' higher education. The chapter focuses on the transition *from* the earlier form of distance education, which was largely associated with and led by dedicated distance universities, *to* the current form of online higher education, which operates and is discussed more and more frequently in mainstream higher education contexts, such as traditional campus-based universities. The particular 'paradigm shift' rhetoric that emerged during that transition will be discussed, and its discursive effects on distance education practices in open universities will be analysed. The main argument is that the rhetoric, as a widespread academic discourse, has generated and continues to perpetuate a 'gap' between learning theories and instructional practices in the open university settings—where current distance education practices have arisen from a unique course of historical development but which are now subjected to 'paradigm shift' rhetoric being imposed from outside. The implications for networked learning (NL) research and practice will be discussed, and several suggestions will be made, whereby the NL community might develop a more balanced and critical discourse about online higher education.

To effectively articulate the argument, it is necessary to conceptually separate the notions of distance education (DE) and online higher education (HE). I will first define DE and then differentiate it from the more recent phenomenon of online HE by emphasising two interrelated aspects, namely, its *pedagogical historicity* and *contextual specificity*.

Distance Education and Online Higher Education and Networked Learning

Although 'it is difficult to arrive at one definition' (Schlosser and Simonson 2010, p. 34) and forms of distance education (DE) are varied across diverse educational levels and contexts, there are two shared elements in general DE practice that have long served to distinguish it from conventional, face-to-face education. The first

---

[1] Rhetoric: The art of effective or persuasive speaking or writing, especially the exploitation of figures of speech and other compositional techniques—language designed to have a persuasive or impressive effect but which is often regarded as lacking in sincerity or meaningful content (Oxford Dictionaries 2016).

component is the separation of teacher and learner, while the second is the use of technological media to unite teacher and learner (Keegan 1996; Moore 1973). In DE practices, teaching and learning activities are *both* technologically mediated and pre-planned through institutional, often 'industrialised', instructional design and production processes (Peters 2007). Unlike online HE, which is a more recently emerged educational phenomenon mainly arisen by the popularisation of the Internet and other ICTs, DE has developed through a long history, during which it has been influenced by a variety of social and political pressures. In fact, the origin of DE dates back to the mid-1800s (Larreamendy-Joerns and Leinhardt 2006). The first US correspondence programme, Anna Eliot Ticknor's *Society to Encourage Studies at Home*, was launched in 1873 (Agassiz 1971; Bergmann 2001), and by the end of the 1800s, a number of correspondence programmes were provided by elite universities (and intellectuals) in both the USA and the UK (Storr 1966).

The Open University of the United Kingdom (UKOU) was established in 1969, and over the subsequent decade, 20 other open universities and autonomous DE institutions were established in around 10 countries, with a particular stated aim: to provide university-level education opportunities to students considered *underserved* by traditional institutions (Perraton 2000). Specialising in distance teaching and DE research, those universities strongly differentiated themselves from campus-based universities and developed institutional identities based on the efficient and cost-effective production and delivery of independent correspondence study programmes, with a strong focus on affordability for students (Guri-Rosenblit 2009; Peters 2008). From its emergence, the academic field of DE research has focused on using a range of technological media to support distance learners, usually in ways driven by per-ceptions of those learners as underserved or disadvantaged, and DE institutions have extensively concerned themselves with the pedagogical implications of the distance between teachers and learners (Lee 2017). The notion of DE in this chapter consciously embraces that unique *pedagogical historicity*: recognising that the ways in which DE practices have developed and been shaped make them a historical product, which may not be readily changeable.

DE can also be conceptually separated from online HE by considering its *contextual specificity*. DE is a term that narrowly refers to those education practices situated in specific institutional contexts (such as open universities), whereas 'online HE' nowadays more expansively refers to diverse forms of learning and teaching activity mediated or facilitated by ICTs (sometimes only partially) within essentially any HE setting (Edwards 1995; Kanuka and Brooks 2010; Swan 2010). Notwithstanding the distinctions emphasised above, in recent years the advent of online HE has heralded radical changes in the general perception of DE. Previously, in the broader HE discourse, there had been a prevailing perception of DE as a second-rate, peculiar or otherwise abnormal education: mainly due to the lack of direct interaction (i.e. contact) between teachers and learners (Rumble 2001). That lack of interaction was criticised as the 'Achilles' heel' of DE programmes (Hülsmann 2009), and it seems to be a core reason why DE received little attention from general higher educators or educational researchers. Educational (or instructional) technologists, whose emphasis was largely on the educational implementation of emerging new technologies, also paid little attention to the original DE contexts, where it was more 'affordable' or 'accessible' technologies that tended to be taken up. For example, the personal computer (PC) was, for some time, not considered affordable or accessible even for the general public; while educational technologists were 'early adaptors' ahead of that general public, DE institutions were comparatively cautious due to their focus on programme accessibility and affordability for the 'disadvantaged' or otherwise underserved. Over time, the rapid uptake of PCs and the wide circulation of broadband technologies have increasingly provided the broad population with access to more cost-effective, many-to-many communication tools. In that technological context, the interactive potential of the Internet is increasingly perceived as a driving force behind pedagogical innovation both in DE and in face-to-face instruction (Harasim 2000; Kanuka and Brooks 2010).

The concept of 'online higher education' (i.e. higher education practices mediated or facilitated by ICTs) has rapidly emerged, and it has been repeatedly stated that online HE will bring radically different theoretical and pedagogical approaches into HE practices and so improve them (Adams 2007; Harasim 2000; Swan 2010). It is instructive to consider in detail one specific example anchored in the prevailing discourses of online HE context. In 2000, Harasim published an article entitled *Shift happens: Online education as a new paradigm in learning*, where she drew a clear conceptual boundary between online HE and other forms of HE (for Harasim, DE is conflated into those 'other forms') and sought to provide a comprehensive overview of pedagogical characteristics distinctive to online HE. Harasim argued that, because innovative networking technologies enable many-to-many communication to happen 'any time and any place', even using a small degree of online networking (e.g. e-mail and computer conferencing) would enhance the quality of learning. That argument was taken to be valid in both face-to-face or DE contexts. Importantly, the development of the discourse of online HE has not been led by traditional DE communities; instead, it has been driven by other scholarly communities and business-oriented groups, including those concerned with general HE, private HE provision and innovation in instructional technology. As a result, in this developmental process of conceptualising online HE and its discourses, the unique features of DE (i.e. its pedagogical historicity and contextual specificity) have not been fully considered and discussed. Additionally, the pedagogical differences between online HE and DE practices have come to be somewhat narrowly explained: as a product of the distinctive features of Internet technologies and their advantages in comparison to other DE media (such as postal correspondence, television and radio).

One consequence is that online HE has become conceptualised and characterised as interactive and collaborative due to the communicative features of the Internet, that is, as an innovative form of social learning practice (Garrison and Kanuka 2008). DE, on the other hand, has been conceptualised as being limited to individualised learning practices (Schlosser and Simonson 2010). Consequently, online HE was initially regarded as superior to DE and, over time, has been seen as preferable even to face-to-face education (Garrison and Kanuka 2008). Alongside a gradual proliferation in the educational use of ICTs for supporting connection and collaboration among learners and teachers, different academic communities and theories have rapidly emerged, developed and sought to obtain academic legitimacy and popularity.[2] Prominent examples are computer-supported collaborative learning (e.g. Dillenbourg et al. 1996; Stahl et al. 2006), *networked learning* (e.g. Goodyear et al. 2004; Dirckinck-Holmfeld et al. 2012) and a range of social constructivist instructional design theories (e.g. Jonassen 1991; Jonassen et al. 1995). The remainder of the chapter considers how those newly emerging and fast-circulating discourses about *general* online HE, which stridently legitimate social constructivist learning approaches and denigrate the more individualistic pedagogical approaches often used in DE, have affected and continue to affect DE practices in *specific* open university contexts. It is important to stress immediately that the aim of the chapter is not to criticise any particular set of learning theories (or the research communities committed to advancing those theories) and nor is it to develop broad claims about the current status of online HE research and practice. Rather, the chapter carefully demonstrates how common assumptions about theoretical and technological development in *general* online HE, which are based on somewhat tacit 'progressive' views of human history, are serving to widen the distance between learning theories and instructional practices in specific DE institutions.

A Theoretical Framework

To elaborate my argument, it is first necessary to clarify the meaning of two important underpinning notions: discourse and theory. Throughout the chapter I follow a Foucauldian conceptualisation of those notions. Foucault's approach to discourse can be distinguished from a more general 'linguistic' approach that focuses on analysing language at the conversational or dialogical levels; instead, discourse in Foucault's works (1985, 1990, 1995) refers to taken-for-granted assumptions or beliefs, which are shared among people in contemporary society or within a particular community (Gee 1996; Hook 2001; Mills 2004). Dominant discourses operate as effective systems of thought within a society: exerting discursive power upon that society by imposing particular ways of thinking, talking and behaving upon its members and, consequently, setting limits on what can be thought, discussed and practised. From this Foucauldian perspective, dominant academic discourse can be effectively understood through the lens of Bourdieu's term *habitus* (Bourdieu 1993). Habitus, in a simple sense, refers to the culture of an academic field—or 'the logic of practices' in the field—which often carries unchallenged or hidden contradictions. That 'culture' or 'logic' produces a 'conditioned and conditional freedom' for members of the academic field, such as researchers (Bourdieu 1990, p. 53). That is, habitus generates 'things to do or not to do, things to say or not to say, in relation to a probable "upcoming" future' (i.e. regulations or possibilities) in a particular academic field—such as the field of philosophy in Bourdieu's own analytic work (Bourdieu 1990, p. 53). In this sense, it can be argued that the habitus of a particular

---

[2] That issue of popularity will be discussed in more detail later in the chapter.

academic field plays an equivalent role in that research community to the rules that dominant academic discourse plays.

'Theory', in a more traditional sense, can be defined as a set of descriptive, predictive and sometimes prescriptive claims about a certain social phenomenon; its explanatory function helps its users understand their world and so guides their practices in particular ways (Bennett and Oliver 2011; Popper 1963; Trowler 2012). The production of theories is neither straightforward nor explicit—instead, it involves complex disciplinary relations, interests and practices, and the question of 'what is a legitimate theoretical claim?' is usually controlled by dominant discourses in the academic field at the time the theory is under examination. From the perspectives both of Bourdieu (1990) and Foucault (1995), therefore, disciplinary knowledge (i.e. 'theory') is neither objective nor a universal truth; instead, it is a subjective and historical (or social) product created and validated within some particular academic field. Although 'theoretically' theory is supposed to be open to any attempts at refutation, at some point a given theory comes to establish an academic legitimacy, and thereafter it is difficult to challenge or to refute that theory. One reason for that difficulty is that academic practices (e.g. research) are always underpinned by theories, which serve to condition *what* is researched, *how* it is researched and what can be *seen* and *learned* from research (Foucault 1977). To Foucauldian scholars, therefore, it is more important to examine the dominant discourse than to focus on specific aspects of theory itself. The purpose of doing so is to understand 'how and under which conditions has a certain theory emerged and become legitimate' and in doing so to open up certain theoretical assumptions to a process of revalidation.

In the next section, I will elaborate one particular paradigm shift rhetoric in online HE. Thus, I will give a close look at how the paradigm shift discourse shapes other theoretical claims in one academic text (Harasim 2000). That paper provides a useful illustrative example for several reasons. Firstly, the text states some assumptions explicitly that may remain tacit in other published arguments. Secondly, the fact that the paper is published in one of the early volumes of *Internet and Higher Education*, which is regarded as one of the most influential journals in the field of online HE—and is also broadly read by, and contributed to, scholars in other relevant academic circles including general HE and instructional technology—suggests that this text may not only *reflect* but also *influence* dominant discourses in the particular education context. Lastly, focusing on that single academic text at that moment in the argument is a strategic methodological decision to effectively analyse the discourse and its discursive product, which cannot be directly analysed. The aim is to clearly demonstrate, within the limited space in the chapter, how the discourse shapes a number of rhetorical or unproven claims about online HE and its practice. A brief overview of the development of the early DE theories, which is quite different to the common account of the theoretical evolution of online HE (or general online education), will subsequently be deployed. In doing so, the basis of some of Harasim's rhetorical claims will be weakened, while, more broadly, the dominant 'progressive' view of the theoretical and technological development of DE will be brought into question.

A Paradigm Shift Rhetoric in Online Higher Education

In 2000, in an article entitled *Shift happens: Online education as a new paradigm in learning,* Linda Harasim, a Canadian scholar well-known for her writing on online HE, proclaimed that a paradigmatic shift *had happened* in HE. It is worth examining the rhetorical mechanisms by which Harasim seeks to substantiate that assertion.

Affirming online HE as a new paradigm in learning, Harasim begins the article by quoting a short passage from Thomas Kuhn's *The Structure of Scientific Revolutions* (1970):

> The proponents of competing paradigms practice their trades in different worlds...
> Practicing in different worlds [they] see different things when they look from the same
> point in the same direction... [B]efore they can hope to communicate fully, one group or the
> other must experience the conversation that we have been calling a paradigm shift.
> (p. 150 in Harasim 2000)

Subsequently, the article presents an overview of the development of online HE oriented around several historical milestones (such as the invention of the World Wide Web in 1992) and significant 'firsts' in online HE activities that contributed to the paradigmatic shift (such as first totally online course in adult education in 1981 and first online programme for executive education in 1982). She summarises the relatively short history of online HE to the point of writing as follows:

> In its vibrant 25-year history, online [higher] education has tackled tough questions and
> developed various models to try to understand how new methods of learning and teaching
> can be *effective, exciting,* and relevant. But while developments in the 1980s and 1990s
> prepared for a *revolution* in the field of education, most of the *noise* generated in the media
> questioned the value and quality of online [higher] education and expressed the concerns of
> some faculty who felt they would be displaced by less well-trained staff. [emphasis added]

In the passage above, Harasim characterises online HE positively as 'a revolution in the field of education', while she describes questions or concerns about online education more negatively, for example, as 'noise'. Throughout her article, Harasim persistently uses progressive words such as 'new' (37 times alongside different nouns such as paradigm, understanding, approach, modes, forms, methods, etc.), 'change' (17 times) and 'shift' (16 times) to emphasise how online HE is fundamentally and paradigmatically different from traditional face-to-face HE and DE. Harasim's favourable attitude towards online HE is also explicit in her linguistic deployment of the terms 'effective' and 'exciting', used to characterise those pedagogical changes in HE facilitated by the adoption of ICTs. While many readers will no doubt readily recognise such rhetoric, it is worth emphasising that this positive attitude towards online HE commonly appears in other literature on online education published around the same time as Harasim's article (cf. Clark 2001; Huang 2002; Kekkonen-Moneta and Moneta, 2002).[3]

---

[3] For example, Clark (2001) discussed the advantages of online learning environments to provide more learner-centred learning experiences by stimulating learner collaboration and discussion, and

Harasim's article defines online HE education rather expansively: as 'new modes of educational delivery, new learning domains, new principles of learning, new learning processes and outcomes, and new educational roles and entities' (p. 45). The following passage from the article clearly separates online HE from DE:

> Online education is not the same as distance education, although it shares some of the same attitudes. Both are any place, any time, and largely text-based. However, the critical differentiating factor is that online education is fundamentally a *group communication* phenomenon. In this respect, it is far closer to *face-to-face* seminar-type courses. (p. 49–50) [emphasis added]

By contrasting two pedagogical approaches that higher educators have adopted when implementing ICTs in their instructional practices, Harasim again stresses the essence of the 'new learning paradigm' in online HE, by which is meant some form of 'collaborative' or 'constructivist' learning:

> Ironically, the technological solutions provided by the Web also introduced new problems or exacerbated existing ones [...] Two basic models of online courses thus emerged: one based on collaborative learning and interaction, and the other based on publishing information online [...] The second, based on *the old model of transmission of information* or *lecture mode* seemed to flourish during the late 1990s, but then its weaknesses became evident. At the same time, new tools and environments customized for education based on educational interaction and collaboration were emerging. (p. 52) [emphasis added]

This passage clearly implies the recognition that the learning paradigm shift in HE is much more complex than simply adopting ICTs. Harasim next advocates, therefore, a collective effort to 'intentionally' shape the paradigmatic shift in HE and transform HE practices, through designing online courses based on the pedagogical principles suggested by this new learning paradigm:

> Humans have experienced several paradigmatic shifts, but they have never intentionally shaped them. Today, we have the unique opportunity and responsibility to engage in designing, at least to some degree, the world that we, and future generations, will inhabit. (p.52)

Seemingly, such a call seems to indicate that, in fact, the paradigm has not yet shifted—so inevitably calling into question the validity of Harasim's earlier claim that online education has shifted the learning paradigm in HE. Nevertheless, without explicitly addressing those contradictions, Harasim goes on to reinforce her earlier argument: by presenting a large set of empirical data collected from her own research project on the *Virtual-U*, one of the first Web-based learning environments in which over 15,000 students and 220 instructors participated in over 439 courses in 1999. Harasim mentions that 100% of Virtual-U courses incorporated some form of networking and collaborative learning activities, argues that students actively participated in those activities and then claims that these courses produced entirely new learning patterns in HE. Based on similar descriptive data from the same project, Harasim further insists that students in online course produce more personally meaningful knowledge by collaborating in groups; the implication she seeks to

---

Kekkonen-Moneta and Moneta (2002) presented their comparative case study result that suggests online education fosters higher-order learning compared to lecture.

draw is that the educational role of online instructors is not to provide knowledge but to facilitate the process of collaborative knowledge construction among students. In her conclusion, Harasim reaffirms that the learning paradigm shift 'happens' as online education *matures* in HE and that, as a result, traditional learning and teaching processes and outcomes are transformed into new ones based on a new paradigm of *collaborative networked learning*:

> The convergence of the computer network revolution with profound social and economic changes has led to a transformation of education at all levels. The new paradigm of collaborative networked learning is evident in the new modes of course delivery being offered, in the educational principles that frame the educational offerings, the new attributes that shape both the pedagogies and the environments that support them and that yield new educational processes and outcomes. (p. 59)

Notwithstanding the dubious consistency of the argument about paradigmatic change, since 2000 this article has been continuously cited—thus amplifying Harasim's impetuous conclusion and normative claims through repetition and reinforcement throughout much other literature concerned with online HE. For example, Nachmias (2002) cites the above excerpt from Harasim's conclusion when he proposes a research framework for Web-based instruction that includes a research focus on 'shifts and paradigmatic changes in pedagogical practice resulting from the implementation of the new technologies' (p. 215). Daly et al. (2004), in their article about teacher learning, also use Harasim's explanation about the close relationship between a new learning paradigm and new communication technologies, on the basis of which they argue that teachers need to transform their pedagogies alongside the current educational changes facilitated by the new learning perspectives and technologies. Papastergiou (2006), similarly, cites Harasim's article along with several other online education 'pioneers'. She does so as part of an argument stating that ICT technologies support the implementation of a social constructivist approach to learning, which they do by providing communication and knowledge sharing tools and thereby 'enabling the creation of online learning communities for construction of shared knowledge across barriers of space and time' (p. 595). Papastergiou goes on to argue that those technologies can transform the traditional educational processes of HE and to claim that applying constructivist learning approaches in face-to-face instruction is difficult, if not impossible, without using ICTs.

As mentioned earlier in the introduction, this chapter seeks to position such claims about the 'paradigm shift' more critically: as one of several rhetorical but dominant academic discourses that have discursive effects, in particular of widening the gap between learning theories and instructional practice in particular DE institutions. To further that argument in light of the analysis of Harasim's paper, it is instructive to highlight the Kuhnian notion of *paradigm* on which Harasim draws and to contextualise it within the theoretical framework of this study. Kuhn's original notion of *paradigm* is, in fact, closely related to Foucault's concept of *discourse*—i.e. a system of thoughts that decides legitimate knowledge, thoughts and statements in each society—as well as to Bourdieu's term *habitus*, which decides a logic of practices in an academic community. Kuhn (1970) uses the term *paradigm* to refer to a system of inquiry shared by the members of a certain scientific community: the 'sets of rules and standards about truth—what is to be studied, why, and how' (Popkewitz and Brennan 1997, p. 300). That is, paradigmatic understandings decide whether a certain inquiry will be considered scientific or not. Kuhn's account of paradigm *shifts*, moreover, focuses on *incommensurable* differences between old and new paradigms.

Kuhn's (1970) argument denies the absoluteness of a single paradigm but instead illustrates that a multiplicity of paradigms contest fields of science at any given moment. In other words, scientific communities with different paradigms pursue their investigations in different, or even conflicting, ways at the same historical moment. Similarly, from a Foucauldian perspective, there are always multiple 'competing' discourses in a particular society, among which it is the *dominant* discourse that regulates the production of legitimate knowledge and the members' practices (Foucault 1995). Note how both the Kuhnian and Foucauldian arguments suggest that the emergence of a new paradigm does not necessarily mean that other discourses, including previously dominant ones, immediately fade away and entirely lose their discursive power within the given society. A paradigmatic shift in science, in fact, does not simply happen by the birth of a new paradigm or the advent of an individual theory, but it involves a series of phases in which the new paradigm is transformed into dominant normal science (Kuhn 1970). From this perspective, the Kuhnian paradigm 'shift' can be understood as congruent with a Foucauldian focus on 'discontinuity' or 'rupture' in social history (Foucault 1985). Neither a shift nor a rupture takes place under a certain social group's direction to change through intentional planning; instead, these events emerge from complex discourse and knowledge relations and developmental phases.

Paradoxically, however, the way in which the term paradigm shift has migrated into broader social sciences is in line with the usage highlighted in the above analysis: it is often used as a prescriptive notion that implies a volitional change, contrasting with Kuhn's original definition of paradigmatic change. Stickney (2006), for example, observes that *paradigm shift*, as a discourse in teacher education, is often rhetorically associated with descriptions of global, societal trends and that it is frequently used on that basis to legitimise authoritarian educational policies or to normatively legitimate campaigns within the local level of school context. Stickney further argues that the paradigm shift rhetoric is misused in diverse school reform projects, where it is utilised as a powerful tool to force teachers to develop a unified identity—as change agents who actively and collectively participate to realise top-down reform initiatives in their schools. Interestingly, in this context, the notion of paradigm shift has itself, in turn, seemingly become a dominant discourse leading educational change and exerting influence upon teachers' beliefs and practices.

Harasim's work provides a useful illustrative example of how Kuhn's concept of paradigm (or paradigm shift) has lost its original legitimacy and rather become adopted as a legitimating rhetoric in online HE. Crudely used, that rhetoric contributes to the oversimplification of complex changes in social practice whose genesis is multifaceted, that is, influenced by multiple factors at different contextual levels, both at local and global level. In the present example, the paradigm shift rhetoric, in the process of unsophisticatedly contrasting DE as old learning paradigm (one that is teacher-centred and non-interactive) and online HE as new paradigm (one that is learner-centred and interactive), fails to consider the pedagogical historicity and contextual specificity of DE. Paradigm as a rhetorical academic discourse has lost its descriptive power; instead, it exerts a discursive power by prescribing right, effective or legitimate ways of designing online courses and being an online instructor.

A Distance Between Theories and Practices

As mentioned earlier, this chapter analyses the discursive effects of the paradigm shift rhetoric on DE practices in specialist 'open university' settings. The previous section illustrated how paradigm shift rhetoric generates certain pedagogical and theoretical claims about online HE—ones that, among other things, raise the status of collaborative and constructive learning theories and disparage 'old' pedagogical approaches to DE. Building on that foundation, the present section problematises 'progressive' assumptions about the historical development of online HE theories, which are commonly advocated as some sort of 'evolution' in general learning theories. Against that general 'evolutionary' view, the section counterposes, once more, the divergent contextual specificity and pedagogical historicity of DE theory and practice.

Let us begin by considering how the 'historical development' of learning theories is typically presented in accounts of online HE. Once again, the account is congruent with the work of Harasim (2012), but analogous accounts can easily be found elsewhere in the literature (e.g. Koschmann 1996; Swan 2005). Jones's (2015) work, concerning a development of NL research in post-compulsory level, also provides a good summary of the general theories of learning, which is complemented by some of the alternative views of learning.

How people learn has always been an important question in education; it is assumed that only if we know how people learn are we able to teach them or to effectively design learning experiences (Bransford et al. 2000). At present, the dominant bodies of literature on online HE literature largely follow a broadly constructivist understanding of how people learn—regarding learning as 'an active process of constructing rather than acquiring knowledge, and instruction is a process of supporting that construction rather than communicating knowledge' (Duffy and Cunningham 1996).

Not very long ago, however, behaviourist learning theories (e.g. Skinner' programmed instruction) and cognitivist learning theories (e.g. Wittrock's generative learning model) dominated most education contexts. Skinner in his article, *The science of learning and the art of teaching* published in 1954, argued that programmed instructional materials should include small steps of desirable behaviour changes, ask frequent questions and offer immediate feedback and allow for individual self-paced approaches. He also advocated that the aversive, oppressive and often corporal behaviour control techniques prevalent in his time be replaced by 'scientific methods', such as the systematic analysis of learning and the optimal arrangement of reinforcement for desired behaviour. Behaviourist learning theorists (e.g. Watson, Thorndike and Skinner) focused on making instruction individually tailored and designed to maximise its instructional 'effectiveness': that is, to provoke positive behavioural changes (Harasim 2012). Later, Wittrock's (1992) generative learning model defined learning as acquisition of factual information and suggested that people learn new knowledge by generating connections between new information and their prior knowledge. Cognitivist learning theorists were interested in learners' internal mental process of knowledge acquisition, based on various information-processing models (Harasim 2012). From the vantage point of this cognitivist learning approach, effective teaching provides a learning task meaningful to individual learners and carefully organises and presents materials as ordered chunks: ordered from simple to complex and so as to build on prior memory.

During the period of the 1990s–2000s, there was an important pedagogical change in general education contexts: a move from cognitivism to constructivism (Bruner 1986; Piaget 1973; Von Glasersfeld 1984; Vygotsky 1978). This transition is mostly explained with respect to an epistemological or philosophical shift from objectivism to constructivism (e.g. Jonassen 1991; Swan 2005; Vrasidas 2000). In this account, whereas objectivists believe that the world is structured and knowledge is objective and external to the knower, constructivists argue that the world is constructed in each individual's mind and knowledge is subjective. That is, constructivist learning theories are fundamentally based on constructivist views about knowledge and knowing. The core ideas of constructivist learning theories are that i) when we encounter a new idea or experience, we either assimilate it into our existing knowledge or accommodate it by restructuring and developing our previous framework of understanding (Piaget 1973), and that ii) people construct their own understanding of the world through interacting with their environments and creating meaning from personal experiences (Vygotsky 1978). Learning—an active process of constructing knowledge by interacting with other people and environments—is, therefore, not an individual process but a social practice (Wenger 1998).

In parallel, the development of instructional technologies has been taken as an opportunity for the theorising of social learning or collaborative learning, with a focus on how to design constructivist learning environments and support students within them (Hillman et al. 1994; Koschmann 1996; Paavola et al. 2004). To cite one example, social constructivist learning environments are set up as being those that 'engage learners in knowledge construction through collaborative activities that embed learning in a meaningful context and through reflection on what has been learned through conversation with other learners' (Jonassen et al. 1995, p. 12). Thus, it is suggested that teachers and instructional designers might focus on developing interactive and collaborative environments rather than controlling behaviours and outcomes and prescribing information into sequences (Swan 2005). For example, Garrison and Anderson (2003) propose the *Community of Inquiry* model whose three key factors are environmental: designing for cognitive presence, social presence and teaching presence. This model does not suggest a prescriptive or procedural approach to instructional design but identifies particular instructional strategies and teaching behaviours that might foster the development of 'community' among learners. Scardamalia and Bereiter's (1994) *knowledge building* framework, similarly, conceptualises learning as a collaborative knowledge building process and carries the implication that a focus of education for the knowledge age should be to engage children in that knowledge building process. Scardamalia (2002) identified 12 principles of knowledge building that might comprise successful collective inquiry processes and suggested that teachers become guides or facilitators, allowing students to have a collective responsibility, as a knowledge building community, for their own learning.

From a broader theoretical perspective, the *computer-supported collaborative learning* (CSCL) research community has been committed to advancing collaborative learning theories from its inception. That group of researchers have tried to better understand 'how people can learn together with the help of computers' (Stahl et al. 2006, p. 409) and how to design technologies to support learners' collective meaning making or knowledge building processes (e.g. Dillenbourg et al. 1996; Scardamalia and Bereiter 1994). *Networked learning* (NL), which is defined as 'learning in which information and communication technology is used to promote connections: between one learner and other learners, between learners and tutors; between a learning community and its learning resources' (Goodyear et al. 2004, p. 1), is another research community that shares with CSCL a commitment to collective collaboration in learning (Jones 2015). It is within that same general historical narrative of the development of learning theories that the current ideas and approaches prevailing in the academic field of 'online HE' are also deeply situated. As shown in the preceding section, online HE is commonly associated with the 'new' constructivist learning paradigm, whereas 'other' forms of DE are devalued on the basis that they are based on 'old' paradigms such as behaviourism, cognitivism or objectivist epistemological views. It is my intention here to briefly present a different narrative about the theoretical development of DE—to problematise the oversimplified conceptual boundaries between online HE and DE, which may be caused by the 'progressive' views of a one-directional move from ignorance to enlightenment, a move which has already been critiqued by other thinkers with regard to other fields[4] (e.g. Foucault 1995).

Early scholars in DE (e.g. Charles A. Wedemeyer and Michael G. Moore in the USA, Börje Holmberg in Sweden, Otto Peters in Germany) were concerned to formulate instructional models for independent correspondence study, augmented by different communication media (such as telephone tutoring). Because learning in correspondence study programmes is fundamentally organised around

---

[4] In a relevant field of educational technology, such critique of the progressivism often appears as a form of counter-arguments or criticisms against 'technological determinism or essentialism' as well as blind 'enthusiasm or boosterism' towards new technologies (e.g. Jones 2015; Selwyn 2013). Although these critiques will not be directly discussed in this chapter in order to closely maintain my focus on the paradigm shift rhetoric, it is worth noting that these critiques provide meaningful insights for understanding the present problem in this chapter in a broader and deeper sense.

knowledge-transmitting or broadcasting activities targeted towards individual learners, who independently complete guided reading or other exercises, it is often associated with the behaviourist-cognitivist learning theories (e.g. Anderson and Dron 2011; Jonassen et al. 1995). However, counterintuitively, the original DE instructional models devised in the 1960s–1970s did not take their inspiration from the popular behaviourist paradigms of that time. Instead, many essential elements of early DE models emerged from quite separate analyses of unique and inherent contextual characteristics of DE practices. For example, the industrial production model for DE of Peters (1967) arose from a practice-oriented recognition that, in DE, all teaching and learning materials and activities need to be carefully planned, organised and clearly presented before courses are provided to students. Peters (1967) took inspiration from industrial production, applying analogous insights and techniques (about formalised divisions of labour, mechanisation, mass production, economies of scale and so on) into DE production and delivery processes, for the purposes of increasing both cost-effectiveness and teaching effectiveness. Peters' model was perceived as having great practical utility to DE contexts, and it was on that basis that it was taken up as an organisational model for many DE institutions, including the Open University in the United Kingdom, and indeed it is still utilised in many DE institutions (Garrison 2000).

In addition, it should be recognised that distance learners in early correspondence study programmes were mostly adults with limited access to face-to-face HE. Therefore, many of the critical elements of the early instructional models (e.g. autonomy, dialogue, structure) took more inspiration from the instructional design practices of 'adult education' (i.e. andragogy in Knowles 1985), rather than the behaviourist-cognitivist learning theories being discussed across formal education settings, including both K-12 and HE (Anderson 2013; Moore 2013). The adult education literature is the foundation, for example, of Wedemeyer's (1981) independent study model, which emphasises student-centred or self-directed learning. It is also closely connected to Holmberg's teaching-learning conversation model—originally a guided didactic conversation model—which emphasises relational qualities and promotes the view that 'feelings of personal empathy and personal relations between learner and teacher support motivation for leaning and tend to improve the results of learning' (Holmberg 2007, p. 69). Building upon Wedemeyer's independent study model, Moore (1990) developed the theory of transactional distance, which seeks to illustrate the relationships between three instructional components: course structure, teacher-learning dialogue and learner autonomy. According to that model, DE can be retrospectively seen as providing experiences aligned simultaneously with behaviourism, cognitivism *and* constructivism learning, with the divergence of emphasis located around the particular difference in transactional distance in the situation (Moore 2013).

Although several technologies (such as TV and radio) had been introduced and utilised to augment teaching effectiveness, DE practices remained largely wedded to independent correspondence study and industrial production models until the 1990s. In the early 2000s, the rapid development of ICTs and their educational applications started to be seen by DE institutions as providing opportunities for improving, although not necessarily revolutionising, their DE practices. At the same time, however, this situation resulted in a rapid increase in the size of the online HE enterprise, which began to be perceived by many social groups as attractive market- able commodities (Harting and Erthal 2005), and subsequently, new online HE pro- viders (competitors from the DE institutions' perspective) emerged: such as online universities using advanced ICT infrastructures and aggressive marketing strategies and well-known campus-based universities starting to provide more programmes online. In this context, the growing scholarly emphasis on constructivist-informed pedagogical practices began to exert pressure on DE institutions for adopting new models of instructional production and delivery (Ice 2010). Yet, since that time, large DE institutions, including many open universities, have experienced a notice- ably *slower* adoption of ICTs—compared to the new online HE providers that origi- nated in the Internet era—and DE institutions have particularly struggled to implement social constructivist learning paradigms (Bates 2008).

One critical barrier to technological and pedagogical change that DE institutions have experienced is related to their adherence to the *cost-effectiveness* principle, set out earlier in the chapter. Since their development, DE institutions have gained cost advantages by using particular pedagogical models and affordable technological media, with the ultimate aim of providing access to the disadvantaged (Hülsmann 2009; Perraton 2000; Rumble 2004; Woodley 2008). For that reason, the issue of the growing digital divide has been extensively discussed in open university contexts, even while it has been far less salient in general HE discourse (Guri-Rosenblit 2009). The focus of that discussion is the question of who benefits and who is mar- ginalised when educational institutions adopt ICTs. On the basis that there has been a large group of people in both developed and developing worlds who do not have access to the Internet—a situation which remains true down to the present—distance educators have tended to take a principled stance that moving towards online deliv- ery might necessarily reduce the accessibility of DE (Bolger 2009; McKeown et al. 2007).

In addition, it is worth emphasising that the forms of practice prevalent in DE continue to be influenced by quite different contextual situations from those preva- lent in much traditional HE teaching. In particular, social learning theories tend to carry assumptions about class sizes, students' ability and willingness to undertake active collaboration and tutors' quasi-autonomous organising and facilitating skills that seem incommensurable with the standard practices of DE from the point of view of its practitioners. Even if implemented, the likely implication would be an increase in the cost of DE to students and a simultaneous decrease in the degree of flexibility of programme delivery and learner independence, which are typically considered essential for successful DE practice (Holmberg 1995). Those arguments have been explicitly made in the DE literature. For example, Battalio (2007) argues that distance learners, with their many other responsibilities, may be unable to devote the time required for collaborative learning components and that they might therefore prefer the structure of traditional 'independent' DE to that of online 'col- laborative' HE. In a similar vein, it has been suggested that those who are already well-prepared (with a high academic language level) and well-connected (having access to the Internet) are those most likely to benefit from online HE (Spronk 2001). It has been a source of persistent regret that 'DE [has] faded into the mainstream and the World Wide Web [has] failed to provide worldwide learning as had been hoped' (Baggaley 2008, p. 49) and also that in online HE only particular 'slices of the population [are] being included and other more substantial slices being excluded' (Bolger 2009, p. 305). Kanuka and Brooks (2010), having set out an argument of that nature, conclude that, in DE contexts, the three components of interactive learning, flexible access and cost-effectiveness cannot be achieved in the same DE programme all at once. As a consequence of that specialist discourse, distance educators tend to narrowly perceive ICTs as either a tool for advanced, independent and personalised learning or as a mechanism for facilitating extended access to educational materials, rather than as a tool for interactive social learning (Garrison and Cleveland-Innes 2010; Harris 2008; Peters 2003).

Discussions: Implications on Networked Learning Research and Practice

The development of ICT and its appropriation within educational contexts has provided educators with numerous opportunities for altering their practice—though the extent to which those opportunities have been recognised, realised or even desired is a matter for debate. Online HE is certainly one of the many opportunities via which the adoption of new technologies has brought about significant changes in HE practice, though the extent to which it has realised the pedagogical potential of the Internet and achieved more radical forms of across-the-board innovation in HE is, again, a matter for debate. The innate aspiration for *radical*, technology-based pedagogical change in the field of online HE has inevitably produced many academic discourses that boost and promote new ways of thinking, talking and acting among their adherents and that aim to influence all higher educators. The paradigm shift rhetoric in this chapter is one example of those dominant academic discourses serving a progressive purpose in the field: one that has normalised and legitimated a new pedagogical approach, based on constructivist learning theories, by setting up that approach as opposed against the 'old', by which means behaviourist-cognitivist learning theories. This type of legitimating rhetoric constitutes the habitus in the field of online HE at the present moment. It generates and circulates particular academic norms and rules that determine what research questions, theoretical frameworks, research methodologies and even research findings are legitimate: that is, the rhetoric conditions research practices and academic discussion in the field.

In order to achieve its aims—which resemble, in an evangelical missionary manner, an objective to move HE into some 'sacred' place—the academic community of online HE has extensively focused on generating one single belief that can guide online HE practices. In the course of effectively articulating a normative direction of movement, the projected discourse in that field has tended to overgeneralise online HE practice (i.e. pedagogical activities mediated by ICTs) and to oversimplify the advocated change (i.e. a move from behaviourism-cognitivism to constructivism).

One consequence is, I suggest in this chapter, that the rhetoric of the field has served to dismiss the diversity of the form and valid historical origins of online HE, the complexity of pedagogical change and the specificity of each online HE context (where the prescribed change may be appropriate or not). In other words, the academic field—by projecting a dichotomised conceptualisation of DE as the 'old', ineffective and to be discarded and online HE as the 'new', effective and desirable—has failed to embrace the pedagogical historicity and contextual specificity of DE. Another consequence is that many open universities[5] have adopted the Internet as an instructional medium without managing to bring about radical changes in their pedagogical principles. As a result, in many open university contexts, there has been an increasing gap between those theoretical ideals being advocated from outside and the mundane pedagogical practices, which have arisen from a unique course of historical development and which have proven not so readily changeable. Nevertheless, this theory-practice gap has not obtained much scholarly attention from HE researchers, whose academic works tend to be regulated by those dominant discourses that have caused the problem in the first place.

At this moment the NL community, having relatively mature theoretical ideas and ample evidence of successful empirical interventions in particular settings, is taking the opportunity to be reflective upon our own practice. The title of the present volume, *Networked Learning: Looking Back – Moving Forward*, is one indicator of that. In that vein, the present chapter seeks to highlight one neglected type of research site whose experiences and narrative differ substantially from those prevalent within the NL community. Accounting for the gap highlighted in this chapter will involve carefully unpacking some of the taken-for-granted assumptions underlying our research practices, thereby perhaps to some extent (re-)developing our scholarly identity as a community. While NL is sometimes understood externally as simply a common theoretical framework pertinent to the understanding of online HE contexts, NL as a community has at least two distinctive merits compared to other scholarly groups in that landscape (such as CSCL). I will argue that those unique characteristics, which the community has maintained and developed throughout its history, provide the potential for NL to serve as a particularly useful vehicle to address the issues discussed in the chapter.

The first merit I wish to highlight relates to the scope and focus of NL research. The NL community has originally emerged from, and has mainly focused on, the post-compulsory education contexts specifically. As one of its 'founding documents', *Towards E-Quality in Networked E-Learning in Higher Education: A Manifesto Statement for Debate* (2002)[6] articulates that the vision of the NL community is 'of a higher education where access and connection are championed and where lifelong learning is truly and effectively supported'. Even though there are some similar rhetorical claims that can be found in many other documents of a similar type, generated by other communities in online HE (such as a great emphasis on

---

[5] An empirical study on one open university in Canada concerning the same problem is presented in my doctoral dissertation (Lee 2015).

[6] This document was produced for the ESRC research seminar series, entitled Understanding the Implications of Networked Learning for HE.

collaboration and co-construction of knowledge and subsequent claims about the relationship between teachers and learners), the manifesto clearly demonstrates that the community's shared concern lies in the accessibility and quality of HE.[7] Given that the NL community has already established considerable in-depth knowledge and expertise on the general HE sector and its underlying mechanisms, I would argue that it is a good moment for the community to turn its attention to more specific, and perhaps more challenging, HE contexts: ones for which NL has not hitherto been considered an appropriate pedagogical approach. In addition, given its long-held concern with the accessibility of HE, NL is well-placed to consider the context-specific and historically emergent practices of DE. In other words, there is more potential for the development of joint understanding between the NL research community and DE practitioners than between the latter and other communities of more evangelical researchers.

The second merit I wish to highlight, then, concerns the nature of NL as a conscious, self-organised research community. NL as a community has strived to maintain and remember (to remind its members) a unique identity and culture based around the notion of *critical scholarship*. One example of how that identity is articulated can be found in McConnell, Hodgson and Dirckinck-Holmfeld's (2012) historical overview of the community:

> The development of networked learning has largely been influenced by understanding of developments in technology to support learning alongside thinking stemming from the traditions of open learning and other radical pedagogical and humanistic educational ideas from the likes of Dewey, Freire, Giroux, and Rogers. (p. 4)

Two points can be discerned within that account. Firstly, NL is not a single theoretical unity, and secondly, the NL community has not been constituted as being about the imposition of a particular pedagogical standpoint; instead, the community has tried to welcome and open diverse alterative theoretical or conceptual ideas including overtly critical ones (see also Jones 2015). One natural consequence of those points is that the community has had a laudable awareness of the complexity of social change, the implications of political agendas and the diverse motivations driving particular pedagogical changes: 'implementing pedagogical changes and institutional learning environments is always a political process first and only secondly pedagogical' (Hodgson et al. 2014, p. 7). From this perspective, I argue that the NL community can consciously choose to avoid being polluted by the dominant rhetoric of online HE but, instead, to critically question these commonly held assumptions in online HE. Consequently, we as a community should seek to collectively generate more balanced and nuanced discourses of online HE, which can overcome the unhelpful conceptual dichotomy between the old DE and the new online HE. Of course, one prerequisite for that critical task is for the NL research community to consciously reconsider some of its taken-for-granted assumptions.

---

[7] It is important to note that, in recent years, NL practices have been changing and expanding into diverse formal and informal educational settings and are no longer circumscribed to the context of HE (see Carvalho and Goodyear 2014; Ryberg and Sinclair 2016).

References

Adams, J. (2007). Then and now: Lessons from history concerning the merits and problems of distance education. *Studies in Media & Information Literacy Education, 7*(1), 1–14.

Agassiz, E. C. (1971). Society to encourage studies at home. In O. Mackenzie & E. L. Christensen (Eds.), *The changing world of correspondence study* (pp. 27–30). University Park: Pennsylvania State University Press.

Anderson, T., & Dron, J. (2011). Three generations of distance education pedagogy. *International Review of Research in Open and Distance Learning, 12*(3), 80–97.

Anderson, W. (2013). Independent learning: Autonomy, control, and meta-cognition. In M. G. Moore (Ed.), *Handbook of distance education* (3rd ed., pp. 86–103). New York: Routledge.

Baggaley, J. (2008). Where did distance education go wrong? *Distance Education, 29*(1), 39–51.

Bates, T. (2008). Transforming distance education through new technologies. In T. Evans, M. Haughey, & D. Murphy (Eds.), *International handbook of distance education* (pp. 217–236). Bingley: Emerald.

Battalio, J. (2007). Interaction online: A reevaluation. *The Quarterly Review of. Distance Education, 8*(4), 339–352.

Bergmann, H. F. (2001). The silent university: The society to encourage studies at home, 1873-1897. *New England Quarterly, 74*(3), 447–477.

Bennett, S., & Oliver, M. (2011). Talking back to theory: The missed opportunities in learning technology research. *Research in learning Technology, 19*(2), 197–189.

Bolger, M. (2009). Globalization: An opportunity for the "uneducated" to become "learned" or further "excluded"? In U. Bernath, A. Szücs, A. Tait, & M. Vidal (Eds.), *Distance and e-learning in transition: Learning innovation, technology and social challenges* (pp. 303–310). London: ISTE Ltd.

Bourdieu, P. (1990). *The logic of practice*. Cambridge: Polity Press.

Bourdieu, P. (1993). *The field of cultural production*. Cambridge: Polity Press.

Bransford, J. D., Brown, A. L., & Cocking, R. R. (2000). *How people learn: Brain, mind, experience, and school*. Washington, DC: National Academy Press.

Bruner, J. (1986). *Actual minds, possible worlds*. Cambridge: Harvard University Press.

Carvalho, L., & Goodyear, P. (Eds.). (2014). *The architecture of productive learning networks*. New York: Routledge.

Clark, J. (2001). Stimulating collaboration and discussion in online learning environments. *Internet and Higher Education, 4*(2), 119–124.

Daly, C., Pachler, N., & Lambert, D. (2004). Teacher learning: Towards a professional academy. *Teaching in Higher Education, 9*(1), 99–111.

Dillenbourg, P., Baker, M., Blaye, A., & O'Malley, C. (1996). The evolution of research on collaborative learning. In E. Spada & P. Reiman (Eds.), *Learning in humans and machine: Towards an interdisciplinary learning science* (pp. 189–211). Oxford: Elsevier.

Dirckinck-Holmfeld, L., Hodgson, V., & McConnell, D. (Eds.). (2012). *Exploring the theory, pedagogy and practice of networked learning*. Berlin: Springer Science & Business Media.

Duffy, T. M., & Cunningham, D. J. (1996). Constructivism: Implications for the design and delivery of instruction. In D. H. Jonassen (Ed.), *Handbook of research on educational communications and technology* (pp. 170–198). New York: Scholastic.

Edwards, R. (1995). Different discourses, discourse of difference: Globalisation, distance education and open learning. *Distance Education, 4*(1), 27–39.

Foucault, M. (1977). In D. F. Bouchard (Ed.), *Language, counter-memory, practice: Selected interviews and essays*. New York: Cornel University Press.

Foucault, M. (1985). *The history of sexuality, Vol. 2: The use of pleasure*. (trans: Hurley, R.). New York: Vintage. (Original work published 1984).

Foucault, M. (1990). *The history of sexuality, Vol. 1: An introduction*. (trans: Hurley, R.). New York: Vintage. (Original work published 1976).

Foucault, M. (1995). *Discipline and punish: The birth of the prison.* (trans: Sheridan, A.). New York: Vintage. (Original work published 1977).

Garrison, D. R. (2000). Theoretical challenges for distance education in the 21st century: A shift from structural to transactional issues. *International Review of Research in Open and Distance Learning, 1*(1), 1–17.

Garrison, D. R., & Anderson, T. (2003). *E-learning in the 21st century: A framework for research and practice.* New York: Routledge.

Garrison, D. R., & Cleveland-Innes, M. F. (2010). Foundations of distance education. In M. F. Cleveland-Innes & D. R. Garrison (Eds.), *An introduction to distance education: Understanding teaching and learning in a new era* (pp. 13–25). New York: Routledge.

Garrison, D. R., & Kanuka, H. (2008). Changing distance education and changing organizational issues. In W. J. Bramble & S. Panda (Eds.), *Economics of distance and online learning: Theory, practice, and research* (pp. 132–147). New York: Routledge.

Gee, J. P. (1996). *Social linguistics and literacies: Ideology in discourses* (2nd ed.). London: Taylor & Francis.

Goodyear, P., Banks, S., Hodgson, V., & McConnell, D. (2004). Research on networked learning: An overview. In P. Goodyear, S. Banks, V. Hodgson, & D. McConnell (Eds.), *Advances in research on networked learning* (pp. 1–11). Dordrecht: Kluwer Academic Publishers.

Guri-Rosenblit, S. (2009). Distance education in the digital age: Common misconceptions and challenging tasks. *Journal of Distance Education, 23*(2), 105–122.

Harasim, L. (2000). Shift happens: Online education as a new paradigm in learning. *Internet and Higher Education, 3*(1), 41–61.

Harasim, L. (2012). *Learning theory and online technology: How new technologies are transforming learning opportunities.* New York: Routledge Press.

Harris, D. (2008). Transforming distance education: In whose interests? In T. Evans, M. Haughey, & D. Murphy (Eds.), *International handbook of distance education* (pp. 417–432). Bingley: Emerald.

Harting, K., & Erthal, M. J. (2005). History of distance learning. *Information Technology, Learning and Performance Journal, 23*(1), 35–43.

Hillman, D. C. A., Willis, D. J., & Gunawardena, C. N. (1994). Learner-interface interaction in distance education: An extension of contemporary models and strategies for practitioners. *The American Journal of Distance Education, 8*(2), 30–42.

Hodgson, V., de Laat, M., McConnell, D., & Ryberg, T. (Eds.). (2014). The design, experience and practice ofnetworked learning. London: Springer.

Holmberg, B. (1995). *Theory and practice of distance education* (2nd ed.). London: Routledge.

Holmberg, B. (2007). A theory of teaching-learning conversations. In M. G. Moore (Ed.), *Handbook of distance education* (2nd ed., pp. 69–75). Mahwah: Erlbaum.

Hook, D. (2001). Discourse, knowledge, materiality, history: Foucault and discourse analysis. *Theory & Psychology, 11*(4), 521–547.

Huang, H. M. (2002). Toward constructivism for adult learners in online learning environments. *British Journal of Educational Technology, 33*(1), 27–37.

Hülsmann, T. (2009). Access and efficiency in the development of distance education and e-learning. In U. Bernath, A. Szücs, A. Tait, & M. Vidal (Eds.), *Distance and e-learning in transition: Learning innovation, technology and social challenges* (pp. 119–140). London: ISTE Ltd.

Ice, P. (2010). The future of learning technologies: Transformational developments. In M. F. Cleveland-Innes & D. R. Garrison (Eds.), *An introduction to distance education: Understanding teaching and learning in a new era* (pp. 137–164). New York: Routledge.

Jonassen, D. H. (1991). Objectivism versus constructivism: Do we need a new philosophical paradigm? *Educational Technology Research and Development, 39*(3), 5–14.

Jonassen, D. H., Davidson, M., Collins, M., Campbell, J., Haag, B., & B. (1995). Constructivism and computer-mediated communication in distance education. *American Journal of Distance Education, 9*(1), 7–26.

Jones, C. (2015). *Networked learning: An educational paradigm for the age of digital networks.* Cham: Springer.

Kanuka, H., & Brooks, C. (2010). Distance education in a post-Fordist time: Negotiating differ-ence. In M. F. Cleveland-Innes & D. R. Garrison (Eds.), *An introduction to distance education: Understanding teaching and learning in a new era* (pp. 69–90). New York: Routledge.

Keegan, D. (1996). *The foundations of distance education*. London: Croom Helm.

Kekkonen–Moneta, S., & Moneta, G. B. (2002). E–Learning in Hong Kong: comparing learn-ing outcomes in onlinemultimedia and lecture versions of an introductory computing course. *British Journal of Educational Technology, 33*(4), 423–433.

Knowles, M. (1985). *Andragogy in action*. San Francisco: Jossey-Bass.

Kuhn, T. (1970). *The structure of scientific revolutions* (2nd ed.). Chicago: University of Chicago Press.

Koschmann, T. (1996). Paradigm shifts and instructional technology. In *CSCL: Theory and practice of an emerging paradigm* (pp. 1–23). Mahwah: Lawrence Erlbaum Associates.

Larreamendy-Joerns, J., & Leinhardt, G. (2006). Going the distance with online education. *Review of Educational Research, 76*(4), 567–605.

Lee, K. (2015). Discourses and realities of online higher education: A history of [Discourses of] Online Education in Canada's Open University (Doctoral dissertation, University of Toronto (Canada)).

Lee, K. (2017). Rethinking the accessibility of Online HE: A historical review. *Internet and Higher Education, 33*, 15–23.

McConnell, D., Hodgson, V., & Dirckinck-Holmfeld, L. (2012). Networked learning: A brief his-tory and new trends. In Dirckinck-Holmfeld et al. (Eds.), *Exploring the theory, pedagogy and practice of networked learning* (pp. 3–24). New York: Springer.

McKeown, L., Noce, A., & Czerny, P. (2007). Factors associated with internet use: Does rurality matter? *Rural and Small Town Canada Analysis Bulletin, 7*(3), 1–15.

Mills, S. (2004). *Discourse* (2nd ed.). Florence: Routledge.

Moore, M. (1990). Recent contributions to the theory of distance education. *Open Learning, 5*(3), 10–15.

Moore, M. G. (1973). Towards a theory of independent learning and teaching. *Journal of Higher Education, 44*, 661–679.

Moore, M. G. (2013). The theory of transactional distance. In M. G. Moore (Ed.), *Handbook of distance education* (3rd ed., pp. 66–85). New York: Routledge.

Nachmias, R. (2002). A research framework for the study of a campus-wide web-based academic instruction project. *Internet and Higher Education, 5*(1), 213–229.

Oxford Dictionaries. (2016). In English Oxford Living dictionaries. Retrieved from https://en.oxforddictionaries.com/definition/rhetoric

Paavola, S., Lipponen, L., & Hakkarainen, K. (2004). Models of innovative knowledge communi-ties and three metaphors of learning. *Review of Educational Research, 74*(4), 557–576.

Papastergiou, M. (2006). Course management systems as tools for the creation of online learning environments: Evaluation from a social constructivist perspective and implications for their design. *International Journal of E-Learning, 5*(4), 593–622.

Perraton, H. (2000). *Open and distance learning in the developing world*. London: Routledge.

Peters, O. (1967). Distance education and industrial production: A comparative interpretation in outline. Retrieved from http://www.c3l.uni-oldenburg.de/cde/found/peters67.htm

Peters, O. (2003). Learning with new media in distance education. Handbook of distance educa-tion, 87–112.

Peters, O. (2007). The most industrialized form of education. In M. G. Moore (Ed.), *Handbook of distance education* (2nd ed., pp. 57–68). Mahwah: Lawrence Erlbaum.

Peters, O. (2008). Transformation through open universities. In T. Evans, M. Haughey, & D. Murphy (Eds.), *International handbook of distance education* (pp. 279–302). Bingley: Emerald.

Piaget, J. (1973). *The child and reality: Problems of genetic psychology*. New York: Viking.

Popkewitz, T. S., & Brennan, M. (1997). Restructuring of social and political theory in education: Foucault and a social epistemology of school practices. *Educational Theory, 47*(3), 287–313.

Popper, K. (1963). *Conjectures and refutations*. London: Routledge and Kegan Paul.

Rumble, G. (2001). Re-inventing distance education, 1971?2001. *International journal of lifelong education, 20*(1–2), 31–43.

Rumble, G. (Ed.). (2004). Papers and debates on the economics and costs of distance and online learning.Oldenburg: Bibliotheks-und Informationssystem der Universität Oldenburg.

Ryberg, T., & Sinclair, C. (2016). The relationships between policy, boundaries and research in networked learning. In T. Ryberg, C. Sinclair, S. Bayne, & M. de Laat (Eds.), *Research, boundaries, and policy in networked learning* (pp. 1–20). Cham: Springer International Publishing.

Scardamalia, M., & Bereiter, C. (1994). Computer support for knowledge-building communities. *The Journal of the Learning Sciences, 3*(1), 265–283.

Scardamalia, M. (2002). Collective cognitive responsibility for the advancement of knowledge. In B. Smith (Ed.), *Liberal education in a knowledge society* (pp. 67–98). Chicago: Open Court.

Schlosser, L. A., & Simonson, M. (2010). *Distance education: Definition and glossary of terms* (3rd ed.). Charolotte: IAP.

Selwyn, N. (2013). Distrusting educational technology: Critical questions for changing times. Routledge.

Skinner, B. F. (1954). The science of learning and the art of teaching. *Harvard Educational Review, 24*(1), 86–97.

Spronk, B. (2001). *Globalisation, ODL and gender: Not everyone's world is getting smaller.* Cambridge: International Extension College.

Stahl, G., Koschmann, T., & Suthers, D. (2006). Computer-supported collaborative learning: An historical perspective. In R. K. Sawyer (Ed.), *Cambridge handbook of the learning sciences* (pp. 409–426). Cambridge: Cambridge University Press.

Stickney, J. (2006). Deconstructing discourses about 'new paradigms of teaching': A Foucaultian and Wittgensteinian perspective. *Educational Philosophy and Theory, 38*(3), 327–371.

Storr, R. J. (1966). *Harper's university: The beginnings.* Chicago: University of Chicago Press.

Swan, K. (2005). A constructivist model for thinking about learning online. Elements of quality online education: Engaging communities, *6*, 13–31.

Swan, K. (2010). Teaching and learning in post-industrial distance education. In M. F. Cleveland-Innes & D. R. Garrison (Eds.), *An introduction to distance education: Understanding teaching and learning in a new era* (pp. 108–134). New York: Routledge.

Trowler, P. (2012). Wicked issues in situating theory in close-up research. *Higher Education Research & Development, 31*(3), 279–284.

Von Glasersfeld, E. (1984). An introduction to radical constructivism. The invented reality, 1740.

Vrasidas, C. (2000). Constructivism versus objectivism: Implications for interaction, course design, and evaluation in distance education. *International Journal of Educational Telecommunications, 6*(4), 339–362.

Vygotsky, L. S. (1978). *Mind in society.* Cambridge: Harvard University Press.

Wedemeyer, C. (1981). *Learning at the back door: Reflections on non-traditional learning in the lifespan.* Madison: University of Wisconsin Press.

Wenger, E. (1998). *Communities of practice: Learning, meaning, and identity.* New York: Cambridge University Press.

Wittrock, M. C. (1992). Generative learning processes of the brain. *Educational Psychologist, 27*(4), 531–541.

Woodley, A. (2008). But does it work? Evaluation theories and approaches in distance education. In T. Evans, M. Haughey, & D. Murphy (Eds.), *International handbook of distance education* (pp. 585–608). Bingley: Emerald.

Chapter 5
Variation in Students' Perceptions of Others for Learning

Maria Cutajar

Abstract This chapter presents a description of variation in students' perceptions of human others as contributors to their networked learning experiences. This description attends to the considerable boundary crossing tacitly implied in an invitation to networked learning for students who are used to classroom-based lectures. This description of variation is the result of phenomenographic research which sought to understand different students' perceptions as distinct simultaneously related. Students' perceptions are constituted in terms of an open and inclusive hierarchical structure comprised of three qualitatively distinct ways of perceiving human others as contributors to learning in a formal networked learning environment. Distinct perceptions of other students and of teachers are proposed as in pairwise alignment. Perceptions are emphasised as fluid and situationally bound in practice. No less there is the suggestion that in deepening awareness students and teachers gravitate towards becoming teachers and learners for each other. This description may serve agents and actors of networked learning to positively assess their views, to acknowledge and accommodate diversity and to constructively work towards increasingly sophisticated ways of understanding and approaching learning with and through human others using networked technologies.

Introduction

In networked learning (NL) practice, the emphasis on human relations for learning beyond engagement with learning materials using information and communication technologies (ICT) is a significant shift from the prevalent classroom-based lecture which students are used to. Teachers are assumed to take a less prominent position permitting students to experience learning through active participation in cooperative and collaborative activities with others (McConnell et al. 2012). Theoretically, students are envisaged not only driving their own learning but also supporting each

M. Cutajar (✉)
Department of Computing & IT (Junior College), University of Malta, Msida, Malta
e-mail: maria.cutajar@um.edu.mt

© Springer International Publishing AG, part of Springer Nature 2018   79
N. Bonderup Dohn et al. (eds.), *Networked Learning*, Research in Networked
Learning, https://doi.org/10.1007/978-3-319-74857-3_5

other's learning through openness and willingness to positively work together on learning tasks towards the common goal of everyone's learning (McConnell et al. 2012). But active student participation in cooperative and collaborative activities for learning is not to be taken for granted. As such, NL is a considerable "boundary crossing" (Ryberg and Sinclair 2016). In expending effort towards the development of what is theoretically projected as a learning network bringing together students and teachers as human players together on the stage for learning, there is the implied assumption of students seeing learning value in others and in taking up activities and interactivities with them for learning. But how and what exactly are students seeing of human others as part of their NL experiences? Putting it in another way, what is the variation in students' perceptions of teachers and other students as contributors for learning in a NL environment?

This chapter reports on qualitative research which sought to understand the different ways students perceive human others as contributors to their learning in a NL environment and moreover to understand these differences in distinction and in relation to each other. Such an understanding is considered important as it acknowledges divergences. It does not dismiss students' inactivity as tacitly seems to be the case when in practice students do not live up to expectations. It is the resultant description of an attempt seeking a constructive logical explanation to observed convergence and divergence from intended inter-human interaction for learning in the NL space. Such an understanding of students' perceptions of others as contributors to learning in a NL environment is considered important for informing NL design and practice striving for positive student connectedness to human others as well as non-human resources for learning.

The chapter is made up of three sections. The first section briefly sets out the challenges of the NL approach in foregrounding the social aspect of learning alongside the cognitive perspective. This section highlights reported disparity in human responses to the challenge of being an active agent for learning and for teaching in the NL setting, further clarifying the contribution of this research to the NL field. The second section presents details of the research which led to the proposed mapping for understanding variation in students' accounts of teachers and other students as contributors to their NL experiences. This section incorporates in it a brief description of the framing research methods to facilitate contextualisation of findings. The third section extends the discussion of the original report (Cutajar 2014a). Students' perceptions are emphasised as emergent in alignment and in misalignment to theoretical assumptions on a continuum denoting discernment of responsibility for learning.

The Challenge of Human Agency for Learning and for Teaching

In NL practice, the process of teaching and learning is declared to be created by students' active participation in cooperative and collaborative activities for learning (McConnell 2000). The students are reckoned to interact with the learning materials and moreover with human others for learning. The teacher is construed as taking a less prominent position (McConnell et al. 2012) permitting students to experience learning in a "community of inquiry" (Garrison and Anderson 2003) wherein students are envisaged in connectedness by way of strong and weak ties (Jones et al. 2008) actively supporting each other's learning and mutually fostering a learning network (Goodyear and Carvalho 2014). In a NL environment, it is not so much about the technologies and the types of connections as it is about the promotion of connections for learning: "between one learner and other learners; between learners and tutors; between the learning community and its learning resources" (Goodyear et al. 2010 p.1).

By emphasising the changed attitude to teaching and learning away from classroom didactic lecturing practices, NL specialists seek to explicate the role of the teacher and emphasise the expected activeness of the students as significant elements of the learning network (McConnell et al. 2012; Goodyear et al. 2010). From a first-person standpoint, directly and indirectly NL researchers and practitioners give their own descriptions about who the teacher is and the expectation of being a student in the NL setting. The teacher is found variously described as "e-moderator" (Salmon 2004), "tutor" (Open University H80x postgraduate course guidebooks), "facilitator" (Jones and Steeples 2002) and "convenor" (Lancaster University e-Research & Technology Enhanced Learning doctoral programme handbooks). Identified terms generally signal a teaching attitude which is shifted from that of the teacher as disseminator of knowledge, underlining the changed role of the teacher as highlighted time and again in NL literature. Recently, Jones (2015) called attention to the restructuring of the teacher's role when the lecturer moves to the NL environment, and McConnell et al. (2012) borrowed the terminology "resource person and co-learner" to characterise the teacher's role in the NL setting. In each of their portrayal of variation Khan (2015), Shah (2014) and Lameras et al. (2012) suggest that the use of networked technologies for teaching is a challenge not uniformly embraced by all teachers. And in a thought-provoking stance, Jones (2015) questions whether there is the explicit need of the teacher figure in a NL environment involving mature adult students. Indeed, in trying to gain an understanding of the "complexities of praxis" in online learning communities for the case of postgraduate professional learners in a formal NL context, de Laat and Lally (2004a) enumerated teaching presences in online exchanges. Drawing on the work of Garrison et al. (2000) they identified teaching presence relating to design and organisation, facilitation of discourse and direct instruction. They put a spotlight on the tutoring processes being taken up by the students themselves in a NL environment. De Laat and Lally (2004b) even followed this up by qualitative research investigating three active students' recollections of the "tutoring processes" they engaged themselves in.

On the other hand, students are observed variously described as "participants" (Salmon 2004), "peers" (McConnell 2000) and "co-learners" (Open University H80x postgraduate course guidebooks). Considering that teaching and learning as two facets of the same teaching and learning process, it is unsurprising that labels associated with the student are observed complementing those tied to the teacher. Whereas teacher-related terminology appears as descriptive of teaching practice, student-related terminology seems to be expressive of student's positioning vis-à-vis other students and/or the teacher within the NL setting. This drift is caught in the NL literature by studies addressing students' identity in NL spaces. From their personal experiences as teacher and learner, Boon and Sinclair (2012) point to identity (together with language, engagement and time) as barriers understood to turn into enablers through "the transformative journey we embark when we enter into networked learning environments" (p. 276). Linking their reflection on practice to literature claims they emphasise NL as inciting "the dislocation of the individual – lecturer or student – from familiar structures and frameworks for teaching and learning" (p. 278). They conclude that immersion in NL environments compels one to rethink and maybe redefine the presentation and representation of self. Also from an insider's standpoint, Mann (2010) draws attention to what has long been recognised in other inter-human communication contexts as the need to know who the others are for attuning one's behaviour accordingly. Explicitly or not, other researchers also reference this relativity (Jones 2016; Davis 2014; Koole 2012; Jones et al. 2008). There is advanced an acknowledgement of the perception of others as impacting one's identity and self-positioning in the NL environment therefore tying to the relational bearing of NL. Implicitly, they underscore the importance of gaining an understanding of perceptions of *human* others as players for learning when learning is proposed in connectedness to human others as much as to content material and other non-human resources such as in NL. The research findings described in the next section reflect a research attempt to shed some light in this direction.

In its ideal the practice of NL is described as democratic and inclusive wherein equity reigns, inspiring relational dialogue and critical thinking (Ryberg et al. 2012) sought by all. The premise is that active responsibility of learning and teaching is shared among participants. But in actual practice, the situation emerges from empirical research (such as that of Nicolajsen 2014; McConnell 2006; Goodyear et al. 2005; Jones and Bloxham 2001) somewhat amiss of this idealism (Cutajar 2014b, Ryberg and Sinclair 2016). For a student, the experience of relating to human others for learning using networked technologies is frequently reported as problematic (such as the case of Ozturk and Simsek (2012), and Krüger (2006)). In a review of the literature, Cutajar (2014a) elaborates on the persistent picture of contrasting views and contradictions when considering the students' views of learning using networked technologies. Inter-human relations for learning which form the basis of the NL approach are many times reported to be celebrated by some students simultaneously signalled as a source of difficulty and tension by others. Meanwhile, holistic investigations of teachers' teaching using networked technologies (such as the aforementioned Khan (2015), Shah (2014) and Lameras et al. (2012)) convey arrays of perceptions. And from her investigation of students' learning using networked technology, Cutajar (2017) also advances a spectrum embodying different ways how a student might experience NL. Boon and Sinclair (2012) maintain that "networked learning is not only itself a threshold concept, but is also a site where threshold concepts abound" (p. 275). They comment that NL turns "educational orthodoxies on their heads" compelling the reconsideration of what teachers and students do and the relationships between them.

In practice NL is not so much the ideal it is theoretically envisioned (Cutajar 2014b). The research findings described in the next section too attest to discrepancies between theory and practice in considering human others as players for learning in a NL environment. But they are also an attempt to understand them. The attempt is to understand qualitatively different student perceptions of other students and the teacher as contributors for learning in the NL environment as all legitimate, potentially helping to trace out paths perhaps leading to better attempts putting theoretical conceptualisations of NL into practice and contributing to its further development.

Mapping Differences in Students' Perceptions of Human Others for Learning

The phenomenographic results described in this section form part of a larger research project exploring differences in students' lived experiences of NL as an encompassing phenomenon. A critical dimension of variation which emerged from that study is the "Self-positioning in relation to others for learning" or what is labelled as "a social proficiency". This part of the research follows up on this finding. The objective of this part of the study was to obtain an understanding of the qualitative distinctions in students' perceptions of human others within this larger picture of lived NL experiencing, therefore an answer to the question "What are the qualitative differences in students' perceptions of teachers and other students as contributors for learning in a NL environment?"

In agreement to phenomenographic goals, distinctions were sought both in separation and in relation to each other. The research objective was to obtain a description of variation from the students, and moreover, in acknowledgement of variation, a description of different perceptions as legitimate forming a coherent whole transcending persistent reports of contrasting viewpoints when probing the students' perspective (Cutajar 2017).

Research Context and Research Participants

This configuration of differences in students' perceptions of others as contributors to their NL experiences was generated through phenomenographic analysis of the verbatim transcripts of 32 students' accounts after a 10-week NL experience which was incorporated as an integral part of the programme of studies they were reading at a large further education college forming part of a Maltese higher education complex. More details about the online course incorporating individual, cooperative and collaborative activities are provided by Cutajar (2014a). The participants were 16- to 18-year-old students studying computing as a non-major subject in their aspiration for entry into university courses. The group of participants made up a purposive sample reflecting an even spread across the three student groups subdividing the student cohort, the online activeness when on course and the end-course assessment scores. Gender balance was not achieved in this sample, but the gender ratio attained by the female representation in the sample (28% (7/25)) compares well to this representation in the cohort (22% (15/68)). Signed consent was sought from the participants, their guardians and the college principal.

Research Methods

During individual interviews, the participating students were asked to describe how they went about learning online, why they went about doing things the way they described, how they viewed the teacher and other students of the course and what they saw themselves getting out of the online course experience. All interviews were held at some available relatively quiet spot on the busy college campus at a time indicated by the participant.

Analysis of verbatim transcripts of interview recordings was taken up when finished with all the interviews. Prior to the iterative process of reading through the data collective towards the next set of categories of description, listening to interview recordings helped initial familiarisation with the data hence permitting attention to the finer details of the conversations which were not captured in the verbatim transcripts. During the first three iterations of data analysis, a preliminary task annotating the transcripts was taken up. Phenomenographic analysis does not incorporate coding in the sense of content analysis (Marton 1986), but it does incorporate the annotation of the pool of data (Åkerlind 2005). Qualitative data analysis software was used to help manage, annotate, search and retrieve the collection of transcribed accounts. But the iterative process for producing the outcome space was entirely a manual effort.

The iterative process of doing phenomenographic analysis was spread across 8 months. Whereas initially perceptions of teachers and the perceptions of students were configured as two separate hierarchies, progressively these were merged first into a two-pronged structure and finally stabilised as a single linear hierarchy wherein perceptions of teachers and students are represented as tightly coupled in pairwise alignment. That is, although in their account participants were found to generally consider other students and teachers in separation, considerations emerged as tied and complementary, acknowledging teaching and learning as two sides of the same process.

Reliability was as much as possible built into this research study through the development of a detailed record (Cutajar 2014a) of the whole research process. It needs to be pointed out that the researcher was also the online course tutor, and up to a few weeks before the interviewing period the researcher was one of the contact teachers for the concerned student cohort as well. This is acknowledged as potentially a limiting factor for generating rich students' accounts of lived experience. But fieldwork proved that more significant for encouraging participating students to speak their mind is the pre-established positive inter-human relationship between students and teacher simultaneously the researcher.

Through the iterative process of phenomenographic analysis, there was a directed effort to stay as close to the raw data as possible at all times by frequently referring back to it. In doing phenomenography, reliability is not sought in the sense of replicability of results but pursued in the sense of consistency and predictability of findings (Åkerlind 2005). In acknowledgement of the inevitable constrained context of this study, it is also noted that in doing phenomenography, the research boundaries are not gatekeepers of the reach and transferability of results as would be the case when assuming a positivistic research perspective but a question of the degree of partiality of results (Åkerlind 2005).

A preliminary form of validity was obtained by involving a professional translator to proofread the Maltese-to-English translations done in-house of excerpts from participants' accounts which were brought forward to support claims. Pragmatic validity as "the extent to which research outcomes are seen as useful and … meaningful to their intended audience" (Åkerlind 2005, p. 330) was sought through the involvement of an experienced "critical friend" teaching within the same institutional context of the research. Apart from technical support and serving as a sounding board through the course of the research venture, this research "participant" was presented with the preliminary findings leading to a discussion meeting a few days later. Communicative validity as the extent to which "research methods and final interpretation are regarded as appropriate by the relevant research community" (Åkerlind 2005, p. 330) was also sought through the presentation of the work to teaching practitioners in the local institutional context, professional educational researchers and online teaching practitioners (by way of conference presentations and seminars) and continues to be pursued by its presentation to the wider research and educational community (through peer-viewed publication).

Research Findings

The phenomenographic description of differences (and commonalities) in students' accounts of their perceptions of others as contributors to their NL experiences was configured by three qualitatively distinct, simultaneously related categories. This depiction has the student viewpoint expanding with deeper discernment of academic role or active responsibility for learning (influenced also by surrounding context). Figure 5.1 is an adaptation of the original graphical representation of the outcome space. For this revised representation, an elliptical rather than the original trapezoidal form is used for picturing the categories; moreover, the bounding lines of categories are now presented as fading to better communicate the fuzziness fusing the different categories of description and the beyond. This logical structure forms a whole picture albeit not losing sight of the constituent categories of which it is made up. In this graphical representation, the categories of description are emphasised as hierarchically inclusive. Although considered

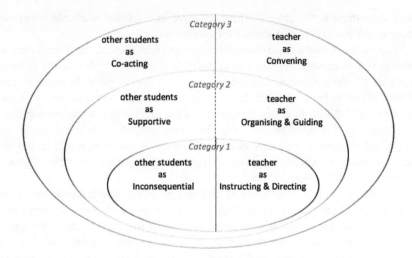

Fig. 5.1 Student's perceptions of others for learning adapted from Cutajar (2014a)

as complete, in phenomenographic research terms, the picture is necessarily open (Marton and Booth 1997).

Referentially, the perception of others as contributors to learning in formal NL experiencing is set out as going from other students contributing in an indirect way as other unconnected learners on the same study course, and the teacher as providing for all there is to learn; to other students contributing to personal learning through the visibility of their online learning activity and interactivity, and the teacher organising and guiding the students' learning monitoring exchanges and explaining issues when students do not manage to sort them out between them; to other students contributing by mutually supporting each other's learning through dialogue and collaboration, and the teacher organising, facilitating and convening activities for learning.

Structurally, students' perceptions expand from a foregrounding of other students as in separation from personal learning, and the teacher as the source for obtaining learning material and direction for students' learning; to a foregrounding of other students as a knowledge resource, and the teacher as an organiser and guide to students' learning; to a foregrounding of other students as significant co-actors co-producing and co-creating knowledge, and the teacher as a leading member of the learning group.

Category 1

For a student aligning to this category, the focus is on the student-resources relation, wherein the resources are expert provision. The teacher is the source of all there is to learn, the provider of learning materials particularly course-notes and tutorial activity work and the point of contact for answering any difficulties. In aligning to this category of description, the student talks about engaging in reading the teacher's notes in isolation possibly out of sync from other students, and all learning activity revolves around what is provided by the teacher. Learning is taken to be the individual student's "business" as set out by the teacher and away from other students:

> Because I feel that I only have to log in, do my work and that's it. Others can do the same. They can do whatever they like. It goes like that, you know. (T26:5)

> Because if beforehand you [teachers] used to give us the HW in class, and correct it in class, and did everything in class. Now we don't have so, all that time, because now everything is available through the vle. (T3:6/7)

> Normally I don't work with others … I do all my work alone and don't really ask to the others about it. We all done it. (T23:4)

In private conversation, the student may be found consulting with trusted close others to answer that occasional question that arises while doing what is reckoned to be solicited by the teacher. But in general, other students are not perceived to have anything to do with the student's personal learning. The student does not see support coming from other students contributing to his/her learning and the organising and guiding act of the teacher as does the student of the next category:

> First I used to read the notes, print them out at home, highlight the important items and bring everything together … Then we used to have the homework. Where I got stuck I used to check the notes, or check it out with my classmates. At the time there was Peter. Or, I ask you [teacher] during class time. (T16:1)

> if [the student] comes across some difficulty you [the teacher] first let us struggle on our own and then if we [students] still have a problem we look you up. (T9:6)

Category 2

This category of description has the student focusing on both the student-teacher relation and the student-student relation. The teacher is not only perceived as the provider of learning material but also as organiser of learning activities, supervising students' activities, acting the "guide at the side". The teacher is considered as intentionally providing space for students to actively manage and control their learning though still an overruling authority monitoring students' work. This perception of the teacher encompasses the former perception in that the teacher is still acknowledged to be the provider of learning material and missing from the stage centre but the student aligning to this category of description now also discerns the teacher in the shadow contributing to students' learning by organising and guiding students' learning activities, only occasionally joining the students at the centre of the stage to explain issues which students cannot somehow sort out between them and to appraise their exchanges. Other students are recognised as contributors to learning by way of their visibility engaged in online learning activity and interactivity. They are now recognised as contributing to personal learning: they are a source for accumulating information and/or obtaining pointers to sources of information; they are a reference point for asking questions when encountering difficulties in study such as a problem the student cannot solve or some detail in the course-notes which the student cannot understand; and a way for obtaining other perspectives of the subject content:

> the notes are online. Then at the same time you get to see the questions of others. The information they uploaded. Like this you have it all. (T9:4)

> We are doing the same things and we are working on the same things as well. I mean you see what others learnt, what you learnt, you put it all together and then the teacher checks that it is correct. On one occasion I had a problem as well and I talked to people whom I didn't know and I never met in my whole life. (T24:5)

The student of this category stresses other students' commitment towards his/her personal learning but in contrast to a student aligning to the next category shows no sign of concern with fellow students' learning:

> for example, I ask my classmates a question and they give me this answer, this answer, this answer, many possibilities of the answer ... the teacher can join in the conversation and say that "here you made a mistake" and possibly corrects many students all together, not one student but simultaneously four or five students who are involved in that conversation ... you need to be certain of what you're doing. Obviously, the teacher is not going to tell you rubbish. (T15:7)

Rather than any notion of collaboration is projected a co-operative attitude for learning together. Tied to this category surfaces a "trading" attitude when thinking about how other students contribute to personal learning in a NL environment:

> I mean you obtain the opinion of your classmates as well. If there is something which you don't know and he knows it, he's going to help me. And if at the end of the day he doesn't know something – something you're going to find him for sure – and you know it, you're going to help him out. You have the perspectives of all other students as well. (T15:5)

In distinction from the previous category, the student is now aware of others as contributors to his/her learning but s/he is not so much conscious, comfortable and willing to likewise be a facilitator to others' learning.

Category 3

From the participants' accounts, this category of description has the student focusing on the student-teacher relation and the student-student relation but different than the previous category the two-way communication is emphasised going beyond strict personal learning interest in relating to others for learning. There is now observed a concern for others' learning as well as for personal learning. This aspect of relating to others qualitatively differentiates this perception of others in learning from that set out by the previous category. Students are perceived to be contributing to each other's learning beyond co-operation to co-produce and collaborate in problem-solving and facilitating each other to understand issues at hand:

> Because, what I did not find on the Internet perhaps somebody else has this website which is better than mine, and he unearths more. Then we put everything together. Then, obviously, we pep it up to make it as presentable as possible and present it (to others). You upload it to show it to other students who did not work on the same task. They get to know more, even they get to learn more ... even the fact that you have that freedom, you are going to give your opinion to others, they are going to listen to you, if they disagree with you they are going to tell you. Where you can improve they're always going to help you. And ... the fact that there are other people who accept your opinion helps as well. You are going to engage in research and with your help in doing research you are going to help others. And that really helped me. (T35:4/5)

There is now advanced a sense of trust in the reciprocity of others to facilitate learning beyond personal gain within the learning group:

> We ended up switching on – doing a Skype call together to work there, and to explain it to each other bit by bit. ... Even the fact that another person helped me and I could help another person with that help ... there were also some who understood better how the program worked. And then with all the information we generated between us we could join up to help others. (T35:6)

Correspondingly, the teacher is also trusted as convening learning in ways which accommodate and favour students. This perception of the teacher goes beyond the perception tied to the previous category wherein the teacher needs to keep track of students' activities to ensure reliability of exchanges. In aligning to this category, the student sees all human players (including other students, the teacher and himself/herself) as facilitating learning in a positive manner even if the teacher continues to be deemed as that superior other:

> More like a student who is more knowledgeable. You [the teachers] are more like a student's friend rather than a teacher because you want to choose things which (students) enjoy and are interactive not something like you have to do the homework. And there are positive connotations not negative ones. (T25:7)

> wherever you go you are going to respect her as a teacher but even in e-learning the teacher is going down to your level, she is going to help you understand things your own way. You can consider them as your friends who are trying to help you understand the subject more, and how to get things working. This is how I consider the teacher in e-learning mostly. (T35:7)

Towards Greater Empowerment Through Shared Responsibility for Learning

The students' perceptions of others as contributors to their NL experiences evolve from a focus on the resources and behind them the teacher as the means of instruction and direction for what there is for learning and others as extra indirect learning

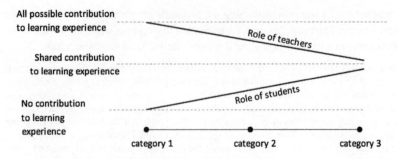

Fig. 5.2 Expanding perception of others copied with permission from Cutajar (2014a)

support means; to a focus also on the teacher and other students as a means for personal learning – albeit the teacher's support organising and guiding is presumed superior and more reliable than other students' contributions which also support learning but may possibly be ill-informed or sketchy; to a focus also on the teacher and other students as a means for all students' learning co-acting and co-creating knowledge through online cooperation and collaboration. There is developing discernment of the students as significant players for learning. The perceived contributions for learning of teachers and of students are configured by this phenomenographic study as emerging through two critical themes of expanding awareness which are the role of the teacher and the role of the student, that is active responsibility for learning.

Figure 5.2 is an attempt to capture the development of expanding perception of teachers and other students as contributors to learning in the NL setting in terms of these two themes. Not shown in this representation is the self-perception of the student as player for learning as well which, from participants' accounts, appears to be at par with the perception of other students. With expanding awareness, the configured themes or "dimensions of expanding awareness" (Åkerlind 2005) gravitate towards convergence but do not quite so realise it. In greater elaboration of perception, students are increasingly recognised as constructively taking on teaching processes yet the teacher remains that superior teaching agent. The most elaborated form of perception constituted by this research upholds de Laat and Lally's (2004b) supposition that in a NL situation, teachers and students fully contribute to the organisation and regulation of learning activities even though the teacher continues to hold a "*status apart*" (p. 166, italics in original text).

These findings are a logical representation of qualitative differences in students' perceptions of human others as contributors in NL experiencing arising from students' accounts. They attest to the theoretical deduction of teaching going from "Teaching as Telling" to "Teaching as Facilitation" and correspondingly learning shifting from "Learning as Listening" to "Learning as Doing" (Goodyear and Ellis 2010). They propose a constitutive outlook wherein the agents for teaching and learning are in a generative dance; therefore, while accommodating de Laat and Lally's (2004a, b) descriptions of elaborated roles and strategies co-operating and collaborating with others for learning as individuals and as a learning group, it also calls to attention more restricted viewpoints of inter-human relations depending on what is discerned of the learning situation at a given time within a specific encompassing context.

This description of variation in the students' perceptions of others as contributors to their learning in a NL environment is considered to help explain contrasting views of student's identity projections and self-positioning in the NL environment which we find in existing literature on students' experiences of NL. It goes beyond highlighting the problem of relating to human others for learning by providing a logical map for understanding the variation in students' accounts of their way/s of seeing human others as contributors to their learning in a NL environment. Students who somehow are observed not following on the cues of design for NL (to co-operate and collaborate with others in activities for learning) are not ignored in this representation. Students' perceptions of others and evidently their self-positioning is dependent on the discernment and perhaps acceptance of responsibility for learning. These are set forth by the continuum of the teacher role and student role going from divergence towards convergence as represented in Fig. 5.2; towards shared contribution to learning and equity of learning contribution in the ideal. In convergence of roles, NL participants are projected as teachers and learners for each other. It is with regard to such an idyllic state of empowerment that Jones's (2015) questioning of the need of a teacher figure in the NL environment is seen to make sense. Perhaps, it is in expectation that mature learners have a greater disposition to deep discernment (Moon 1999) that Jones explicitly poses this question specifically for "when dealing with adult learners" (p. 71). This expectation explains why NL is seen most often taken up in formal and informal learning contexts involving professionals.

This phenomenographic outcome also denotes an open range of different ways how students may go about perceiving others as contributors to their learning in a NL setting. Therefore, this portrayal does not deny the limitlessness of human perception. This goes beyond the elucidation of the existence of difference between conceptual thought and actual practice when considering human agency for learning using networked technologies. It emphasises the unboundedness of the expectation that in practice students don't necessarily take up NL as planned (Goodyear and Carvalho 2014) and from personal observation not even teachers when encouraged by the institution to incorporate networked technologies in their professional practice. Students who are used to classroom-based traditional lectures cannot be expected to switch to active learning and non-prescriptive teaching methods using networked technologies overnight although the possibility is not excluded. All this signals the need for NL design and implementation to accommodate different possible interpretations of human relations for learning therefore transcending contemplation of contrasting views in students' lived NL experiences. This also flags the need for research investigating how provision may in practice be more open in the sense of constructively supporting students with different viewpoints of human agency in learning permitting them to all thrive, possibly become more empowered through shared responsibility for learning in a formal learning environment employing

networked technologies; which environment is increasingly becoming more popular and in demand matching the needs of technologically connected diverse learners
of all ages.

Concluding Remarks

In this chapter was set out the outcome of a phenomenographic investigation exploring variation in students' perceptions of teachers and other students as contributors
to their NL experiences. Qualitative differences were configured in this research by
three distinct and hierarchically inclusive categories structured by the emergent
broadening awareness of all human constituents as significant sources of learning
through the responsibility of teaching processes they are discerned as sharing. These
findings suggest a forward deepening development of human perception yet again
agree to the possibility of shifts to more, or less, elaborated standpoints on the continuum of critical themes – teacher and student roles – depending on what is discerned in the specific situation. This constitutive description provides an explanation
to theoretical conceptualisations of human agency in the NL context. It underscores
that human agency for learning is not to be taken for granted. Simultaneously, this
description highlights and gives an explanation to diverges in actual practice both in
between identified perceptions and the theoretical expectation in NL practice that is
the assumption of students' active engagement co-operating and collaborating with
human others in activities for learning. This research outcome is considered as an
important contribution to the knowledge base of research on NL offering a constructive viewpoint of different interpretations of teachers and other students for learning
not as in contrast to each other but in coherence to each other. This may prove useful
to positively encourage students to rethink human actors as agents for learning in
their experiences of NL, therefore facilitating development as networked learners.

This research outcome based on the accounts of a group of young barely adult
students in a specific post-compulsory education setting is not generalizable to other
contexts and other educational levels. Perception, akin to experiencing, is situationally and temporally located (Marton and Booth 1997). The phenomenographic
strategy employed for taking forward this research further emphasises the partiality
of the research outcome. Further research is needed to investigate this aspect of
sociality in other contexts and at different education levels. Extended investigative
work looking into the "affordances" of deepening awareness of human agency for
learning influencing sociality may also help to address the suitability of NL as a
pedagogical approach in different teaching and learning contexts perhaps giving
reason to the greater adoption of NL in contexts which involve mature adults most
often in continued professional development (CPD) and/or professional practice
(Cutajar 2014a). Mature students are generally considered as more capable of
reflection and reflexivity (Moon 1999) and of having amassed substantial amount of
knowledge and experience than younger learners such as the barely adult 16–18-year-
old students of this study who are popularly considered immature and inexperienced.

Nevertheless, perhaps, in actual formal NL practice teachers will always be considered as holding the greater share of responsibility as contributors for learning. But, it remains important to work for greater awareness of the potential and consequent benefit for all players contributing to learning. That is, even if in the formal NL setting the ambition for seamlessness between teachers and learners is somewhat utopic, it is still a useful aspiration that may be approached by finding ways encouraging deeper discernment of shared contribution for learning such as through the outcome of this research, and the ensuing learning benefit entailed.

Acknowledgements The research work disclosed in this publication was partially funded by the Malta Government Scholarship Scheme.

I also acknowledge Professor Paul Ashwin for his supervision during the development of this research work.

References

Åkerlind, G. S. (2005). Phenomenographic methods: A case illustration. In J. Bowden & P. Green (Eds.), *Doing developmental phenomenography*. Melbourne/Sydney: RMIT University Press.

Boon, S., & Sinclair, C. (2012). Life behind the screen: Taking the academic online. In L. Dirckinck-Holmfeld, V. Hodgson, & D. McConnell (Eds.), *Exploring the theory, pedagogy and practice of networked learning*. New York: Springer.

Cutajar, M. (2014a). *Qualitative differences in post-compulsory pre-university Maltese students' accounts of their networked learning experiences*. Ph.D, Lancaster University, Lancaster, UK.

Cutajar, M. (2014b). *Phenomenography for researching aspects of networked learning: beyond the match of underlying values and beliefs*. Paper presented at the 9th International Conference on Networked Learning 2014, Edinburgh.

Cutajar, M. (2017). The student experience of learning using networked technologies: An emergent progression of expanding awareness. *Technology, Pedagogy and Education, 26*(4), 485–499.

Davis, J. (2014). *Dimensions of identity and the student experience of networked learning*. Paper presented at the Ninth International Conference on Networked Learning Edinburgh, Scotland.

De Laat, M., & Lally, V. (2004a). Complexity, theory and praxis: Researching collaborative learning and tutoring processes in a networked learning community. *Instructional Science, 31*(1–2), 7–39.

De Laat, M., & Lally, V. (2004b). It's not so easy: Researching the complexity of emergent participant roles and awareness in asynchronous networked learning discussions. *Journal of Computer Assisted Learning, 20*(3), 165–171.

Garrison, D. R., Anderson, T., & Archer, W. (2000). Critical inquiry in a text-based environment: Computer conferencing in higher education. *Internet and Higher Education, 2*(2–3), 87–105.

Garrison, D. R., & Anderson, T. (2003). *E-learning in the 21st century: A framework for research and practice*. London: RoutledgeFarmer.

Goodyear, P., & Carvalho, L. (2014). Networked learning and learning networks. In L. Calvalho & P. Goodyear (Eds.), *The architecture of productive learning networks*. New York and Oxon: Routledge.

Goodyear, P., & Ellis, R. A. (2010). Expanding conceptions of study, context and educational design. In R. Sharpe, H. Beetham, S. De Freitas, & G. Conole (Eds.), *Rethinking learning for a digital age*. Oxon: Routledge.

Goodyear, P., Jones, C., Asensio, M., Hodgson, V., & Steeples, C. (2005). Networked learning in higher education: Students' expectations and experiences. *Higher Education, 50*(3), 473–508.

Goodyear, P., Banks, S., Hodgson, V., & McConnell, D. (Eds.). (2010). *Advances in research on networked learning*. Dordrecht: Kluwer Academic Publishers.

Jones, C. (2015). *Networked learning*. Cham: Springer International Publishing.

Jones, C. (2016). *Experience and networked learning*. Paper presented at the 10th International Conference on Networked Learning, Lancaster, UK.

Jones, C., & Bloxham, S. (2001). Networked legal learning: An evaluation of the student learning experience. *International Review of Law, Computers & Technology, 15*(3), 317–329.

Jones, C., & Steeples, C. (2002). Perspectives and issues in networked learning. In C. Steeples & C. Jones (Eds.), *Networked learning: Perspectives and issues*. London: Springer-Verlag.

Jones, C. R., Ferreday, D., & Hodgson, V. (2008). Networked learning a relational approach: Weak and strong ties. *Journal of Computer Assisted Learning, 24*(2), 90–102.

Khan, S. H. (2015). Emerging conceptions of ICT-enhanced teaching: Australian TAFE context. *Instructional Science, 43*(6), 683–708.

Koole, M. (2012). *A Social Constructionist Approach to Phenomenographic Analysis of Identity Positioning in Networked Learning*. Paper presented at the Networked Learning 2012, Maastricht, Netherlands.

Krüger, S. (2006). *Students' Experiences of e-learning: a Virtual Ethnography into Blended Online Learning*. Paper presented at the Networked Learning Conference 2006, Lancaster.

Lameras, P., Levy, P., Paraskakis, I., & Webber, S. (2012). Blended university teaching using virtual learning environments: Conceptions and approaches. *Instructional Science, 40*(1), 141–157.

Mann, S. (2010). A personal inquiry into an experience of adult learning online. In P. Goodyear, S. Banks, V. Hodgson, & D. McConnell (Eds.), *Advances in research on networked learning*. Dordrecht: Kluwer Academic publishers.

Marton, F. (1986). Phenomenography - A research approach investigating different understandings of reality. *Journal of Thought, 21*(2), 28–49.

Marton, F., & Booth, S. (1997). *Learning and awareness*. Hillsdale: Lawrence Erlbaum.

McConnell, D. (2000). *Implementing computer supported cooperative learning* (2nd ed.). London: Kogan Page.

McConnell, D. (2006). E-learning groups and communities. Maidenhead: Open University Press.

McConnell, D., Hodgson, V., & Dirckinck-Holmfeld, L. (2012). Networked learning: A brief history and new trends. In L. Dirckinck-Holmfeld, V. Hodgson, & D. McConnell (Eds.), *Exploring the theory, pedagogy and practice of networked learning*. New York: Springer.

Moon, J. A. (1999). Reflection in learning & professional development: Theory and practice. oxon: RoutledgeFalmer.

Nicolajsen, H. W. (2014). Changing the rules of the game: Using blogs for online discussions in higher education. In V. Hodgson, M. De Laat, D. McConnell, & T. Ryberg (Eds.), *The design, experience and practice of networked learning*. Cham: Springer International Publishing.

Ozturk, H. T., & Simsek, O. (2012). *Of Conflict in Virtual Learning Communities in the Context of a Democratic Pedagogy: A paradox or sophism?* Paper presented at the 8th International Conference of Networked Learning, Maastricht, Netherlands.

Ryberg, T., & Sinclair, C. (2016). The relationships between policy, boundaries and research in networked learning. In T. Ryberg, C. Sinclair, S. Bayne, & M. de Laat (Eds.), *Research, boundaries, and policy in networked learning*. Cham: Springer International Publishing.

Ryberg, T., Buus, L., & Georgsen, M. (2012). Differences in understandings of networked learning theory: Connectivity or collaboration? In L. Dirckinck-Holmfeld, V. Hodgson, & D. McConnell (Eds.), *Exploring the theory, pedagogy and practice of networked learning*. New York: Springer Verlag.

Salmon, G. (2004). *E-moderating: The key to teaching and learning online* (2nd ed.). Oxon: RoutledgeFalmer.

Shah, U. (2014). Teacher's use of learning Technology in a South Asian Context. In V. Hodgson, M. De Laat, D. McConnell, & T. Ryberg (Eds.), *The design, experience and practice of networked learning*. Cham: Springer International Publishing.

Chapter 6
Inequality as Higher Education Goes Online

Laura Czerniewicz

Abstract With the promises of networked learning as a base, this chapter describes changes in the higher education (HE) sector, using inequality as a frame. It provides a brief overview of particular aspects of the reconfiguring landscape where education itself has become intrinsically digitally mediated and disaggregation an important trend. It notes the global shift online and locates the MOOC trend in the broader curriculum provision terrain. Other important considerations include the ways that globalisation and marketisation are playing out, including in terms of the geopolitical differences and contested power relations. The paper then reviews the rise in inequality across the world, noting the UK's position in Europe and the extreme situation in South Africa, as well as the different approaches in an information age to addressing inequality: through market-led and commons-led approaches. Therborn's equality/inequality framework is then used to interrogate this increasingly online Higher Education (HE) landscape using three types of inequality: vital inequality, resource inequality and existential inequality. Vital inequality shows how educational inequality is a life-and-death issue. Resource inequality includes a range of capitals: economic disparities (e.g. costs of data and availability of connectivity), discrepancies of cultural capital (e.g. digital literacies), and the value of institutional capital as new forms of certification jockey for legitimacy. Existential inequality, the most neglected, comprises five dimensions: self-development, autonomy, freedom, dignity and respect. Considerations here include issues of virtual representation, discoverability and visibility online, as well as the skewed geopolitics of knowledge, ironically worsened in an open access context. The chapter ends with a call for critical research, inequality-framed experimentation, policy and advocacy. It argues for theorised explorations of the fluid intersection between inequality and the digital as well as for innovations in the development of new commons-based business models.

L. Czerniewicz (✉)
Centre for Innovation in Learning and Teaching, University of Cape Town,
Cape Town, South Africa
e-mail: laura.czerniewicz@uct.ac.za

© Springer International Publishing AG, part of Springer Nature 2018   95
N. Bonderup Dohn et al. (eds.), *Networked Learning*, Research in Networked
Learning, https://doi.org/10.1007/978-3-319-74857-3_6

Introduction

Ever since the concept of networked learning was first articulated and a community manifesto developed, considerations towards equality and inclusion have been foundational. As the 2002 manifesto stated, the vision for networked learning is of a higher education where access and connection are championed; indeed an expressed core principle was explicitly to support democratic processes as well as diversity and inclusion. It was also noted that networked e-learning has significant potential for widening access and participation in higher education and for promoting social inclusion. In the years since these principles were spelt out, they have become entrenched and extended to include the concepts of critical engagement and critical pedagogy (Ryberg and Sinclair 2016) and within a seminal text in the field, it has been argued that networked learning inexorably refers to politics too (Jones 2015).

This chapter is a contribution to these aspects of networked learning, those which are aligned with the political and the critical. The questions of social inclusion mooted at the start of the community's existence form the focus of this paper on inequality in the online arena. The chapter opens with a brief overview of the changes in the higher education landscape; describes an equality/inequality framework suitable for this discussion; considers some of the key questions and implications at the global, institutional and course levels through this inequality lens; and finally asks questions and make suggestions for how these issues of inequality in HE could be addressed going forward.

The fact and nature of a changing, digitally-mediated landscape in higher education has become familiar. Those academics working in the traditional formal sector have seen an initially slow shift and then a more recent acceleration to online education. What has been particularly illuminating, at least from an inequality point of view, is how MOOC-related models have been explored and trialled. In particular, disaggregation and changing monetisation models have been critical developments in the tertiary landscape as technology has percolated through the entire system. Where the norm has been for all components of the educational process to be paid for by fees and subsidies, with students receiving a complete package of content, support, assessment and certification through a quality assured platform, now the entire, single "package" has unbundled. Each different aspect can be provided separately, and different elements may be paid for separately through, for example, "freemium" models whereby some parts are free and some are paid for. This has come to mean that universities may not be quite the central players that they have assumed themselves to be. They have become only one of the players in the sector and are now jostling with information and communication companies and private online companies (both long standing and new), publishers who are becoming education providers and digital media and telecommunications companies, as well as with mobile providers (Olds 2013).

While 2012 may have been the "year of the MOOC", those innovations were solely in the non-formal online educational arena; what has crystalized since then is that the entire system is going online, or at the very least become blended. At the same time, there has been a distinct blurring of the previously implacable barriers between the formal and the informal educational sectors, with credit transfers having broken through the barrier. It was therefore no surprise in 2015 when even Forbes and The Economist flagged the centrality of online education for society as a whole (Barack 2014; Morrison 2015).

In the USA, online provision has thus far been offered mainly by private companies, but this trend is decreasing globally, with public and residential universities moving rapidly into the online sphere (Allen and Seaman 2015), and MOOCs, to the surprise of many, not disappearing. MOOCs and MOOC-type offerings continue to grow in number and are being provided by a range of organisations with different agendas around the world (ICEF 2014, Shah 2015). One of the most significant aspects of online education – especially from a global south perspective – is its global rather than local orientation. Students are no longer merely locally based but potentially based anywhere at all, and the rising global middle class (especially in developing countries) is ear-marked as potential learners for online providers everywhere. This aligns neatly with the view of education as an export; examples are numerous – even a recent JISC report talks about scaling up online education for the global marketplace. This also means, from a learning perspective, that all higher education is digitally mediated – it is a matter of "how much" rather than "if" as there is no longer a dichotomy between an "online classroom" and the "traditional classroom". The implications are profound in terms of digital literacies, diversity of learners, cultural capital, language and a plethora of other learning considerations as digital affordances infiltrate the educational experience.

Inequality

At the same time as the rise of online in higher education, equality and inequality have become sources of pressing global disquiet with, for example, the World Economic Forum reporting that the second most concerning trend in the world today is widening income disparities. Numerous lenses and explanations abound as inequality receives much needed attention. This chapter draws on Therborn's work, one especially valuable for education as he expounds beyond resources and matters of economics when explaining inequality, being mindful both of individual and collective actions and about the systemic arrangements which predicate inequality. His definition of equality is crisp: the "capability to function as a human being" (Therborn 2013). He considers human beings in three ways – as organisms, as actors and as persons – and aligns these versions of humans to three different types of inequality, respectively, vital inequality, resource inequality and existential inequality (2013), as explored later in the chapter.

How does inequality get measured? One accessible measure is the Palma ratio, which divides the richest 10% of the population's share of gross national income by the poorest 40%'s share. The most extreme case of inequality is South Africa where the 2 richest people in the country have wealth equal to the poorest 50%, i.e. 2 people hold the same amount of wealth as 26.5 million people (South Africa, in fact, has the worst inequality in the world). However, inequality is not exclusively a global south problem. It is interesting to note the position of the UK, for example, in relation to the income distribution of the OECD countries: out of 30, it is ranked 4th most unequal. It is the most unequal nation in Europe – the richest 10% of households in the UK hold 44% of the wealth, while the poorest 50% hold 9.5%. The USA, of course, is even more unequal. (https://www.equalitytrust.org.uk/scale-economic-inequality-uk).

How might these issues link to technology? For many, the possibilities of technology promise solutions to addressing inequality. While there is unlikely to be a direct causal or determinist relationship, there can be no question that technology – most significantly the Internet – could and should be a major part of combating inequality (la Rue 2011). It is therefore surprising that popular reports on educational technology rarely, if ever, mention of equality or inequality.

Debates about equality in information societies are of course long standing. Mansell (2013) has framed the issue succinctly – the prevailing, dominant social imaginary is market-led, and the alternative is "open" or commons-led. This conflict "leads to major problems for stakeholders in deciding which policies or mix of policies and strategies, is most likely to facilitate progress towards more just and equitable information societies" (Mansell 2013). This is not necessarily an either-or scenario – a hybrid situation prevails, and history has shown that a completely public-led and government-funded approach does not necessarily lead to equality. The challenge therefore lies in its balancing these approaches.

And yet the market-led approach is dominant. Educational technology funding is growing – it reached $1.87 billion in 2014 – and it has become global in scope and reach. The counter-narrative is the democratic "open" movement, epitomised by the Cape Town Open Education Declaration (2007) which states that "each and every person on earth can access and contribute to the sum of all human knowledge". It is however of note that that the commons movement as a counter-narrative has not received the same amount of attention as the market-led approach and that new models and structures in this paradigm are less evident.

The tensions manifest in these imaginaries are underscored by the austerity environment which typifies higher education in many contexts. An Oxfam report argues strongly that there is a need to take back control of public policy and that at least 20% of government funding should be spent on education; however, between 2008 and 2012, more than half of developing countries reduced spending on education (Seery and Arendar 2014). The many scholars and students in institutions where transformation and decolonization is the predominant discourse are emphatic that "transformation will not happen without a recapitalization of our institutions of higher education" (Mbembe 2015). The question is, therefore, how a values-led hybrid ecology of digitally mediated educational provision can be shaped that strikes a strategic balance between state support and private sector provision to prioritise and enable equality in higher education.

Vital Inequality

Returning to Therborn, if one considers education in terms of vital inequality, could it be regarded as a "life-and-death" issue as he suggests? Of course it could, given that that poor people are less likely to be educated (Seery and Arendar 2014) and that educated people generally live longer (Meara et al. 2008) – even parents of college graduates live longer (Friedman and Mare 2014; Ingraham 2014). It is also not irrelevant that more complex indices of poverty alleviation now incorporate educational deprivation as one of the major indicators (Noble and Wright 2012). In South Africa, such issues are critical with equality in education being understood not simply in terms of access as entry, but in terms of access to success. Only 25% of students graduate in regulation time, and more than half of students who enrol in universities never graduate, even accounting for students who take longer than 5 years, or who return after dropping out. The situation is further complicated by racial considerations, with completion rates among white students being on average 50% higher than among black African students, and only about 5% of apartheid category black and coloured youth succeeding in any form of higher education (Council for Higher Education 2013).

The early days of MOOCs saw some visionary discourses about the democratisation of higher education (Agarwal in Palin 2014), as well as somewhat hyperbolic claims for the possibilities for online education to solve poverty (Friedman 2013). Many academics were naturally dismissive of such grand statements, and indeed research has shown that: MOOC students are predominantly highly educated and employed; more often men than women, more educated than the general population (especially in BRICS [term for the loose grouping of Brazil, Russia, India, China, South Africa] and other developing countries); largely from developed countries, and generally older where they are from developing countries (Christensen et al. 2013; Palin 2014). Other studies – based on very large data sets (40,000 online students in nearly 500,000 courses) – have shown that online learning is more challenging, especially for males, younger students, black students, and students with lower grade point averages (Xu and Jagger 2014). Online education then certainly presents marked challenges, and these challenges are exacerbated in under-resourced contexts, where solutions need to be particularly pragmatic.

However, it is disturbing that by emphasising the problems, and rejecting the potential opportunities, there has been a concomitant rejection of the possibilities that these innovations still present. There is an imperative to reorientate the discussion and return the focus to how the emergent landscape of educational technology and digitally mediated higher education can address the needs of the disadvantaged and enable social inclusion (Franco Yanez 2014). There is also a need to draw policy attention – both at institutional and at government levels – back to social and public imperatives, which have been eclipsed by the commercial possibilities of online education. Although there is a small body of innovative literature and research into the new forms of provision in challenging or fragile environments with disadvantaged students (e.g. Dillahunt et al. 2014; Franco Yanez 2014; de Waard et al. 2014;

Moser-Mercer 2014; Nkuyubwatsi 2014; Liyanagunawardena et al. 2013; Nyoni 2013; de Boer et al. 2013), the answer to the question "how can online education (including MOOCs) help less privileged people to learn and/or gain an acknowl-edged education?" has not yet been found. Similarly key questions remain: which forms of blended and online education can best serve the social and economic inter-ests of developing countries and of the disadvantaged in unequal societies; and how can advances in online education (and successful online education providers) have a positive competitive effect on educational practices in public and residential higher education institutions?

Resource Inequality

Inevitably a discussion about resources is a discussion about power and its contesta-tions – who has access to which resources, and in which configurations: economic, material and infrastructural. When considering resource inequality in an educational context, Bourdieu's categories are additionally helpful as they shift beyond the financial and economic capital to include cultural capital as either "institutional", i.e. qualifications, or "embodied", i.e. abilities or dispositions. However, infrastruc-ture remains the essential starting point. In a global climate where resources are in short supply, assumptions about even basic resources such as electricity are often misguided. Internet connectivity remains the exception, not the rule, and location is key – rates of internet access within the population continue to be largely deter-mined by levels of development, with North America enjoying 84% connectivity, while sub-Saharan Africa has only 13% connectivity (Internet.org 2014).

Within this climate, mobile connectivity seems to provide a solution to the prob-lem of inequality. However, rates of mobile device ownership and subscription do not necessarily translate into opportunities for connectivity, as it is the data that determines access, not the device. Mobile data affordability when calculated at 5% of monthly income is still low, with 53% of the population in sub-Saharan Africa able to afford only 20 MB of data – only just enough for SMS and email. Entry-level connectivity is estimated at 100 MB per month, maturing connectivity at 500 MB, and full connectivity at a level where online education becomes viable is estimated at 2GB per month (Internet.org 2014). This has many implications for learning design for mobile and the assumptions which can be made about smartphones.

There are also differing views in developed and developing countries on the pur-poses of connectivity. In developing countries, people tend to have more practical requirements, using connectivity for personal development, as opposed to devel-oped countries, where people tend to view it as more of a convenience. Forty per-cent of respondents in developing countries state that connectivity has "improved their earning power" – compared with just 17% in developed countries – and 39% have experienced a "significant transformation in their access to education" because of connectivity (Global Bandwidth Index December 2014).

All of this means that student populations have become more differentiated, delivery models have become more diverse and there is wider differentiation of cultural capital. Yet, despite flexible learning becoming more mainstream, the literature has shown that the sector has not been successful at accommodating part-time, flexible and nontraditional students, and universities are not well organised to support them. This is not only a learning design issue, but a systemic, institutional problem. In South Africa, for example, more than 50% of the student population within the sector is part-time and has been for some time (Buchler et al. 2007) with implications at the institutional, social and personal level. The idea of a homogenous student body or a typical online learner has been shattered as has the fantasy of the "digital native". This perfect online learner is apparently someone who has a strong academic self-concept; is competent in the use of online learning technologies, particularly communication and collaborative technologies; understands and engages in social interaction and collaborative learning; possesses strong interpersonal and communication skills; and is self-directed (Dabbagh 2007). The much more stark and sobering reality, as captured in Beetham's (2015) research, is of very differentiated learner engagement with the digital world, digital skills which are shallower than previously thought, the many contradictions hidden in "digital native" stories, the minority of active knowledge creation and sharing, activities typically introduced by educators and consumer practices and populist values dominating the digital space, with many feeling excluded or worse (Beetham 2015).

Just as embodied cultural capital is an issue pertaining to inequality, institutional capital in the form of certification is an equity issue. New forms of provision often lack legitimacy, and certification therefore does not carry value but and may even carry a form of a stigma. This is a moving target and may shift with time; if it does change, it may offer real promise for those in need of legitimate and valued certification. For many in developing countries, this – rather than issues of access, sophistication or even context – is the crux of the matter as it is certification which helps with employability. Until the issue of verifiable certification for free online courses can be resolved, many argue that there will not be much traction in the online learning arena (de Hart 2014).

Existential Inequality

According to Therborn, existential is the most neglected type of inequality. He identifies five main areas where existential inequality manifests, namely, self-development, autonomy, freedom, dignity and respect. These, of course, pertain directly to the work of educators. In the higher education sector, they involve issues of power and agency, for both academics and students, and they manifest at different levels across the sector and disciplines, within and across institutions and within qualifications, curricula and courses. They are about the nature of relationships and about who makes decisions.

It is in this area of inequality that the extent of the resentment towards changes in the global landscape is most stark. As Mbembe (2015 p.21) warns, "The rescaling of the university is meant to achieve one single goal – to turn it into a springboard for global markets. The brutality of this competition is such that it has opened a new era of global Apartheid in higher education. In this new era, winners will graduate to the status of "world class" universities and losers will be relegated and confined to the category of global bush colleges".

This antipathy has manifested most visibly in attitudes towards MOOCs, where critiques include the nature of money, power and condescending attitudes, the exclusion of epistemological world views due to practices ingrained in social realities and questions regarding who the real beneficiaries are. The criticism of neocolonialism has been levelled (Altbach 2014), elaborated forcefully by the view that evangelical arguments and self-appointed saviours of the less civilised rule the airwaves on the global front (Sharma 2013). Such condemnation extends to larger trends such as the globalisation of knowledge, where Gregson and others (2015) have identified the dangers of a flattened "coca-colonisation" of knowledge, and there have been calls for the decolonization of the university, and "pluriversalism, via a horizontal strategy of openness to dialogue among different epistemic traditions" (Mbembe 2015). The digital in education extends issues of inequality and privilege into the online space, given that the virtual and the material are indivisible and integrated.

Addressing these concerns involves the reshaping of networks, the redrawing of provider-recipient relationships and the shifting from a broadcast model where the "rest" of the world is the customer to a participatory model. There is a need to reduce the digital production gap, reshape the read-write web and move away from the consumer culture (Brake 2014; Schroeder 2011) towards a model where access means being able to participate not simply to receive.

The wish for more participation and equality online is undermined by the fact that most content online originates from the global north (Flick 2011). Ironically the open access policies which predominate in Europe and the UK have made this more difficult for developing countries, as it means that online content from the global south cannot be found amidst the large volumes of content flowing from the north. This is problematic, as online representation matters for knowledge, for learning and for existential equality – what is found online shapes what comes to be known. In addition, legally enabling two-way engagement through the use of open licences for remixing and adaptability is essential – anything else is simply another version of the broadcast model. Furthermore, user experiences online should be respected, and user-generated content should be owned by users.

This is not to say that the global north should not be generating content, but rather that fostering partnerships and collaborative relationships regarding new kinds of provision is essential. Tensions in new kinds of relationships surface issues of mutuality and reciprocity, as Bowles (2015, n.p.) says, "To recognise digital learning as the practice that networks small higher education institutions to global circuits of influence and profit, we need to think about … this strategic withholding of reciprocity". She then asks, "What are the obligations for care that should accompany the power to impose curriculum from one place on learners at another? What are the implications for longer term sustainability of research-led teaching in smaller institutions around the world?"

When considering inequality – especially in education – it is impossible to avoid language, especially in the virtual sphere. Eighty percent of all online content is in one of ten languages: English, Chinese, Spanish, Japanese, Portuguese, German, Arabic, French, Russian or Korean. In order to make the internet relevant to 80% of the world, it would require content in at least 92 languages (Internet.org 2014). Other equity considerations in global online education relate to the extraordinary diversity of students now being the norm; and courses increasingly diverse in terms of backgrounds, cultures and ethnicities. While "good diversity" can be enriching, "bad diversity" reinforces inequality. This surfaces the need for critical learning design for diversity in the online space, the reviewing of principles of cultural inclusion (Marrone et al. 2013) and the leveraging of research into design for large-scale provision (Kulkami et al. 2015).

The emergence of new online business models is increasing opportunities for access. Global access needs to be matched by increased access, and new forms of certification are not trivial in a rapidly changing world – they provide new forms of opportunities for some groups and value for teacher education, professional development and lifelong learning. However, in considering these new opportunities to succeed, it is necessary to distinguish between equity of access and equity of outcomes. Equal opportunities and outcomes in higher education depend crucially on supportive institutional environments and cultures, appropriate curricula and learning and teaching strategies and effective induction and mentoring (Badat 2015).

The challenges of success in online and distance education provision are significant, and the value of fully online courses as part of full qualifications has yet to be shown. Ultimately, success online requires resources, scaffolding and flexibility, and the role and extent of blended formats is unproven. The cost of providing the care and support necessary in online education needs to be measured against success.

Conclusion

Issues of inequality pervade the entire higher education landscape – this is undeniable. For those in the critical networked learning community, the question then is how to ensure values-based pedagogically shaped online learning in an austerity environment and a hybrid higher education ecology.

There is a need for critical research, inequality-framed experimentation, for equity-driven policy and for advocacy. Critical must be understood in all senses: necessary and important; asking difficult, argumentative questions; surfacing power relations. Policymakers appreciate research-based evidence, and it is necessary more than ever before to be researching the changing environment and theorising scholarship. Theory needs to help in understanding the landscape, as changes happen before implications can be understood, and by then new practices are in place. New forms of business models which support a commons approach require experimentation – this approach is weakened at present, and requires much more attention and support. There is a need to innovate with emergent forms of provision, with the specific intent to exploit the affordances of technology to support the needs of the disadvantaged. If one understands policy to mean the allocation of goals, values and resources (Codd 1988), then policy matters more than ever given that it shapes an enabling environment. In addition, advocacy is required to remind, enlighten and challenge decision makers.

If issues of inequality and inclusion are accepted as crucial and if it is agreed that there are critical absences in the global online higher education landscape, then what is needed are communities of policy, research and practice by a range of parties to find shared values-led solutions to ensure educational equality for all.

References

Allen, E., & Seaman, J. (2015). *Grade level: Tracking online education in the United States*. Babson Survey Research Group and Quahog Research Group, LLC Retrieved from www. onlinelearningsurvey.com/reports/gradelevel.pdf

Altbach, P. (2014). MOOCs as neo-colonialism: Who controls knowledge. *International Higher Education*, (Spring), 5, 7.

Badat, S. (2015). *Social Justice in Higher Education: Universities, State, and Philanthropy*. Presented at The Advancement and Financing of the Social Justice Mission of Higher Education Institutions: A Symposium, Cape Town.

Barack, L. (2014). Higher education in the 21st century: Meeting real-world demands Economist Intelligence Unit research report, The Economist.

Beetham, H. (2015, April). *What is blended learning?*. Seminar presentation, Bristol UK. BIS. (2013). Literature Review of Massive Open Online Courses and Other Forms of Online Distance Learning.

Bowles 2015 "Stones Only" blog post available at http://musicfordeckchairs.com/blog/2015/05/16/stones-only/

Brake, D. (2014). Are we all online content creators now? Web 2.0 and digital divides. *Journal of Computer-Mediated Communication, 19*, 591–609.

Buchler, M., Castle, R., Osman, R., & Walters, S. (2007). *Equity, access and success: Adult learners in public higher education (triennial review)*. Pretoria: Council for Higher Education.

Christensen, G., Steinmetz, A., Alcorn, B., Bennett, A., Woods, D., & Emanuel, E. (2013). *The MOOC phenomenon: Who takes massive open online courses and why?* Working Paper. University of Pennsylvania. Retrieved from http://papers.ssrn.com/sol3/papers.cfm?abstract_id=2350964

Codd, J. (1988). The construction and deconstruction of education policy documents. *Journal of Educational Policy, 3*(3), 235–248.

Council for Higher Education (2013). *A proposal for undergraduate curriculum reform in South Africa: The case for a flexible curriculum structure. Report of the Task Team on Undergraduate Curriculum Structure*. Pretoria.

Dabbagh, N. (2007). The online learner: Characteristics and pedagogical implications. *Contemporary Issues in Technology and Teacher Education, 7*(3), 217–226.

de Hart, K 2015, in Czerniewicz 2015 in Open Education an international perspective ,available at https://www.slideshare.net/laura_Cz/oep-scotland-19-march

De Waard, I., Gallagher, M., Zelezny-Green, R., Czerniewicz, L., Downes, S., Kukulska-Hulme, A., & Willems, J. (2014). Challenges for conceptualising EU MOOC for vulnerable learner groups. In *Proceedings of the European MOOC Stakeholder Summit* (pp. 33–42).

DeBoer, J., Stump, G., Seaton, D., & Breslow, L. (2013). *Diversity in MOOC students' backgrounds and behaviors in relationship to performance in 6.002 x.* Presented at the Sixth Learning International Networks Consortium Conference.

Dillahunt, T., Wang, Z., & Teasley, S. (2014). Democratizing higher education: Exploring MOOC use among those who cannot afford a formal education. *IRRODL, 15*(5), 177–196.

Flick, C. (2011). *Geographies of the world's knowledge.* Oxford: Convoco.

Franco Yanez, C. (2014). *DeMOOCratization of education? Massive Open Online Courses, opportunities and challenges: Views from Mexico, Thailand and Senegal.* Retrieved from www. norrag.org/fileadmin/Working.../Working_Paper__8_Franco.pdf

Friedman, T. (2013). Revolution Hits the Universities. *New York Times.* Retrieved from http://www.nytimes.com/2013/01/27/opinion/sunday/friedman-revolution-hits-the-universities.html

Friedman, E., & Mare, R. (2014). The schooling of offspring and the survival of parents. *Demography, 51*(4), 1271–1293. https://doi.org/10.1007/s13524-014-0303-z.

Global Bandwidth Index December 2014 (2014). Juniper Networks.

Gregson, J., Brownlee, J., Playforth, R., & Bimbe, N. (2015). *The Future of Knowledge Sharing in a Digital Age: Exploring Impacts and Policy Implications for Development Jon Gregson, John M. Brownlee, Rachel Playforth and Nason Bimbe March 2015* (IDS EVIDENCE REPORT No. 125). Institute of Development Studies. Retrieved from http://opendocs.ids.ac.uk/.../ER125_TheFutureofKnowledgeSharinginaDigitalAge.pdf

ICEF 2015, Global review maps the state of MOOCs in 2014, ICEF Monitor, 19 Jan 2015, http://monitor.icef.com/2015/01/global-review-maps-state-moocs-2014/

Ingraham, C. (2014, July 31). Want to live longer? Send your kids to college. *Washington Post.* Retrieved from http://www.washingtonpost.com/blogs/wonkblog/wp/2014/07/31/want-to-live-longer-send-your-kids-to-college/

Internet.org (2014). *State of Connectivity 2014: A Report on Global Internet Access.* Retrieved from https://fbnewsroomus.files.wordpress.com/2015/02/state-of-connectivity_3.pdf

Jones, C. (2015). *Networked learning: An educational paradigm for the age of digital networks.* Berlin: Springer.

Kulkarni, J., Cambre, C., Kotturi, Y., Bernstein, M., & Klemmer, S. (2015). Making distance matter with small groups in massive classes. In *CSCW: ACM Conference on Computer-Supported Cooperative Work*, Vancouver, BC, Canada: CSCW.

La Rue, F. (2011). Report of the Special Rapporteur on the promotion and protection of the right to freedom of opinion and expression, Human Rights Council Seventeenth session § Agenda item 3.

Liyanagunawardena, T., Adams, A., & Williams, S. (2013). The impact and reach of MOOCs: A developing countries' perspective. *Elearning Papers, 33.*

Mansell, R. (2013). Imagining the internet: Open, closed or in between. In F. Girard & B. Perini (Eds.), *Enabling openness: The future of the information society in Latin America and the Caribbean.* Ottawa: IDRC.

Marrone, M., Mantai, L., & Luzia, K. (2013). MOOCs – what's cultural inclusion got to do with it? In *Electric dreams.* Sydney: Macquairie University Sydney.

Mbembe, A. (2015). Decolonizing Knowledge and the Question of the Archive (Text for lecture at Wits). WISER. Retrieved from http://wiser.wits.ac.za/system/files/AchilleMbembeDecolonizingKnowledgeandtheQuestionoftheArchive.pdf

Meara, E., Richards, S., & Cutler, D. (2008, March). The gap gets bigger: Changes in mortality and life expectancy, by education, 1981–2000. *Health Affairs.* https://doi.org/10.1377/hlthaff.27.2.350.

Morrison, N (2015) The EdTech Trends To Look Out For In 2015 in Forbes Jan 1, 2015, available at https://www.forbes.com/sites/nickmorrison/2015/01/01/the-edtech-trends-to-look-out-for-in-2015/#5d91b8ce19ba.

Moser-Mercer, B. (2014). MOOCs in fragile contexts. In *European MOOCs Stakeholders Summit*. Retrieved from http://inzone.fti.unige.ch/Media-Upload_Xvc78HxeZ34xv/Kcfinder/files/MOOCs%20in%20Fragile%20Contexts.pdf

Noble M, Wright G. (2013). Using indicators of multiple deprivation to demonstrate the spatial legacy of apartheid in South Africa. *Social Indicators Research*, 112, 187–201.

Nkuyubwatsi, B. (2014). A cross-modal analysis of learning experience from a learner's perspective. *The Electronic Journal of eLearning, 12*, 195–205.

Nyoni, J. (2013). The viral nature of massive open online courses (MOOCs) in open and distance learning: Discourses of quality, mediation and control. *Mediterranean Journal of Social Sciences, 4*(3), 665.

Olds, K. (2013). *European MOOCs in Global Context*. available at http://www.aca-secretariat.be/fileadmin/aca_docs/images/members/Kris_Olds.pdf, 10 October 2013

Palin, A. (2014, March 9). MOOCs: Young students from developing countries are still in the minority. *Financial Times*. Retrieved from http://www.ft.com/cms/s/2/8a81f66e-9979-11e3-b3a200144feab7de.html#axzz3Zr1w1HfF

Ryberg, T., & Sinclair, C. (2016). The relationships between policy, boundaries and research in networked learning. In T. Ryberg et al. (Eds.), *Research, boundaries, and policy in networked learning, research in networked learning*. Cham: Springer International Publishing.

Schroeder, R. (2011). The three cultures of post-industrial societies. *Sociological Focus, 44*(1), 1–17. https://doi.org/10.1080/00380237.2011.10571385.

Seery, E., & Arendar, C. (2014). *Even it up: Time to end extreme inequality*. Oxfam. Retrieved from www.oxfamamerica.org/static/media/.../even-it-up-inequality-oxfam.pdf

Shah, D (2015) By The Numbers: MOOCS in 2015, Class Central December 21, 2015, https://www.class-central.com/report/moocs-2015-stats/

Sharma, S. (2013). A MOOCery of Higher Education on the Global Front. Retrieved from http://shyamsharma.net/a-moocery-of-global-higher-education/

The Cape Town Open Education Declaration. (2007). Retrieved from http://www.capetowndeclaration.org/read-the-declaration

Therborn, G. (2013). *The killing fields of inequality*. Cambridge: Polity Press.

Xu, D., & Jaggars, S. (2014). Performance gaps between online and face to face courses: Differences across types of students and different academic areas. *The Journal of Higher Education, 85*(September/October), 633–659. https://doi.org/10.1353/jhe.2014.0028.

Part II
New Challenges: Designs for Networked Learning in the Public Arena

Chapter 7
Hybrid Presence in Networked Learning: A Shifting and Evolving Construct

Apostolos Koutropoulos and Suzan Koseoglu

Abstract Despite the rapid growth of open online courses (namely, MOOCs) in recent years, a fundamental question is still being debated widely in the education community: how to design and deliver these MOOCs in a way that is not based on, what Freire terms, a banking model of education, in which the teacher has traditionally been the central authority. The goal of this chapter is to examine current conceptions of ways of being in teaching and learning environments through the lens of "presence," and we identify a different type of being, a different "presence," which we term hybrid presence. Instead of a single facilitating role that might be connoted by a teaching or teacher presence, we propose a presence which stems out of authentic relationships among, what Rheingold terms, esteemed co-learners. Along with our proposed hybrid presence, we propose a handful of design principles for designing learning environments that foster this hybrid presence among esteemed co-learners.

The proliferation of massive open online courses (MOOCs) is no doubt one of the most talked about and debated educational phenomena of this past decade (e.g., Friedman 2012; Hyman 2012; Yuan and Powell 2013), and it is at the core of many of these discussions where we situate our argument. The hype surrounding MOOCs pushes educators to think critically about the purposes and structures of traditional education, both residential and online, structures which some types of MOOC of this time period are replicating. In addition, open online courses are remarkably easy to access, providing a free educational opportunity for anyone who has the resources and skills necessary to participate in a networked environment. The disruptive, or revolutionary, potential of MOOCs in higher education is often tied to notions of educational equity.

A. Koutropoulos (✉)
Applied Linguistics Department, University of Massachusetts Boston, Boston, MA, USA
e-mail: a.koutropoulos@umb.edu

S. Koseoglu
Teaching and Learning Innovation Centre, Goldsmiths, University of London, London, UK

© Springer International Publishing AG, part of Springer Nature 2018   109
N. Bonderup Dohn et al. (eds.), *Networked Learning*, Research in Networked
Learning, https://doi.org/10.1007/978-3-319-74857-3_7

However, as Farmer (2013) argued, there is not yet sufficient evidence to suggest that MOOCs "are a '[d]isruptive [i]nnovation' that will resolve issues of access and cost" in higher education. First, as Bali (2014) noted, MOOCs are "the next logical step" in the evolving landscape of online education (p. 44), which is important to consider in our discussions on the potential and future of MOOCs. We believe ignoring this opens the doors to misinterpretation of the MOOC phenomenon (i.e., the hype about MOOCs) and misinforms the potential trajectories of open online courses. Second, classifying MOOCs as a single entity is problematic, as there are significant variations in MOOCs in terms of educational vision and overall course structure (Bali 2014; Bayne and Ross 2014; Ross et al. 2014). Third, we argue that issues of access and equity cannot be addressed simply by putting free content on the web. In order for learners to benefit from this *educational opportunity,* to be full participants, and to take advantage of these free offerings, they need, at the very least, to have a certain level of proficiency in various literacies and to be self-motivated. These are, by and large, traits generally acquired through formal education. Finally, there is a need to further examine the meaning of disruption in education. We argue that real change in education is a collective effort that *evolves* as a result of the interaction between social, economic, political, and cultural realities of a society or community. In other words, education as a public good is not as flexible a domain as consumer products or services to be "disrupted" as a result of a single action, product, or philosophy (Kim 2010; Knoll 2009).

Instead, we propose to direct our attention to innovations that are much smaller in scale: pedagogical innovations that may go unnoticed in everyday practice. We believe the future success of open online courses lies in how well we foster meaningful and memorable learning experiences through effective pedagogies and learning design. Yet, as Bayne and Ross (2014) argued, "[pedagogy] has been noticeably under-represented" in the MOOC discourse (p. 4). Furthermore, teachers' roles in MOOCs are "both significant and neglected" (2014, p. 18).

In this chapter, we build on Bayne and Ross's (2014) call for a need to focus on MOOC pedagogy as a highly visible, demanding, situated, and emergent practice by examining and building from the construct of teaching presence. We start from looking at teaching presence as creating a meaningful and receptive relationship with learners. We also place a spotlight on the diversity of teacher roles in openly networked environments. We then discuss the notion of "learners as teachers" and how this reframing calls for a reconsideration of these two distinct presences: learner presence and teacher presence. Reconsidering these two, we then add to this a third presence that is a hybrid of the two. This hybrid presence is particularly useful to consider in networked MOOCs, in which connections learners make (i.e., with other learners, their course convenors/facilitators, and resources) and the community resulting from those connections are at the heart of the educational experience (Goodyear et al. 2004). Finally, through the lens of hybrid presence, we suggest four interrelated learning design principles: *prepare to cede authority, embrace plasticity, be present with fellow learners*, and *leave assessments at the door*.

All the learning design principles we propose highlight approaches that are responsive to the affordances of connectivity and diversity on the World Wide Web.

In the first principle, *cede authority*, we suggest that MOOC instructors see themselves as convenors of MOOCs and that they see the learners as co-learners in their educational journey. The second principle, *embrace plasticity,* draws attention to the importance of being receptive and responsive to the direction and nature of learner voices in distributed networks. In the third principle, *leave assessments at the door,* we take a critical look into the accreditation of learners and question the value of using traditional assessments in open courses. Finally, in the last principle, *be present with fellow learners,* we suggest using tools that foster mutual empathy and awareness for both learners and teachers to be present in the environment in authentic ways. Each principle is illustrated with specific examples from different types of network-based MOOCs, such as Change11 MOOC, MobiMOOC 2011, Rhizomatic Learning, OLDSMOOC, and UNIV 200: Inquiry and the Craft of Argument.

Teaching Presence

One of the best known frameworks that addresses teaching presence is the community of inquiry (CoI) framework, originally developed by Garrison et al. (2000). The CoI framework was originally developed to make sense of the issues around the nascent online distance education and to also explore that experience. In this framework, teaching presence is defined as "the design, facilitation, and direction of cognitive and social processes for the purpose of realizing personally meaningful and educationally worthwhile outcomes" (Anderson et al. 2001, p. 5). Everything a teacher does to guide and support learners actively, for example, giving directions, organizing or facilitating class discussions, and giving feedback, may be considered part of teaching presence. Hence, within this framework teaching is seen as a directive role. The two other presences of the CoI framework, the ones actively managed by teaching presence, are termed cognitive and social, and they specifically refer to learners exhibiting certain social and cognitive actions. Although social presence, as presented, can be considered as something exhibited by the teacher, there does seem to be a dichotomy in the CoI with regard to the roles of the teacher and the learner. In addition, we observe a separation of cognition and social practice perhaps for ease of discussion and for measurement purposes (e.g., see Arbaugh et al. 2008).

Even though we do not base our conception of *teaching presence* on the CoI framework, it is useful to discuss an important proposed extension to the existing framework here: emotional presence (Cleveland-Innes and Campbell 2012). Cleveland-Innes and Campbell define emotional presence as the outward expression of affect as it relates to the course, the content, the mediating technology, and the individuals in their CoI (Cleveland-Innes and Campbell 2012). However, the emotional and affective aspects are separated from the social presence, where they currently reside in the CoI framework, and they are expanded. The *outward expression* of feeling and affect is important because even though our conception of teaching presence encompasses both empathy and awareness, that needs to be outwardly expressed, which we will explain in our learning design principles.

Aligning with the CoI framework, Pacansky-Brock et al. (2015) conceptualized teaching presence, empathy, and awareness as building blocks of effective facilitation in online learning environments. According to these scholars, teaching presence is a strategy to increase learner engagement—it is part of a method to "humanize online classes." Similarly, Kilgore and Lowenthal (2015) argue that "one thing that often separates a good online course though from a bad one is an active, caring, present instructor who has not forgotten the importance of the human touch" (p. 2), which, according to Ross et al. (2014), could also be extended to the tools we use.

In this work we also advocate for humanizing online classes to make them much more than mere content delivery. However, we argue that teaching presence is more than a collection of facilitation techniques. According to Rodgers and Raider-Roth (2006), teaching presence is tied to the lived experience of teachers; it is a *shifting* and *evolving* process rather than a directly measurable, or an immediately visible, construct. Rodgers and Raider-Roth (2006) note:

> [We view] teaching as engaging in an authentic relationship with students where teachers know and respond with intelligence and compassion to students and their learning. We define this engagement as 'presence'—a state of alert awareness, receptivity and connectedness to the mental, emotional and physical workings of both the individual and the group in the context of their learning environments and the ability to respond with a considered and compassionate best next step. (pp. 265–266)

Thus, teaching presence can be conceptualized as a construct that encompasses *both* empathy and awareness. Further, it can be argued that in an online context, teaching presence is more than synchronicity, direct instruction, direct communication, or visibility through multimedia; rather, it is about creating and maintaining a meaningful and receptive relationship with learners.

The framing of teaching presence through relationships also calls for a need to examine learner presence in the environment as well, because as Rodgers and Raider-Roth (2006) asserted "[t]o be in connection with another human being a person needs to see and be seen by the other" (p. 274). We discuss learner presence next with a particular focus on how traditional views of learner presence are challenged in networked environments.

Learner Presence

Learner presence is not something that appears to have been explored in great depth. We do, however, need something with which to juxtapose teaching presence in order to get a holistic sense of what happens in classrooms. Some aspects of what might fit into a "learner presence" have been explored through the community of inquiry (CoI) framework. The CoI has a distinct teaching presence, but no distinct learner or learning presence. The two presences which interact and provide us with what might have characteristics of a "learner presence" are the social presence and the cognitive presence. Social presence is defined as the ability of learners to project their personal characteristics, both social and affective, thereby presenting themselves as "real people" in the learning community (Rourke et al. 2001). Cognitive presence is defined as the extent to which learners are able to construct and confirm meaning through sustained reflection and discourse (Garrison et al. 2000). These two presences, which explicitly refer to the learner, can be thought of as providing the core of what the CoI authors might consider as applying only to learners.

Learner presence is a proposed extension to the core CoI framework mentioned previously. This extension comes from Shea and Bidjerano (2010) who, in their view, state that there is an element missing from the CoI, namely, the sense of self-efficacy on the learner's part. They connect self-efficacy to learner effort, which leads into the original framework's cognitive presence.

As we noted before, another extension to the CoI framework comes from Cleveland-Innes and Campbell (2012) who propose "emotional presence." Emotional presence is defined as "the outward expression of emotion, affect, and feeling by individuals and among individuals in a community of inquiry, as they relate to and interact with the learning technology, course content, students, and the instructor" (p. 283). In the construct of emotional presence, we see not just the doing aspect of learners that we see in the cognitive and social presences but also the feeling or affective aspect of learning. This proposed expansion of the CoI pushes our understanding of the learner a bit further by separating out the emotional aspects from the social and, by doing so, perhaps giving us a better understanding of the learner. However, the "dualism between the abstract mind and concrete material social practice" was questioned by many scholars (e.g., see Hodgson et al. 2014; Parchoma 2016). Parchoma (2016) further called for approaches that transcend such dualisms and open "new examinations and problematizations" in networked learning.

While the CoI and the proposed expansions, such as *emotional presence* or *learner presence*, provide us with some dimensions of the learner, there is an important aspect that isn't particularly addressed. That aspect is the aspect of power dynamics in a classroom between and among the teacher and the learner. These power dynamics may be real or perceived. For example, while the CoI framework does not exclude learners from exercising teaching presence, it is not the de facto stance of the learners to direct and design for the reaching of learning objectives. In this way we see learner presence, as it currently stands, as a presence where one is being directed and instructed to perform certain things in certain ways. Thus, taking cues from both what is in the CoI and what is not, and for the purposes of this paper, we define traditional learner presence as *the extent to which learners, under external direction by an individual who orchestrates a course, are able to construct and confirm meaning and engage socially and affectively within their learning community.*

It is important to note here that learner presence in traditional classes are typically limited by the boundaries of traditional learning such as time, physical space, and accreditation through formalized assessments (Dron 2016). One other boundary Dron posits is the lecture method. Within a physical environment where rooms are built and arranged in certain ways, where we may have classes in rooms such as large auditoria, the pedagogy is partly dictated to us by the physical environment in which learning takes place. Certain varieties of MOOCs have replicated those structures without critically considering why those structures exist in the first place. However, as Bayne (2016) argued, "[n]etworked learning does not happen 'in' a space; it *produces* space newly"; that is, learning spaces can be emergent, and multiple spaces can coexist and evolve at different times and rates.

Why are we discussing traditional teacher and learner roles and issues with space and boundaries here? Because our understanding of learner presence is much more fluid; it is constantly shaped by learner agency and motivation in networked spaces. It is a construct that is closely tied to *identity*. As we also noted before in this chapter, our understanding of teaching presence is also a fluid construct because it is receptive and responsive to learner presence, with all its complexities. Thus, if the nature of learner presence changes, the nature of teaching presence should change too, and vice versa. For this reason we posit a new and evolving understanding of presence in a networked learning environment: the hybrid presence. We further elaborate on this complex presence in the next section.

Hybrid Presence

Our focus in this paper is *hybrid presence*, a construct that emerges out of authentic relationships in a networked learning environment. Hybrid presence is a presence that is not firmly set in either teacher presence or learner presence but rather somewhere in between. In traditional learning environments, even though we can design with learner-centered pedagogies in mind, there is still an institutional pull toward a central authority. This authority has traditionally been the course instructor, who obtains their power and authority from the institution, and it is this bestowing of power that puts them in the instructor's position. The instructor designs not just the bureaucratic aspects of the course such as goals, objectives, deliverables, and deadlines but also sets the tone and scope of the course and thus frames boundaries that learners may not necessarily be welcomed to surpass. Learners in such environments, even when allowed to play freely and explore, are still being *directed* to do so. This power dynamic maintains a clear separation between teaching and learning roles. All the frameworks we discussed earlier in this chapter on teaching presence illustrate this separation in varying degrees.

In networked learning environments, however, these roles are not always as clear-cut. As Kop et al. (2011) noted, teachers can have complex and multidimensional roles in networked learning including "aggregating, curating, amplifying, modelling … coaching or mentoring" (p. 89). These are also roles which can be adopted by learners in networked MOOCs, such as connected courses (http://connectedcourses.net/) or Rhizomatic Learning (http://rhizomatic.net/). Also through aggregating, remixing, repurposing, and feeding forward—roles that were described by Siemens and Downes (2011) as important for participating in MOOCs—learners can, in fact, shape the course as much as, and perhaps more than, the instructor. Thus, by reframing the role of the learner, and by acknowledging the additional roles of instructors in networked environments, we see a blurring of traditional teacher and learner roles. Indeed, as Cutajar (2016) observed in networked learning "teachers and learners gravitate towards becoming teachers and learners for each other" (p. 1) with growing awareness of one another's potential.

For example, in Rhizomatic Learning (e.g., http://z.umn.edu/rhizo14), while there may have been a weekly prompt from the course facilitator, learners did not necessarily follow the directives of the course facilitators, providing new and unexpected paths to explore the concept of rhizomatic learning. Learners could deviate from the predetermined weekly topic in class discussions and craft their own pockets of participation around topics of mutual inquiry. Furthermore, participants have the capability of extending the duration of the official course. This is something that was observed in Rhizomatic Learning 2014 (rhizo14) when participants started recommending and pursuing topics after the course was formally over (Cormier 2014). As such, learners approach the course directives as suggestions for a given module and interact with fellow participants in both a teaching and learning capacity, leading us to the notion of hybrid presence, one which is fluid and encompasses both teaching and learning presences.

We would like to emphasize that we don't see hybrid presence as simply a mashup of traditional teaching presence and traditional learner presence. While elements of the two overlap, the mix of actions, structure, and power relationships work toward producing a third presence that has elements of the two previous presences while at the same time developing certain unique characteristics of its own (see Table 7.1).

For both learners and course convenors, moving toward hybrid presence is not a straightforward process because it is directly related to identity and belonging in a group or network and real (or perceived) power relations. In other words, hybrid presence is only possible with meaningful connections and participation in

Table 7.1 Moving toward hybrid presence

Teaching presence	Hybrid presence	Learner presence
Directing	Co-directing	Directed
Broadcaster	Broadcasting and receiving	Receiver
Designer	Co-traversing	Assessed
Assessor	Co-designing	Action other-initiated
Self-initiated action	Co-learning	Power dynamic low
Power dynamic high	Negotiated power relationships	Social/self-directed
Social/self-directed	Social/self-directed	Social/other-directed
Enforcer of institutional rules and norms	Mutual inquiry	Limited flexibility
Limited flexibility	Flexible rules and course directions	
	Networked	

community, which members of a networked learning community to start to break down barriers.

Approaching a state of hybrid presence will be different depending on what the starting point is. For a teacher, coming from a traditional teacher presence, moving toward hybrid presence will include thinking strategically. Some learners in the convened networked MOOC may be known to the teacher-convenor already, and therefore those connections might already exist. Some learners will be new, and those connections need to be negotiated and traversed. This is a conscious process because a teacher, perhaps coming from a traditional learning environment with boundaries, should be aware of the power potential that their role carries. In order to accomplish this, teachers will need to provide a sandbox for the community to develop their state of hybrid presence, and in effect *cede authority* of that sandbox, but also provide support structures for learners to successfully develop their identity in this new environment.

Conversely, on the learner side of the equation, some learners, those who already know the instructor, might already have a head start in developing their hybrid presence, while others might not. Other students—described as *category 1 network learners* by Cutajar (2016)—will first, and primarily, focus on the interaction between themselves and the learning materials. However a networked environment means that greater affordances are provided by the enabling of connections not just between learner and course materials but also between the learners and their fellow co-learners; and as learners strengthen those connections with their fellow co-learners, additional connections to entities outside of the community can take root. This process of connecting both within and outside of the community is directly tied a sense of learner identity. Whereas in traditional learner presence, the learner was directed more by a guiding force, was a receiver of information, and was the assessed party (among other qualities), in developing their state of hybrid presence, they are now co-directing their learning, the power relationships are negotiated, and they are much more granular as learners are members of both a larger learning community and smaller sub-communities within that larger community (as their networks develop). They design assessments that work for them, not necessarily taking something that is dictated by the instructor. Hence, we see that the establishment of hybrid presence hinges on establishing, cultivating, and maintaining connections in the network, which require an advanced level of networked literacies (Rheingold 2013). Thus, teachers in a state of hybrid presence should help learners "establish, cultivate and use social connections" (Kehrwald and Oztok 2016); this can be both within the learning community but also outside of the community as resources exist both within the bounds of the networked MOOC and outside it. This breakdown of the barriers between formal and informal learning and the creation of connections should assist learners to develop their own agency, as it meets their own emergent learning needs.

In the next section of this paper, we propose some key learning design principles aligning with hybrid presence, which we believe has significant potential in improving the open course pedagogy.

Learning Design Principles

The MOOC format(s) hold unique challenges for instructors and learners, ranging from course design, to feedback, to the scope and aims of assessment, to copyright considerations (Koutropoulos and Zaharias 2015). Presence, and what it means to be present in the course, is also one of the central challenges. For example, "the low barrier to entry and departure" (Koutropoulos et al. 2012, p. 11) of most open courses can attract a large number of learners who may all have varied and conflicting goals as compared to those of the course designers. Learners may not be interested in completing the course or actively participating in class activities—their movements through the course may not even be visible in the learning environment (deWaard et al. 2011; Kop et al. 2011). However, we believe, as Morris and Stommel (2013) argued, that "meaningful relationships are as important in a class of three as they are in a class of 10,000. In fact, the best pedagogies are co-produced and arise directly from these relationships." Bali (2015) provides some insight on how to approach this seemingly impossible task:

> You cannot possibly know every individual or see every blog post, comment, or tweet. This often means that you will miss some things, and in missing them, miss entire consequences built upon them. So there will also always have to be a humility of "knowing we do not know." (para. 24)

With the humility of knowing we cannot know, and we do not need to know, everything in an openly networked environment, we suggest the following learning design principles as a starting point to design for hybrid presence in a networked learning environment.

Prepare to Cede Authority

In traditional coursework there are various ways in which the instructor of the course is *the* authority of the course. This authority can exist in areas of content, course structure, course flow, course assessments, and, if need be, course-related discipline. This authority sets boundaries for the course and for the learners in that course. Topics, approaches, and ways of knowing outside of those boundaries are not always encouraged, because the instructor might also have a mandate to stay within those boundaries. Individual MOOCs do not exist in highly regimented academic environments, and they are not necessarily part of established curricula. This freedom of entry and exit, and the freedom of learners to explore in a consequence-free environment, may explain the lack of participation reported in the MOOC literature (Koutropoulos and Zaharias 2015), as compared to traditional course participation.

Given this freedom of learners, instead of looking to traditional models of classroom authority to encourage sustained participation, we suggest that MOOC instructors see themselves as convenors of MOOCs and that they see the learners that sign up for the MOOC that they convene not as empty vessels to be filled by new knowledge but as esteemed co-learners (Rheingold 2014) in their educational journey. The course convenor may not be the only one that has a high level of knowledge and understanding of the topic. Since MOOCs attract participants with varied levels of prior knowledge, learning opportunities exist not just from a top-down direction, as we see perhaps in traditional classrooms, but rather they exist in a networked manner where learning opportunities can come from any source.

Ceding control can range from the traditional inclusion of guest speakers to promoting and permitting esteemed co-learners to take control of the course or some aspect of the course. The former example can be seen in action in the Change11 MOOC (http://change.mooc.ca/) where each week promoted different people to the spotlight of the MOOC, while the latter example can be seen in action in Rhizomatic Learning 2014 (http://z.umn.edu/rhizo14) and Rhizomatic Learning 2015 (http://rhizomatic.net/) MOOCs, where learners either took control of the course once the MOOC formally ended (rhizo14) or jumped in and started working on proposed topics for the given week when the course convenor was late in proposing the weekly topic (Rhizomatic Learning 2015). This deviation from the original plan helps cultivate not only learning but also a sense of ownership in the course, which we explain further in our next principle "embrace plasticity."

Embrace Plasticity

As we will discuss further in the next design principle, the distributed nature of expertise in MOOCs requires a shift from designing performance and outcome-based assessments to assessments that encourage self-reflection and connectivity. As such, the direction of learning can be unpredictable and may not align with initial goals and objectives. This uncertainty can, in fact, be a strength in the environment if we allow ourselves to modify the course design based on feedback and learner activity.

Aligning with this theme, Campbell (2014a) once noted that successful learning and teaching calls for a need to "pay attention to surprises along the way, amplify those surprises that go in a good direction, and always value that moment of surprise" (15:37). For example, from a technological perspective, the use of a course hashtag is something that brings together members of a networked community. An example of using a hashtag to bring together a MOOC community on Twitter can be seen in MobiMOOC 2011 (Koutropoulos et al. 2014). By establishing and using a course hashtag, the course convenor allows for the bringing together of a community across many networked spaces. This act enables learners to be active in spaces that they feel comfortable in and does not force discussion on just one sanctioned discussion forum. Hashtags provide a marker that distinguishes posts as belonging to a specific course regardless of the space they are in. This also allows for the creation of subgroups and subnetworks of the main course, allowing them to take the course in a direction that they feel it needs to go. This enables the course convenor, and other co-learners, to be members of both the "main" course community and members of any other community that forms in the course. While the course convenor is usually the person who sets the original hashtag, learners exhibiting a *hybrid presence* in the course can create, use, and disseminate additional hashtags to create and promote sub-communities in the course. In turn, the course convenor can promote such grassroots hashtags in order to raise awareness and contribute to the diversification of the course. Such responsiveness, we believe, is vital to help learners have voice in the environment and feel a sense of ownership in the course design and structure.

Leave Assessments at the Door

One of the potential functions of courses is the accreditation of the learner. Credits for learning can come in many different forms, with some of the popular ones being certificates of participation, college credits, digital badges, diplomas, and professional certifications. In the original instantiations of MOOCs, such as those in *Connectivism and Connective Knowledge* in 2008 and 2011 (CCK08 and CCK11) and *Change MOOC: Education, Learning, and Technology* (Change11), there were no assessments of learning. Learners, in heutagogical fashion, set goals for their own learning and gauged their success based on their own standards. In heutagogy the convenor "facilitates the learning process by providing guidance and resources, but fully relinquishes ownership of the learning path and process to the learner, who negotiates learning and determines what will be learned and how it will be learned" (Blaschke 2012). In later instantiations of MOOCs, the so-called xMOOCs, more traditional forms of assessment, such as multiple choice exams and mini essays, made it back into the what was considered appropriate components of a MOOC, resulting perhaps from the need to offer some mechanism to gauge "completeness" for the purposes of a certification.

Some might argue that the insistence on assessment and certification in these types of MOOCs have given rise to new ways of *cheating*. One recent method of cheating, proposed by Northcutt et al. (2015), involves having multiple accounts in a system in order to harvest the *right* answers to an automated assessment. These right answers are then used by the main account of the user to earn a passing mark (2015). While these learner *innovations* in circumventing assessments in such MOOCs may be viewed by some as academic dishonesty, there may be deeper issues than simply wanting to cheat one's way past the exam. It is possible that assessments themselves are flawed instruments for gauging learning that is occurring in MOOCs. We argue that a better way of designing a MOOC is not with assessment in mind but rather with opportunities for self-reflection, artifacts that make sense to the learners, and the creation of meaningful connections with fellow learners. The course design should afford these opportunities to learners. Instead of using traditional assessment instruments which are out of context in a MOOC environment, it would be better to build learning opportunities that encourage learners to reflect on the process of learning, through tools such as blogs, portfolios, and learner-generated personal learning environments and through project work. By encouraging learners to connect with one another, and to provide non-compulsory critical review of peer's work, MOOCs become much more of a community of learning rather than a mechanism for central learner credentialing.

Examples of such work can be seen in courses like OLDSMOOC (olds.ac.uk) where learners interested in receiving a badge created projects that were relevant to them by using principles learned in the MOOC. Learners who were interested in peer review then submitted their work to a review bank to receive feedback. While badges were dispatched by the course convenors, they were more tokens of participation in *some* aspect of the course, not as a credentialing mechanism, and not as a token of whole course participation. This participation in the course also required something more substantive than reading the week's materials or filling out the answers to a multiple choice exam. Examples of these more substantive measures included weekly reflections, designing and sharing a learning design, offering peer feedback on other's learning designs, remixing open educational resources, and contributing sources to the community toolbox. Hence, badges were more activity-driven rather than based on performance on assessments.

Be Present with Fellow Learners

We suggest thinking about presence as a communal construct in learning environments: it can only exist and develop with relationships. It is vital that we choose, and encourage the use of, tools that might nurture these relationships, because they directly impact the quality and direction of the learning experience. We particularly suggest designing the learning environment around tools that foster mutual empathy and awareness. For example, a welcome video does not necessarily lend itself to mutual empathy as it is often times one-way communication. Blogging, on the other hand, allows for multiple interactions (e.g., interaction with other learners, instructors/facilitators, and content/issue of study) and has the potential to create new and unexpected paths of learning, as we have observed in Virginia Commonwealth University's first MOOC, UNIV 200: Inquiry and the Craft of Argument (www.thoughtvectors.net).

This research writing course was designed around the idea of "launching thought vectors into concept space," that is, the sharing of "lines of inquiry, wonder, puzzlement, and creative desire emerging from individual minds" (Campbell 2014b) in the communal spaces of the web. These spaces, particularly customized learner blogs, were a place for learners to be present on the web in authentic ways (Koseoglu 2016). The instructors of the course also blogged along with learners and encouraged open reflection and transparency throughout the course and beyond. For example, in a blog post titled "Letter to Learner" (http://www.gardnercampbell.net/blog1/?p=2344), Gardner Campbell—one of the course instructors and designers—

reflected on his feelings and reactions in response to a student who raised concerns about the course structure. In doing so, Campbell portrays an instructor who is willing to listen, and respond with empathy and understanding, to students in the course. Thus, the blogging platform provides an outlet to the outward expression of affect, which is important to build meaningful presence as we discussed earlier in this chapter and to engage in democratic conversations between teachers and students. This, we believe, is an approach that is responsive to, and that capitalizes effectively on, the diversity in MOOCs and the connections that could be made in the learning community and beyond. Blogging is also useful to create a learning community where traditional power relationships are deconstructed with mutual respect and readiness to learn from one another (Becker et al. 2014). Note how presence in this context is not an afterthought or an add-on through multimedia; it is, in fact, an inseparable part of the learning process.

Going Forward

In this chapter, we have argued that the disruptive power of MOOCs is not a property inherent in either the instructional design format or the delivery method; rather, we viewed disruption in education as a complex process informed by our educational visions and pedagogy. We then suggested four interrelated design principles (*prepare to cede authority*, *embrace plasticity*, *be present with fellow learners*, and *leave assessments at the door*) to improve the open course pedagogy through the lens of hybrid presence. We described hybrid presence as a fluid and evolving construct that emerges with the breaking down of traditional teacher and learner roles and power structures. We also posited that this process is only possible with meaningful connections and relationships learners and teachers build in a networked environment, which require certain digital literacies, such as networked literacy, and an openness to working with others in public spaces.

The learning design principles we suggest in this chapter should be interpreted as broadly outlined suggestions or roadmaps, as we acknowledge there is a uniqueness in each MOOC and the emergent nature of pedagogical decisions that might impact the learning ecology of a specific MOOC. These principles could also be applicable to smaller, traditional online courses, yet readers should bear in mind the inherent flexibility of MOOCs (e.g., no accreditation requirements, no final grade, etc.) and how that flexibility contrasts with the traditional boundaries of learning. We call for future research that examine the construct of hybrid presence and the principles recommended in this chapter in different contexts, including small-scale online classes, using methods that are appropriate to the complexity and relational nature of teaching. We expect that future research will connect to existing lines of inquiry, and educational philosophies, such as Freire's and Freirean scholars' work on critical pedagogy, as well as lines of inquiry in networked learning environments, both on- and offline.

References

Anderson, T., Rourke, L., Garrison, D. R., & Archer, W. (2001). Assessing teaching presence in a computer conferencing context. *Journal of Asynchronous Learning Network, 5*(2). Retrieved from http://cde.athabascau.ca/coi_site/documents/Anderson_Rourke_Garrison_Archer_Teaching_Presence.pdf

Arbaugh, J. B., Cleveland-Innes, M., Diaz, S. R., Garrison, D. R., Ice, P., Richardson, & Swan, K. P. (2008). Developing a community of inquiry instrument: Testing a measure of the community of inquiry framework using a multi-institutional sample. *The Internet and Higher Education, 11*(3–4), 133–136.

Bali, M. (2014). MOOC pedagogy: Gleaning good practice from existing MOOCs. *MERLOT Journal of Online Learning and Teaching, 10*(1). Retrieved from http://jolt.merlot.org/vol10no1/bali_0314.pdf

Bali, M. (2015). Pedagogy of care—gone massive [Web log post]. Retrieved from http://www.hybridpedagogy.com/journal/pedagogy-of-care-gone-massive/

Bayne, S. (2016). *Campus codespaces for networked learners.* Keynote presented at the Tenth international conference on Networked Learning, Lancaster, UK, 2016. Retrieved from: https://www.youtube.com/watch?v=t0CDKZsWhes

Bayne, S., & Ross, J. (2014). The pedagogy of the massive open online course: The UK view. The Higher Education Academy. Retrieved from https://www.heacademy.ac.uk/sites/default/files/hea_edinburgh_mooc_web_240314_1.pdf

Becker, J., Boaz, B., Campbell, G., Cales, R., Engelbart, C., Gordon, J., Strong, P., & Woodward, T. (2014, June). *VCU's new media cMOOC: Live in concert!* Paper presented at the meeting of New Media Consortium, Portland. Retrieved from https://www.youtube.com/watch?v=ITIoXkyzrYg

Blaschke, L. (2012). Heutagogy and lifelong learning: A review of heutagogical practice and self-determined learning. *The International Review Of Research In Open And Distributed Learning, 13*(1), 56–71. https://doi.org/10.19173/irrodl.v13i1.1076.

Campbell, G. (2014a). Interview by H. Rheingold. Channeling Engelbart: Augmenting human education. Retrieved from http://dmlcentral.net/channeling-engelbart-augmenting-human-education/

Campbell, G. (2014b). Our summer cMOOC: Living the dreams [Web log post]. Retrieved from http://www.gardnercampbell.net/blog1/?p=2260

Cleveland-Innes, M., & Campbell, P. (2012). Emotional presence, learning, and the online learning environment. *The International Review Of Research In Open And Distributed Learning, 13*(4), 269–292. https://doi.org/10.19173/irrodl.v13i4.1234.

Cormier, D. (2014). Rhizomatic learning – A big Forking course [Web log post]. Retrieved from http://davecormier.com/edblog/page/2/

Cutajar, M. (2016). Qualitative differences in students' perceptions of others in a networked learning environment. In S. Cranmer, N. B. Dohn, M. de Laat, T. Ryberg, & J. A. Sime (Eds.), *Proceedings of the 10th International Conference on Networked Learning 2016* (pp. 472–480). Retrieved from: http://www.networkedlearningconference.org.uk/abstracts/pdf/P53.pdf

deWaard, I., Abajian, S., Gallagher, M. S., Hogue, R., Keskin, N., Koutropoulos, A., & Rodriguez, O. C. (2011). Using mLearning and MOOCs to understand chaos, emergence, and complexity in education. *International Review Of Research In Open & Distance Learning, 12*(7), 94–115.

Dron, J. (2016). P-Learning's unwelcome legacy. *TD Tecnologie Didattiche, 24*(2), 72. https://doi.org/10.17471/2499-4324/891.

Farmer, J. (2013). MOOCs: A disruptive innovation or not? [Web log post]. Retrieved from http://mfeldstein.com/moocs-a-disruptive-innovation-or-not/

Friedman, T. L. (2012). Come the revolution. *The New York Times.* Retrieved from http://www.nytimes.com/2012/05/16/opinion/friedman-come-the-revolution.html

Garrison, D. R., Anderson, T., & Archer, W. (2000). Critical inquiry in a text-based environment: Computer conferencing in higher education. *The Internet and Higher Education, 2*(2–3), 1–19.

Goodyear, P., Banks, S., Hodgson, V., & McConnell, D. (2004). Research on networked learning: anoverview. In P. M. Goodyear, S. Banks, V. Hodgson, & D. McConnell (Eds.), *Advances in research on networked learning* (pp. 1–9). Boston: Kluwer Academic.

Hodgson, V., de Latt, M., McConnell, D., & Ryberg, T. (2014). Researching design, experience and practice of networked learning: An overview. In V. Hodgson, M. de Latt, D. McConnell, & T. Ryberg (Eds.), *The design, experience and practice of networked learning* (pp. 1–28). New York: Springer.

Hyman, P. (2012). In the year of disruptive education. *Communications of the ACM, 55*(12), 20–22.

Kehrwald, B., & Oztok, M. (2016). Social presence and impression management: Understanding networked learners' cultivation of learning networks. In S. Cranmer, N. B. Dohn, M. de Laat, T. Ryberg, & J. A. Sime (Eds.), *Proceedings of the 10th International Conference on Networked Learning 2016* (pp. 226–233). Retrieved from: http://www.networkedlearningconference.org.uk/abstracts/pdf/P17.pdf

Kilgore, W., & Lowenthal, P. R. (2015). The human element & MOOC: An experiment in social presence. In R. D. Wright (Ed.), *Student-teacher interaction in online learning environments* (pp. 373–391). Hershey, PA: IGI Global. Retrieved from http://patricklowenthal.com/human-element-mooc-experiment-social-presence/.

Kim, P. (2010). Is higher education evolving? *Educause Quarterly, 33*(1). Retrieved from http://www.educause.edu/ero/article/higher-education-evolving

Knoll, M. (2009). From Kidd to Dewey: The origin and meaning of 'social efficiency. *Journal of Curriculum Studies, 41*(3), 361–391.

Kop, R., Fournier, H., & Mak, J. S. F. (2011). A pedagogy of abundance or a pedagogy to support human beings? Participant support on massive open online courses. *International Review Of Research In Open & Distance Learning, 12*(7), 74–93.

Koseoglu, S. (2016). Third learning spaces in open online courses: Findings from an interpretive case study (Doctoral dissertation). Retrieved from University of Minnesota: Twin Cities.

Koutropoulos, A., & Zaharias, P. (2015). Down the rabbit hole: An initial typology of issues around the development of MOOCs. *Current Issues in Emerging eLearning, 2*(1). Retrieved from http://scholarworks.umb.edu/ciee/vol2/iss1/4

Koutropoulos, A., Gallagher, M. S., Abajian, S. C., de Waard, I., Hogue, R. J., Keskin, N. O., & Rodriguez, C. O. (2012). Emotive vocabulary in MOOCs: Context & participant retention. *European Journal Of Open, Distance And E-Learning, 1.*

Koutropoulos, A., Abajian, S., deWaard, I., Hogue, R., Keskin, N., & Rodriguez, C. (2014). What Tweets Tell us About MOOC Participation. *International Journal Of Emerging Technologies In Learning (IJET), 9*(1), 8–21. https://doi.org/10.3991/ijet.v9i1.3316.

Morris, S. M., & Stommel, J. (2013). Pedagogies of scale [Web log post]. Retrieved from http://www.hybridpedagogy.com/journal/pedagogies-of-scale/

Northcutt, C, Ho, A., & Chuang, I. (2015). CAMEO Dataset: Detection and Prevention of "Multiple Account" Cheating in Massively Open Online Courses. Retrieved from: https://doi.org/10.7910/DVN/3UKVOR, Harvard Dataverse, V1.

Pacansky-Brock, M., Leafstedt, J., & O'Neil-Gonzalez, K. (2015, April). How to humanize your online class. Workshop at the 8th Annual Emerging Technologies for Online Learning International Symposium, Dallas (TX).

Parchoma, G. (2016). Reclaiming distributed cognition in networked learning: An inter-subjective, socio-material perspective. In S. Cranmer, N. B. Dohn, M. de Laat, T. Ryberg, & J. A. Sime (Eds.), *Proceedings of the 10th International Conference on Networked Learning 2016* (pp. 113–119). Retrieved from: http://www.networkedlearningconference.org.uk/abstracts/pdf/P03.pdf

Rheingold, H. (2013). Network literacy mini-course. Retrieved fromhttp://rheingold.com/2013/network-literacy-mini-course/

Rheingold, H. (2014). Co-learning about co-learning [Web log post]. Retrieved from http://connectedcourses.tumblr.com/post/102236510955/co-learning-about-co-learning

Rodgers, C. R., & Raider-Roth, M. B. (2006). Presence in teaching. *Teachers and Teaching: Theory and Practice, 12*(3), 265–287.

Ross, J., Sinclair, C., Knox, J., Bayne, S., & Macleod, H. (2014). Teacher experiences and academic identity: The missing components of MOOC pedagogy. *MERLOT Journal of Online Learning and Teaching, 10*(1), 56–68.

Rourke, L., Anderson, T., Garrison, D. R., & Archer, W. (2001). Assessing social presence in asynchronous, text-based computer conferencing. *Journal of Distance Education, 14*(3), 51–70.

Shea, P., & Bidjerano, T. (2010). Learning presence: Towards a theory of self-efficacy, self-regulation, and the development of a communities of inquiry in online and blended learning environments. *Computers & Education, 55*(4), 1721–1731. https://doi.org/10.1016/j.compedu.2010.07.017.

Siemens, G., & Downes, S. (2011). *How this course works* [Website post]. Retrieved from: http://cck11.mooc.ca/how.htm

Yuan, L., & Powell, S. (2013). MOOCs and open education: Implications for higher education, JISC CETIS White Paper. Retrieved from http://publications.cetis.org.uk/wp-content/uploads/2013/03/MOOCs-and-Open-Education.pdf

Chapter 8
Designing an Inclusive Intercultural Online Participatory Seminar for Higher Education Teachers and Professionals

Ilene D. Alexander and Alexander Fink

Abstract How do we design an inclusive, collaborative online learning space to encourage deep discussion, analysis, and practical change in the pedagogical practices of present and future university teachers? How especially do we foster this engagement around "difficult" and "common sense" conversations? With these questions in mind, the authors explore their development of a relational, reflexive, dialogical, and praxis-oriented online learning space as a springboard for co-creation of intercultural teaching and learning knowledge and practice among education professionals. The authors draw on their locations as an experienced educator of future teachers and a graduate student in youth leadership, both rooted in social justice activism and interdisciplinary scholarship to discuss developing a seminar that (1) embodied its content (intercultural, inclusive learning and teaching) in praxis, (2) supported development of networked learning connections between learners, teachers, resources we collectively brought together, and (3) extended to the communities that participants entered daily as teachers and learners. This chapter details the process of co-designing such a seminar, discusses some of the pedagogical processes utilized to promote the co-production of knowledge with participants, and explores the outcomes of these efforts with participants.

Introduction

We have spent our careers working within educational traditions that elevate the importance of connectivity and the co-production of knowledge, two key elements defining networked learning (Beaty et al. 2010). Our experiences as participants in

I. D. Alexander (✉)
Center for Educational Innovation, University of Minnesota-Twin Cities, Minneapolis, MN, USA
e-mail: alexa032@umn.edu

A. Fink
Youth Studies, School of Social Work, University of Minnesota, St. Paul, MN, USA

© Springer International Publishing AG, part of Springer Nature 2018
N. Bonderup Dohn et al. (eds.), *Networked Learning*, Research in Networked Learning, https://doi.org/10.1007/978-3-319-74857-3_8

higher education – as learners and instructors, teaching mentors and educational consultants – shaped our belief that an advanced course exploring inclusive intercultural learning and teaching would greatly enhance professional development for future university instructors in first-level teaching professional development courses. In our learning and mentoring roles, we have observed experienced, well-intentioned teachers fumble or fail in fostering deeply inclusive environments that enable learning for all students in various learning spaces. In our teaching and educational consulting roles, we have learned that creating inclusive intercultural environments requires setting aside many "common sense" teaching practices to consciously create learning spaces that support a broad range of learners when they are with us in a course and when they move into other learning and life spaces rife with messages and practices that marginalize diverse learners and impair learning for many students.

These multiple roles and our shared commitment to social justice philosophies combined with requests from past students and current teaching colleagues prompted us to initially propose the Multicultural Inclusive Learning and Teaching seminar we explore in this chapter. To support broad access to the seminar, we gained Center for Educational Innovation authorization to develop a modified open boundary online course (Kernohan 2013) so that anyone whose higher education role engaged them in working with university and college students would be able to engage the seminar.

In this initial stage, we turned to work by two sets of pedagogical mentors Septima Clark (1962, 1964) and Myles Horton (2003), education director and founding director of Highlander Folk School, respectively, and to Minnesota-based scholars Carolyn Shrewsbury (1987) and Stephen Brookfield (2007), whose feminist and/or critical pedagogies work and writing embody practices established at Highlander. Opening in 1932 as a cultural centre with a focus on leadership among "local people" located in the Appalachian region of the southern US state of Tennessee, Highlander Folk School has always existed as an interracial, intercultural organization, even in times when state legislation banned such gatherings through the 1960s. Work during the initial decade was deeply linked to labour organizing and building of cross-class alliances; from the 1940s onward, civil rights and social justice work have been at the heart of Highlander's work. Horton and Clark both advocated participant-generated education, organization, and leadership. Participants during this rich civil rights era included Rosa Parks and Martin Luther King early in their activism; groups of primarily white college students and full-time teachers from northern US states joining with students and community organizers of colour from southern states to staff of the 1964 Freedom Summer schools and community centres hosting the voter registration efforts; and community leaders training to become teachers in Citizenship Schools that would prepare black voters for successfully passing restrictive voter registration requirements in the segregated US south. Now called Highlander Research and Education Center, the centre remains a place where people pursue Highlander's mission of "com[ing] together to interact, build friendships, craft joint strategy and develop the tools and mechanisms needed to advance a multi-racial, inter-generational movement for social and economic justice".

From these activist teacher roots, we committed specifically to:

1. Incorporate learning practices developed at Highlander Folk School – relational, reflexive and praxis-oriented – to reflect our understanding that classrooms as learning spaces can be "treated as a consciously experienced set of conditions and surroundings, where people can come to understand the nature of society by examining the conflict situations and the crises thrust upon them, in their own personal lives..." (Horton 2003, p. 243).
2. Draw on practices embodied in Shrewsbury's description of the classroom as a networked learning space, "characterized as persons connected in a net of relationships with people who care about each other's learning as well as their own is very different from classroom that is comprised of teacher and students" (1987, p. 6).

In the process of designing, three compelling, emergent questions required our attention as we collaborated with students from previous courses, teaching colleagues, disability resources student services staff and academic teaching and technology consultants:

- How do we design a seminar as an open online learning space where teaching professionals explore rich pedagogical histories, intercultural and inclusive learning theories and boundary crossing practices through dialogical discussions (Coffield and Edwards 2009; Lather 1991)?
- How do we counter repressive tolerance – the practice of allowing all voices to be heard, even if they play on systemically harmful narratives (like racism, sexism, etc.) (Brookfield 2007)?
- How do we wrestle with the pervasive "problem of time" (Wallace 2000) – practitioners' ongoing hope to infuse multicultural learning and teaching practices that is often sidelined by perceptions of them not having enough time to "deal with" classroom diversity or enough support to "get to" the work of building more intercultural learning and teaching practices?

This paper details the process of codesigning such a course, discusses some of the pedagogical processes utilized to promote the co-production of knowledge with participants and explores the outcomes of these efforts with participants. We begin by exploring the course design process, including the background behind goals and aims, pedagogical approach and module design. In the section that follows, we further explore the selection of content, activity, assessment and discussion practices to support creation of an inclusive learning community that would support participants from across disciplines and institutions to co-produce knowledge within and beyond the seminar. Finally, we draw on data collected from the first two iterations of the course to explore outcomes for participants and to address changes we have made based on feedback.

Designing an Inclusive Intercultural Teaching-Learning Space

To begin, we addressed Dee Fink's ideal impact guiding questions: "What would I like the impact of this course to be on students, 2–3 years after the course is over? What would distinguish students who have taken this course from students who have not?" (Fink 2004, p. 10). Our largescale goal for this open online participatory seminar would be to focus on inclusive intercultural learning and teaching with teaching-oriented higher education practitioners (e.g., teachers, student support professionals and pedagogical administrators across disciplines, geographies and cultural and personal identities) working dialogically and collaboratively to develop pedagogical practices agile and robust enough to support the broad range of learners enrolled in our colleges, programs and courses. Further, participants would work together to re-examine and expand individual, collective, collegial and cultural ideas about *what* we teach, *how* we attend to *who* is in the classroom, *when* we address tensions/conflicts, *where* to be transparent and *why* all this matters.

As seminar designers and facilitators, we would amplify three components embedded in the ideal impact goals:

- Action *teacher* as convener, facilitator, participant, advocate, questioner/quester, lecturer, responder, hub, researcher, organizer and specialist roles for all participants.
- Pluralize theories *and* pedagogies in selecting materials, just as we would see students in the plural in terms of demographics, identity, interests and liminality (Burke and Crozier 2012; Waite et al. 2013).
- Foster relationships among all participants through collaboration, co-construction and critical and reflective reflection within dialogue across identities and institutions (Beaty et al. 2002).

Our design practice also built on our experiences within cMOOCs and pMOOCs – connectivist and project-based MOOCs – that each of us participated in as professional development learners (e.g. CMC11, Mooc Mooc, OLDS MOOC, EC&I 831 and FSLT12 and FSLT13). Across these engagements, especially as we reflected on our own experiences of learner and lurking roles in Oxford Brookes' First Steps in Learning and Teaching modules (Waite et al. 2013), we recognized the importance of "lurking learners" – whom we came to identify as *lurners* – as active agents to keep in mind throughout our design process.

From these experiences, we needed to select a virtual learning environment that would allow participants to choose among multiple modes of participation – from enrolled for credit, to badge-earning, to participation in peer discussion within or beyond the open online participatory seminar (OOPS) learning space and on to dipping in for reading, uploading and downloading materials that supported an individual's further *lurning* (the acts of lurking for learning). As a seminar that would include graduate students enrolled for credit as well as practitioners seeking professional development, with both constituent groups newly exploring aspects of inclusive intercultural teaching and learning practices, we sought to build our learning space within a platform where it would be safe to risk exploration and expression of new ideas. For this we selected our university-supported VLE, Moodle, as a place where all who registered for the seminar could access discussion forums, open resources and badge-earning activities including peer exchange and feedback. The addition of a YouTube channel and seminar blog made it possible to share seminar materials in a public, open access mode.

Lastly, to cap this stage of designing for inclusive learning, we adopted a *design for inclusive learning* process. For us, this approach blends work by several scholars on multicultural teaching and learning (Biggs and Tang 2007; Chávez 2007; Gómez 2008; Kaplan and Miller 2007; Wiggins and McTighe 2005). Alongside this, we relied on an inclusion framework offered by CAST, the Center for Applied Special Technology's Universal Design for Learning, which considers how to best serve students with disabilities and extends to course design that "take[s] into account the wide variability of learners in higher education environments" (UDL on Campus n.d.). Design for learning is the base from which we build inclusive inter-cultural learning and teaching practices and spaces. To design backwards, we composed five learning aims to guide us in the basic work of constructing the seminar curriculum and site design (selection of seminar materials, development of discussion forum prompts – which would become the core seminar materials – and constructionist badge activities and creation of frameworks for feedback and assessment):

- **Interact** with – respond to, analyse and discuss – readings in a reflective practice mode, reviewing via multiple lenses, considering diverse perspectives, addressing personal contexts and imagining professional possibilities.
- **Develop** a personal – contextual, robust and dynamic – understanding of MILT through participation in discussion forums and activity workshops.
- **Engage** ideas in multiple ways – spoken, verbal, visual/audio and written – in order to create teaching/learning activities and/or artefacts.
- **Apply** core course design constructs – course alignment, universal design for learning and a range of critical multicultural pedagogical principles – to one's teaching roles and learning responsibilities.
- **Stretch** to create among ourselves – and beyond this course – learning spaces akin to those we seek for our students as we exchange and expand our viewpoints through our new interactions.

In all, for the first run of our seminar, 70 participants signed up in response to our small-scale email and social network postings. They came equally from science, education and liberal arts departments and identified across multiple sexualities, ethnicities, genders, home places, teaching spaces, class backgrounds and family affiliations. More than half of the registered participants ventured into at least two of the six modules, with 13 signing up for credit, which would require ongoing participation in all module discussion forums and completion of the four badge activities, and nearly an equal number of registrants participating regularly in the *lurning* mode. The following list sets out module topics and badge activities:

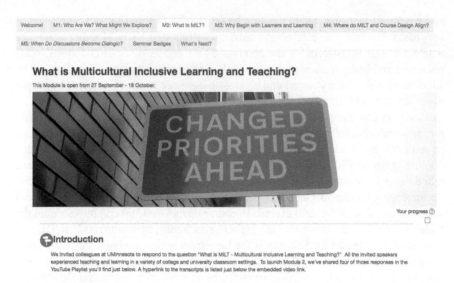

Fig. 8.1 Sample module page

1. Seminar Welcome
2. Who In the World Are We?
3. What is MILT? / Badge 1 – Philosophy Statement
4. Why Begin with Learning and Learners? / Badge 2 – Assignment Design
5. When Do Words Fail Us?
6. How Do Discussions Become Dialogic? / Badge 3 – Discussion Reflection
7. Where do MILT and Course Design Align? / Badge 4 – Course Design

Within each module, we incorporated four sections: *Introduction* to frame a module's topic within learning and diversity science literature, *Information* to showcase 2–3 open resources as seeds for participant-driven content creation through discussion, *Insights* to feature resources expanding the research and practice base in light of participants' contexts and *Activities* as the anchor for each module, linking to a discussion forum, and to badge activity exchanges of artefacts and feedback. Materials within the Introduction, Information and Insights sections included images we selected; meta-essays we composed to synthesize core theory/history/praxis ideas into a 2-page, hyperlinked essay; video-based resources we scripted or invited to showcase intercultural learning and teaching ideas developed within our own networks; and curated texts (articles, blog posts and essays, as well as samples drawn from colleagues teaching materials) that allowed us to embed materials offering an intercultural array of pedagogical voices and approaches (see Fig. 8.1 for a sample module page screenshot). While we designed the full seminar in advance, we also integrated new resources in an emergent design as we learned more about seminar participants through discussion and feedback forums.

Ethos: Community and Climate

There were two main areas of concern guiding the design process: (1) the community and ethos of the seminar and (2) the seminar climate, or learning atmosphere, we hoped to create to support a range of participation and participants. These frameworks are discussed next.

Community and Learning Circles

Our intention was to work within each module as we would within other learning circle spaces (Wallace 2011, p. 12). Learning circles were foundational to Highlander Folk School's praxis in hosting racially (class-, gender-, age-, education- and sexuality-) integrated workshops. Highlander's founder Myles Horton says this of learning circles in a conversation with Paulo Freire:

> "Circle" is not an accidental term, for there is no head of the table at Highlander workshops; everybody sits around in a circle. The job of the staff members is to create a relaxed atmosphere in which the participants feel free to share their experiences. Then they are encouraged to analyse, learn from and build on these experiences. Like other participants in the workshops, staff members are expected to share experiences that relate to the discussions, and sources of information and alternative suggestions. (Horton et al. 1990, p. 150)

Learning circles are first and foremost a gathering of people. They are distinct from a community of practice in that participants do not necessarily share a common craft or profession but rather hold in common goals related to community activism and social change. At Highlander, topical focuses for workshops, typically spanning 3 days, are pre-established in response to current community issues, cultural developments and citizenship concerns in light of civil rights legislation and social and economic justice goals in a US context. Historically, and still, Highlander workshop attendees are people already engaged in such endeavours and recognized in home communities as local leaders who were also small business owners, community organization volunteers and teachers. Participants sought out the workshops to learn more – in realms of ideas and activism – from others pursuing similar goals and facing similar obstacles, to personalize national movements and to return to home communities for cocreating next actions. Highlander's face-to-face workshops feature three learning circles, each a "discussion round" building on the previous one. In planning for two learning circle discussions on a Saturday and one on a Sunday, facilitators would prepare "open-ended questions designed to elicit answers that draw creatively on experiences and interests that participants bring, on a topic that you know is alive for them" (Wallace 2011, p. 13). Thoughtfully scripting questions allows facilitators time for "thinking through what the overall shape and sequence of discussions is going to be, what questions and what texts or videos to [use to] set up questions..., and draft the wording or at least important parts of the wording of the questions with those plans in mind" (Wallace 2011, p. 14). Each round of a learning circle can be structured in multiple ways for multiple learning space formats, with each round sharing this pattern overall: The facilitator poses a question; each participant speaks, building on what they have heard in others' responses; in moving around the circle, participants may also choose to pass at their turn in order to further listen, mull or reflect before speaking. Once all in the circle have spoken, the discussion opens to crosstalk –follow up questions, requests for clarification, amplification of ideas and extended reflection as part of sense-making. In an exchange of stories listened to and ideas expressed (Alexander 2013), participants create what we will describe as "thick thread" discussions in a later segment.

During each of the three rounds, facilitators also take a turn in responding, choosing when and how to enter the crosstalk. Expected to be acute listeners, facilitators are poised to offer follow-up questions, perspective-taking synthesis, resource-sharing examples and personal reflection and/or provide a "discussion inventory" (Brookfield 2011) so that participants attend to conversational elisions and instances of repressive tolerance, as well as trace developments of new ideas and insights. During breaks between rounds, facilitators will act improvisationally to phrase the next round prompts based on their sense of how the discussion is, or is not, unfolding (Elbow 1983; Wallace 2011).

In our seminar, the learning circle concept is acted as a structuring method for writing forum prompts as well as for posing next queries to deepen/expand, or redirect/extend, a forum discussion. Our hope in designing and teaching the seminar from this perspective was that the community-building nature of learning circles would foster a deep co-inquiry in our online learning space. We planned the overall template of Introduction, Information and Insights resources also to align with the 3-part learning circle model, which facilitators often state in a series of shortened questions: *What?*, *So What?* and *Now What?* In each module's forum, we scripted *What?* questions: What resonates for you – in the reading, relative to your experiences? What bubbles up – as you make connections among the readings or to others' postings? We could post-follow-up *So What?* questions within discussion threads: So what might be a way to leverage these ideas – in response to a problem you posed, in further developing a course in your context? So what might be responses of students, of administrators and of a particular author to what you're proposing? So what might happen if you take this other resources or perspectives or contexts into account? Finally, *Now What?* questions could suggest lines of discussion in response to identified problems: Now what actions or collaborations or alliances or further research might you, or we, need to engage to make the change you, or we, have proposed?

Our decision to build the open online participatory seminar with learning circles in mind is supported by contemporary discussion as a way of learning research. Specifically we drew on Brookfield and Preskill (1999), Brookfield (2011), Dennen (2008) and Pentland (2014) as scholars investigating patterns of effective discussion in multiple learning spaces. Each underscores the importance of short, overlapping, dense interactions via comments generated in response to authentic discussion prompts, with Brookfield providing reminders that discussion works when it builds on reflection or reading, when there is room for silent thought, when we recognize that discussion is always culturally grounded and when discussion facilitators accept a responsibility to "intervene to structure true, democratic participation. Otherwise a pecking order of contributors will quickly develop and those who hold power outside the discussion will move to dominate the conversation". Dennen adds that inbuilt practices of metacognitive reflection further support knowledge creation and long-term learning. Pentland adds that discussion practices of high-performing cooperative groups enhance understandings of why or whether to validate or invalidate emergences of consensus and dissent. With Elbow, Wallace, Dennen and Pentland in mind, we recognized our discussion process as improvisation, as we would be asking students to "yes, and" their way into sharing what "bubbled up" in responding to springboard seminar materials, discussion prompts, previous experiences (whether cognitive/affective/embodied, personal/professional/public) and others' words (Sawyer 2004). Learners took this seriously, most conversations taking tones of expanding and seeking understanding and of engaging cognitive and affective thinking/responding, even with contentious issues.

Climate and Safety to Take Risk

While the learning circle structure provided a heuristic, we turned to the scholarship of multicultural teaching and learning to think through how we would design the whole of the seminar in principle and practice. For this, we drew on Alexander's (2007) approach to infusing inclusive intercultural learning and teaching across the entirety of a course and Chávez's six elements of an "empowering multicultural learning environment" (Table 8.1) (and we included an extract of Chávez as a reading early in the seminar as an act of reciprocity, the sixth of Chávez' elements). Within the classrooms she studied, Chávez notes, "teachers worked with all students to create collective, empowering learning experiences that utilized and honoured multicultural realities within a shared and rigorous academic experience" (2007, p. 278).

We incorporated Chávez's elements in the design of the seminar in an effort to build on the cocreative and co-productive elements of networked learning approaches. We fostered the safety of the environment through (1) the modified open boundaries of the course; (2) the framing of the discussion prompts and participation, which invited personal sharing and "yes, and" conversations, rather than confrontations; (3) and modelling of inclusive participation in the forums (Ryberg and Sinclair 2016). Following this, risk-taking was also an aspect of our modelling, wherein we wrote content and recorded videos that shared our personal stories and did this in our forum posts as well. In our selections of content, we focused on congruence between a given topic and the authors/speakers we chose (as well as proactivity in the design and selection of materials), assuring that these folks came from a diverse array of backgrounds, as well as national and international contexts. We hoped to encourage multiplicity by drawing on an array of personal narratives, blog posts and varieties of academic writing in the content. We planned to encourage

Table 8.1 Chávez (2007) elements of an empowering multicultural learning environment

Safety	Respect and support for individuals in making room for respectful confrontation and minimization of the effects of hierarchy
Risk taking	Given the broad range of learning preferences, experiential perspectives and needs related to exploring ideas in a classroom, facilitators and participants work together in an "uncomfortable process of bringing issues and ideas out into the realm of respectful dialogue [which] distinguishes an empowering learning community" (p. 281)
Congruence	Course materials are both consistent with expressed aims and reflect realities of the *broad range* of participants
Proactivity	Proactivity "brings with it a need to utilize a diversity of knowledge, methods, styles, and relationships in various processes" (p. 283)
Multiplicity	Embodied learning, which calls on minds and hearts and physicality and spirit as factors in facilitators' course design, becomes a factor as facilitators infuse courses with "a multiplicity of ways of knowing, knowledge sources, realities, relationships, and experiences" (p. 283)
Reciprocity	Involves learners and facilitators as *stewards* developing new knowledge, rather than as standard bearers guarding knowledge traditions, and as *allies* in the creation of new knowledge and meanings in the interaction of ideas crossing personal, cultural and disciplinary boundaries in cognitive and affective realms

learners to bring their hearts and minds to the work, sharing their own stories and personal experiences, as well as what they have read and seen. Finally, we hoped for participants to become cocreators and co-producers of knowledge as they brought resources they encountered elsewhere into the seminar and reflected on this and our content. The hope was that we would both foster new ideas together and take ideas new and old into practice in our classrooms.

Through this application of Chávez in the design of the seminar, our intention was to promote the connective possibilities of the seminar: of participants to facilitators, participants to each other, participants to content within the seminar and participants and facilitators alike to content outside of the immediate context. Additionally, we hoped to involve participants not only in connecting knowledge and theory in new ways but to build a reciprocal relationship between theory, discussion, co-production of knowledge and practice. This dialogue between theory and practice would ideally also be a dialogue between an array of possibilities and the realities of local contexts: positionality, career status, field specialties and institutional types (Beaty et al. 2010).

Also, as we planned, we knew that the roles each of us would take in the seminar would be based on the practices conveyed in Chávez' matrix. At Module 2 we realized that, though we jointly created, commissioned and/or selected the resources that spurred initial conversation, we were taking on different instructional roles. Ilene often read forum posts through Brookfield's (1998) four lenses of critically reflective teaching (lenses of our own autobiographies as learners, of learners' eyes on the seminar, of peers' observations of our teaching and of the pedagogical literature) as part of providing responses to queries, and in reflecting critically on her own experiences. Alex, with fewer years of experience teaching, often came with his own curiosities and questions that prodded conversation, much like other participants. While we ultimately assigned grades and issued badges, learners provided feedback on each other's work, which they drew on in revising *and* in developing self-assessments using sample instruments. The exchange of feedback as well as the mindful reviewing of it as part of a revision process further fostered a sense of networked peer learning collaboration (Steeples et al. 2002). Rather than prioritizing a traditional student/teacher relationship, this approach joined instructors and participants together as learners engaged in feedback and with multiple roles in assessment loops. Rather than *illuminating the way* or *getting out of the way* (Gómez 2008), we conceptualized an in-between space that would make it possible for us to find *ways into* participating by listening to what bubbled up in us, by lurking within the densely voiced forums, by reflecting on questions that wrangled into place through various threads and by discerning why, when and where to enter the interchange.

Data Digging with Design in Mind

In this section, we present data gathered on the ways our design operated in practice. These data are presented in four sections. The first three are data gathered during the first round of the seminar, which took place in 2015: (1) an examination of the dynamics of the discussion forums that demonstrates the deepening networks of participation as the seminar progressed, (2) feedback from participants on their experiences of the seminar, and (3) an exploration of the experiences of "lurners" – those participants who did not fully participate in badge activities but were present in the seminar nevertheless (Milligan et al. 2013). Though by no means conclusive, these data offer a snapshot of some of the results of our design practices. The fourth section, entitled *Learning in the Redesign*, (4) examines the changes made based on data from the first round of the seminar and the impacts of these changes on the second run of the seminar.

Discussion Forum Graph Analysis

These modes of instructor participation are evident when examining the three graph analysis diagrams (see Fig. 8.2) capturing some discussion dynamics as the seminar progressed. Though the instructors never disappear as nodes within the conversation, participants become more central, with the participants' responses building "thick thread" discussions in patterns of more dense engagement with each other. One participant describes their experience of the changes in discussion over time:

Looking back at my earliest posts [...] I wasn't searching for big ideas; I was looking for minor suggestions and affirmations. In some way, I suspect I'd been infected by the very same apathy and disinterest that I was attempting to avoid. I was convinced that the Big

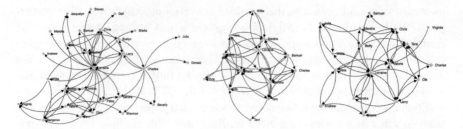

Fig. 8.2 Graph analysis for Welcome, Module 2 and Module 5 discussion forums

Problem (MILT in STEM fields) wouldn't really have any Big Answers. [...] Rather than engaging only in "safe" topics (related specifically to STEM fields or on subjects that I felt experienced in) I began to seek out discussions from people in vastly different fields. I started to grasp onto threads that were less familiar to me and ask myself "what about that? How could I address this in my classroom?" ?" [...] I started to engage more in "yes, and" conversation rather than simply stating my thoughts in essay form. I listened more. (Larry, physics)

In addition to a deeper space for listening, a space for critical, grounded engagement of the topics evolved. The first instance marking potential for such discussions emerges in the *Welcome Module* forum where two threads break from the pattern of participants taking turns to introduce themselves. This forum includes the largest number of "starter" threads with 29 participants offering posts in response to a "What's 'bubbling up' for you as participants drawn to this seminar?" prompt; of those introductions, nearly all featured subject lines with variations of *hello* and *hi*. Overall, this forum functions as a populating of the person-to person network(ing) to be built. The two bolder subject lines – "Hi! (and MILT in science)" and "Hello there!" – are the only two with double digit exchanges within the thread, with 12 and 10, respectively. With the graph analysis clearly mapping out the thickness of these interactions, the qualitative analysis reveals these entries as introducing discussion and epistemological threads that will recur in the seminar – STEM content as not being "culturally 'neutral'" and collectively pushing against "single-story" narratives that often drive disciplinary narratives. While Heather (science) and Robin (social science), who composed the anchor entries in these threads, each carried on in the seminar as lurners, those who wrote in response to these initial posts would continue as active participants in discussion forums, their names often linked in the graph analysis to more central nodes.

Our *Module 2* featured a set of short videos through which university instructors, advisors and staff shared components of their MILT philosophies, and few of the discussion forum posts explicitly referred to the speakers or their ideas. Rather, the nine thick discussion threads mainly revolved around various MILT principles that required teachers to engage in "embracing contraries" (Elbow 1987), which had been the focus of the meta-essay we composed as a secondary text for the module. Elbow posits that good teaching is a challenge specifically because it requires instructors to embrace these contraries: obligations to students, to learning *and* to knowledge to society. Our prompt invited participants to consider how MILT intersected with the contraries in shaping their own – and their disciplines' – principles and practices, whether about classroom climate, content or creating assessments. The graph analysis for Module 2 maps out five primary nodes that gained much multidisciplinary traffic in exploring intersections of loyalties to students and to knowledge and intersections among students' and teachers' roles and responsibilities in creating MILT spaces and knowledge. In this one-to-many, many-to-one networking the two-part theme can also be posed via these two questions: How might teachers and learners bring their "whole selves" to learning? How might we shift teaching and learning principles and practices within disciplines so that the embracing of contraries also embraces MILT?

In *Module 5*, a discussion forum thread critical of a reading we shared (on critical thinking, no less) became a major topic of conversation. Participants were open in their challenges to and extensions of the reading, testing it against their experiences as students and teachers. Further, they shared (more even than in earlier modules) their own resources on the topic, deepening the questions and conversation. In this module, the people-to-resources networking took on its deepest and broadest connections. Finally, across the seminar's six major discussion modules, the seminar evolved into a networked learning space where participants and instructors had the opportunity to share, teach and learn—all grounded in participants' experiences.

Participant Feedback Survey Items

One question in an early-seminar survey invited participants to share perceptions about discussion as a way of learning, asking, "When you participate in class discussions, what tends to get you to 'step forward' into the conversation?" With word cloud visualizations and thematic analysis, we devised a paraphrase characterizing participant responses, which overwhelmingly focused on discussions in the teaching-learning context: *We will appreciate participants' learning and teaching experiences, ideas and questions in conversation.*

At this point, the majority of participants would have previously engaged in face-to-face discussions with multidisciplinary colleagues (typically through earlier participation in "Teaching in Higher Education", the core Preparing Future Faculty course) and would have just read the welcome module's "Characteristics of a Participatory Seminar" meta-essay, which concluded by listing from Dennen (2008) and Pentland (2014) characteristics central to motivating "discussion for learning" in an online environment: inviting dense interactions, diversity of ideas and metacognitive reflection. By the end of the seminar, regularly engaged participants took part in up to six forum and four badge discussions (totalling some 9570 views among ~30 regularly active learner/lurner participants). The six forum discussions, as we've noted above, featured "thick threads" – an average of 9 discussion threads (ranging from 6 to 11) per forum that were sustained by multiple participants stepping forward in multiple ways: extending ideas, adding experiential observations, offering resource, proposing a synthesis of ideas, posing astute questions, linking to

Fig. 8.3 "Step forward" word cloud

materials, inquiring about proposed or possible practices and downloading threads to review more closely or at later junctures.

The comments from participants completing the Critical Insights Questionnaire embedded in the Dialogic Discussions Module (the 5th of 6 modules) affirmed that actions taking place within the seminar supported their initial hopes for "learning through discussion". We asked, "At what moment during the MILT OOPS! have you felt most engaged with what was happening?" The thematic and word cloud responses (Fig. 8.3) prompted us to devise this paraphrase: *We appreciated person-alised postings with people sharing experience, ideas, and learning, especially in badge feedback comments* (Steeples et al. 2002).

One participant identifies the combination of engagement and personalization as "[going] back to Module 1, when we were first forming our OOPS community, and discussions and ideas were first bubbling up from so many places – so many different disciplines, identities, backgrounds, 'I am froms'…" (Ola, agriculture). Another points to peers' experiences as heightening engagement in ways readings alone could not:

> I felt most engaged by the discussion of repressive tolerance in Module 4. Although I didn't actively participate in all of it, I learned a lot from other students' posts. I think this was the one area where a forum discussion most enhanced the learning experience above and beyond what articles alone provide. Reading how different people interpreted different concepts really gave a three-dimensional view of the material. (Samuel, social science)

And of connections made in moving between topical and badge discussion forums, one participant offered this liminal comment about personal professional development:

> If I had completed the Course Design Badge toward the beginning of the semester, it would have looked very different from the final product that I submitted at the end of the semester! I incorporated many of the collaborative learning techniques that we have discussed, and I built in ways for students to self-evaluate their learning practices while at the same time providing me with input on my efficacy as an instructor. I would imagine that after one semester, I would be a much different, and improved, teacher at the postsecondary level. I

would hope that after one semester, my students would be much different, and improved, learners at the postsecondary level as well. In turn, they may go on to become effective instructors themselves, thereby broadening my sphere of influence. (Tara, education)

Another participant remarked on their deepening engagement as linked to two invitations to participants: to build a climate in which it is possible to take learning risks (Chávez 2007) by making use of "yes, and..." discussion tactics (Sawyer 2004):

From this deeper engagement, some new creative thoughts began to develop: thoughts on making safe spaces, thoughts on sharing resources with students, thoughts on new methods of group discussion, thoughts on even developing a curriculum or book on inclusive science history. These thoughts were shaped and guided by my discussion partners and broke me out of my pattern of assumptions. I realized that there was a much broader range of issues to be addressed than even the ones that I had felt were under-valued in my own department. The encouragement and engagement of my colleagues led me down these paths, and I'm still finding others. (Larry, physics)

In the official SRTs (student ratings of teaching), one participant's response to an open-ended question – "It was clear that [Ilene and Alex] were really wanting an honest discussion, not just looking for the 'right answer.'" – reflects our overall sense that we met our goal of creating an online community climate. The selection of course materials, crafting of springboard discussion prompts and our own reflectively honest responding within the forums did invite participants to step forward, to stretch to create the bulk of content by seeking to learn more with and because of one another.

As the centrepiece of our seminar, module and badge forums integrated cognitive and affective, personal and professional, learner and teacher, public and personal dimensions of learning. In coding forum data, we are gaining a greater sense of "how" the participatory foundations worked for those who wrote their presence into the discussions. In preparing for the Fall 2016 seminar, we will be setting up a focus group to learn more about the role the online discussions played within small clusters of student affairs/advising lurners who were active readers within the seminar but then moved into personalized face-to-face discussions beyond the seminar.

That participants quickly developed "thick thread"/"yes, and..." discussion patterns remain heartening as we review feedback data and review quantitative participation data to gain an overall view of discussions. This supports our sense that the seminar supported people-people networked learning within its forums. In addition, preliminary reviews of late modules (on dialogic discussion and course design) point to ways that participants in general carried the conversational substance and practices in their daily teaching learning lives.

Learning from the Lurners

Given our intentions to design a seminar that would serve enrolled students, badge-seekers and "lurking learners" – those we referred to as *lurners* – we made a specific effort to understand the experiences of this latter group. By examining Moodle access logs and participation records, as well as through interviews and other correspondence with lurners, we were able to develop a picture of the ways lurners participated.

The seminar ended with a spectrum of lurners who participated in ways we predicted as well as in ways we did not predict. We had anticipated that lurners might access resources independently and read forum posts. Though we invited their participation, even offering some ways to mark a reading presence (e.g. a discussion comment that might simply state *yes, great point, new idea for me* or *listening in on this conversation was*___), we assumed those adopting lurner roles would not overtly participate in the forums and would likely not participate by seeking badges. However, some lurners did end up taking part in each of these areas.

The majority of lurners did not actively contribute to forums or badge work. They accessed resources and occasionally read forum posts. When interviewed, one such participant shared that she gathered a small group of student affairs professionals at her local university as a "reading group". For each module, this person would download the available resources and share them with group members. Group members would then split the downloaded resources and read them prior to a group meeting. At the group meeting, they would share what they had learned and discuss these readings in the context of their student affairs work. They did this for every module, though they never posted in the forums. When interviewed a year later, this participant shared that group members were continuing to use these resources to design their work with students. Though we expected – and respected – the desires of some to work in these ways, this particular approach made us curious about how to invite this kind of participant to contribute something to the seminar, given the time and energy they were spending thinking about it and the potential value of such contributions to other participants. During the interview, this particular participant suggested creating local meet-up events with specific invitations to those accessing resources but not regularly contributing.

Another group of lurners accessed some of the forums as readers of course materials discussion posts according to the LMS logs and sometimes "popped in" when they were particularly interested in a conversation or set of resources, but otherwise tended to download and read rather than directly engage. When they did post in forums, they were responded to by other more regular participants in the seminar. There were, as is often expected of seminar of this type, several who participated in the early modules and dropped away completely during later modules.

A few lurners did participate in badge activities. One completed work to earn all of the badges, while participating sporadically and unevenly in the regular forum activities. Yet another participant read and responded to the public badge activities of others, but did not actually complete the badges herself. These lurners invested in the seminar, presumably, during parts that most interested them.

Learning in the Redesign

These data led to several changes in the second offering of the seminar, in process at the time of this Fall 2016 writing. This included changing the number and order of modules to (1) better align resources with discussion focuses, (2) change timing across modules in an effort to reduce bottlenecks in workload toward the end of the semester and (3) make content changes relevant to current events. We describe these changes next and discuss their impacts on the course thus far.

Our Spring 2015 seminar had included a penultimate Module 4 titled "When Do Words Fail Us?" with a focus on undergraduate and graduate classroom-based scenarios featuring "flash point" moments raising critical questions beyond the specifics of the individual scenario that would engage seminar participants in critical reflection and discussion regarding interpersonal, cross-diversity, teacher-student or student-student interactions played out in higher education beyond the particular fields/units/disciplines represented in the scenarios. Responses to these scenarios were rich, reflective and detailed across 67 posts in 7 discussion threads. In reviewing the course discussion logs, we found that the points raised actually overlapped with – and therefore drained energy from – what we had intended as the focus for our Module 5 discussion, which was meant to focus on ways to and why to foster dialogic discussions as part of formal and informal discussions in multiple learning spaces. In Module 5, the five threads focusing on the intended discussion were overshadowed by one thread taking on a reading focused on critical thinking. With 23 posts in the critical thinking thread, the other 5 posts in that forum garnered an average of 6 responses, and the proposed what and why of learning space discussions faded away.

When we opened the Fall 2016 seminar, we removed the old Module 4, incorporating its focus on repressive tolerance into other modules, drew on ideas from the scenarios as part of responding to posts in our Learning and Learners module and reorganized the closing Module 5 with new resources and prompts for the focus on dialogic discussions.

Based on data we reviewed from round one of the seminar, feedback from lurners, review of Moodle activity logs and analysis of high- and low-engagement discussion threads, we made modifications that would cut one module and would wrap the seminar with a welcoming section to foster early personalized introductions and a closing section where participants could all reflect on "take-away" understandings, and we could post a document linking to the "for future use" resources noted across the seminar.

The following represents our planned line-up:

0. Seminar Opening: Welcome
1. Who In the World Are We?
2. What is MILT? / Badge 1 – Philosophy Statement
3. Why Begin with Learning and Learners? / Badge 2 – Assignment Design

4. How Do Discussions Become Dialogic? / Badge 3 – Discussion Reflection
5. Where do MILT and Course Design Align? / Badge 4 – Course Design
0. Seminar Closing: What's Next?

Two local learning environment (VLE) infrastructure challenges impacted this second offering of the seminar: one complicated university course registration access for those who wished to enrol for course credit and the second complicated the issuing and activation of guest accounts for those who registered as professional development learners and lurners. Thus, the second round had fewer registrants (45) than the first round (70). Discussion threads this semester remained deep, but there was less overall participation. In each offering of the seminar, conversation has primarily been driven by the ongoing presences of credit earners, rather than by professional development participants and lurners. We wonder whether greater participation in the first round leads to a virtuous cycle, with more lurners finding spaces of interest to enter the conversation when more and expansive conversations were taking place. We wonder, further, whether the combination of the resulting later start for the seminar with the final months of the 2016 US presidential campaign and election impacted seminar participation. We know from personal communication and personal experience that – for this seminar cohort, composed of people engaged already as inclusive intercultural learners and teachers – the social, political and psychological dimensions of the campaign were wearing; commitments to community organizing are even more pressing; and work to address public rhetoric normalizing hate-speech and repressive tolerance regarding racism, xenophobia, Islamophobia and homophobia was unceasing.

Within the registration number of 45 participants, analysis of Moodle logs shows 7 persons as never logging into the platform, 17 persons as occasional visitors, 10 as regular lurners and a further 9 as core participants. The *occasional visitor* group is composed primarily of professional development participants who sometimes posted and responded to others in discussion forums and sometimes perused seminar resources; overall, these participants have logged this "sometimes" pattern of activity for three of the six modules. The *regular lurners* group includes mainly postdoctoral fellows and graduate students who entered the seminar site regularly, primarily to interact with course resources (ranging from 4 to 14 interactions per module, either to review materials or view discussions), and posting in either a discussion or badge forum two or three times. The *core participants* group includes, along with the seven credit-enrolled participants, two professional development participants, Elena and Greta, each full-time lecturers with more than 15 years of classroom experience who also hold department leadership roles. Overall, these two core participants interact with each module – through accessing module resources; accessing, posting and responding in forum discussions; and contributing in varying ways across the badge activity forums. Moodle activity data show Elena and Greta accessing each module approximately 18 times, generally between Sunday and Tuesday. In personal communication Elena has contacted Ilene twice with regard to sharing course materials with others in her department, and once regarding a larger curriculum development for a course shared among multiple instructors. Greta has also spoken with Ilene about her engagement with the seminar, summing up ideas from those conversations within an email message:

> I committed to lurning in OOPs this fall with a goal to do just slightly more than lurn but hoping I would at least keep up enough to do some lurning. I found after the first module that with relatively little investment (i.e., less than an hour) I was getting huge pay-offs. Within just one reading or video I had huge "ah-ha" moments..., or I just had totally new revelations on how I could change my courses to be more accessible and inclusive.
>
> I've also found the course really approachable. At no point have I felt like I've been teaching "all wrong" and harming my students with my "one story" version of [my social science discipline] (which makes me squirm!!). I've felt accepted for my current knowledge and skill level and challenged and supported to take my work a step further, and a step further. I have felt a lot of support and seen great idea-sharing. I have sometimes wanted to dig a bit deeper on issues and wished the online discussions had gone deeper. But, this is honestly a good thing as I cannot commit to having the ability to get into longer, sustained and deep conversations at this point.

As we write, the combination of contextual factors prompted us to accept that this would not become a semester to "undo" the seminar-ending bottleneck in badge activity forums and that we would need to switch the order for our final two modules so that the individual reflection and collective analysis of discussion would come at close the seminar. The following reflects our amended line-up, with bold text indicating a change in order and crossed out text indicating a dropped module:

0. Seminar Opening: Welcome
1. Who In the World Are We?
2. What is MILT? / Badge 1 – Philosophy Statement
3. Why Begin with Learning and Learners?/Badge 2 – Assignment Design
4. **Where do MILT and Course Design Align?/Badge 3 – Course Design**
5. **How Do Discussions Become Dialogic?/Badge 4 – Discussion Reflection**
0. ~~Seminar Closing: What's Next?~~

In moving the "Where do MILT and Course Design Align?" to precede the "How Do Discussions Become Dialogic?" module, our adjusted aim was to provide participants with learning circle space to address the impact of the highly charged US presidential campaign on personal and pedagogical work this semester, to dig a little deeper (as Greta noted) and to join together in understanding ways the cultural political context may impact pedagogical planning for learning spaces in the coming semesters.

From the start, our seminar planning involved acts of curating, collating and considering resources to enact a course design that would address these gaps in inclusive intercultural learning and teaching by supporting aims we've noted at the start of this paper. The seminar data are helping us to understand how we did engage new and experienced university teachers and staff in this area of academic professional development. We are beginning to see where we missed opportunities to strengthen people-material connections, how we might make bridges with lurners and how we make room for large-scale and ongoing world and local events that impact participants' thinking and acting as MILT practitioners.

Looking Forward

During the Fall 2016 iteration of this seminar, Ilene taught a second online seminar in the Preparing Future Faculty curriculum, "Teaching for Learning." This seminar enrolls students whose financial and timing budgets cannot accommodate the in-person PFF teaching course; in redesigning this other online course, Ilene has applied the learning circle practices to structuring and scripting forum discussions and prompts and has infused inclusive intercultural resources into a course structure organized around episodes in a teaching semester. On average, this second seminar enrols 20–25 graduate students whose forum interactions have been more often monologic than dialogic. Based on a first comparison of current and archived discussion records for this online course, the shift to a learning circle approach has enhanced participation with more learners responding to other learners to extend conversations, expand upon ideas and make connections among already posted threads.

As we plan for Fall 2017, our third iteration of this seminar, our clear understandings about the seminar are these: With things already in place for registration and VLE platform access, we can make good use of multiple networks to share what we and our participants have learned as part of recruiting new seminar participants; further, based on what we have learned from the inclusive intercultural seminar and the teaching for learning course, we will finalize a seminar timeline in consultation with past participants. In the proposed reorganization, we will continue to prioritize learning circles as a structuring method: Modules 0, 1 and 2 address the *What?* of our seminar, with Modules 3 and 4 encompassing the *So What (do you make of all this)?* query, and Module 5 plus Seminar Closing making space to explore *Now What?* Further, we will reconfigure the activities, staggering and consolidating them, so that all enrolled participants complete the philosophy and discussion activities while choosing – based on personal interests and teaching contexts – whether to complete an assignment or course design activity. Finally, we will move from issuing badges as micro-credentials to providing personalized letters to recognize individual participants' contributions to and professional development within the seminar. The following represents the new scheme:

0. Seminar Opening: Welcome
1. Who In the World Are We?
2. What is MILT?/Activity 1 – Philosophy Statement
3. Why Begin with Learning and Learners?
4. Where do MILT and Course Design Align?/Activity 2 – Assignment or Course Design
5. How Do Discussions Become Dialogic?
0. Seminar Closing: What's Next?/Activity 3 – Discussion Reflection

In many ways, the US higher education context acted as the core problem launching our research and subsequent course development. Here, professional development linked to teaching and learning is almost entirely optional and then typically addressed through one-shot, hour-long workshops open to all instructors who can be on campus for the sessions, or via departmental mentoring programs for new teaching assistants (doctoral students or postgraduate researchers), or within a 2-day orientation program for new instructors (typically tenure-track instructors with teaching, research, advising and service requirements). Some universities support ongoing teaching centre programming such as semester- or year-long learning communities organized around career stages or emergent instructional practices (flipped classrooms, serial teaching, teaching across difference), monthly open-invitation journal club gatherings, regular social media posting via a centre-generated blog or social media account and course- or certificate-based postgraduate/postdoctoral teaching professional development programming. As an example of the latter option, the University of Minnesota offers both a Preparing Future Faculty Program (which sponsors our seminar alongside three other course offerings) and a Teaching Assistant Professional Development program that include workshops and observations of teaching. A further problem across these offerings is that multicultural, intercultural and inclusive teaching is typically a "problem" to be addressed rather than an integral element of learning and teaching infused across workshops (Connolly et al. 2016).

We are also working with colleagues from the Center for Educational Innovation and the Provost's Faculty and Academic Affairs office to link the seminar to newly formalized professional development programming now open to new faculty and to advanced-standing graduate students and postdoctoral fellows. In these development program schemes, new faculties who completed six professional development sessions from the list of offerings are recognized with a letter (copied to unit chairs and college deans) and reception; and future faculty who will complete eight teaching-related sessions across a matrix of three categories will receive a letter outlining their specific teaching professional development achievements. In linking the seminar to these programs, those engaged in either professional development program will be able to earn one-half of program requirements. The linking should benefit seminar discussion forums and make possible more than one-off professional development engagement related to inclusion.

As our lurners showed us, there is an interest in professional development opportunities of this type. Across the seminars, some lurners used the modules to fuel work place professional development conversations. This demonstrated the ways open participation and open access to resources made it possible to organize learning experiences that generally did not make it back to the seminar forum discussions. Our group of student affairs professionals serves as a good example. They organized a study group, used the resources and discussion to fuel conversations and applied the content and thinking directly to their professional development in student affairs. Our hope – that openly talking about lurners and lurning would remove the shaming that often occurs with the term "lurker" – seems to have created a role for participants in the course that allowed them to take what they wanted and participate when it was useful for them. We see this as a site for future experimentation in networked learning practice, starting with the question: Can we give name to possible forms of participation, legitimize them and, by so doing, invite a more diverse group to participate in our courses, in more diverse ways? While the example group above did not directly contribute back to the discussion forums of the course, their conversations with us at the close of the course influenced the design of the second iteration. Other lurners dipped into the forums in the middle or end of the course and added new perspective. Still others downloaded the content and read the discussion forums, but never contributed directly back to the course. One goal as we design future iterations is to further consider ways to encourage some form of contribution to integrate the ideas of those choosing to be lurkers.

Our experience with this course contributes to a belief that it is important to offer conscious choices of how to participate in the course. As detailed earlier, we invited participants to reflect at the beginning on how they have participated in similar past experiences, how they wanted to participate in this one and what kind of participant they might be. Being a lurner was a legitimated choice about how to participate. In our course evaluations and conversations with others, we are hoping to uncover other ways that folks might want to participate. Whether we create specific titles or roles for these different modes of participation, we imagine that learning more about them will increase our ability to tailor the course to diverse audiences.

This paper detailed the conceptualization, design, ongoing development and outcomes of an open online participatory seminar designed with the intention of involving participants in the co-production of knowledge and class resources to address inclusive intercultural learning and teaching in higher education contexts. Our seminar work has involved acts of curating, collating and considering resources to design a seminar that would support aims we've noted throughout this paper. The seminar data are helping us to understand how we did engage new and experienced university teachers and staff in inclusive intercultural academic professional development. We are beginning to see where we missed opportunities to strengthen people-material connections, how we might make bridges with lurners and how we make room for world and local events that impact participants' thinking about and acting in learning spaces. As the course moves to its third iteration, we anticipate these learnings will translate into a deepening of the pedagogy and content of the course, as well as to the design of other professional development teaching- and learning-related seminars of this nature.

Acknowledgements The authors especially thank Jane O'Brien and Kate Martin for their clear and ongoing support for the development of this seminar, and we remain thankful for the support from Susan Tade, David Lindeman and Chris Scruton, our teaching with technology consulting colleagues. Alex and Ilene owe thanks (and pints) to our 2 July Learning Community, who responded to early ideas and then checked in with us during the beta run. We want to thank Erik Epp for developing the visualizations of networking and nodes within discussion participation data for the Spring 2015 seminar. Finally, we note our deep appreciation of John Wallace as a scholar, community builder and mentor in our personal and professional lives.

References

Alexander, I. D. (2007). Multicultural teaching and learning resources for preparing future faculty in teaching in higher education courses. *New Directions for Teaching and Learning, 111*, 27–33.

Alexander, I. D. (2013). Learning and teaching in other ways. *Journal of the Assembly for Expanded Perspectives on Learning, 19*(1), Article 13. http://trace.tennessee.edu/jaepl/vol19/iss1/13. Viewed 13 Aug 2015.

Beaty, L., Hodgson, V., Mann, S., & McConnell, D. (2002). Manifesto: Towards equality in networked e-learning in higher education. http://csalt.lancs.ac.uk/esrc/manifesto.htm. Viewed 4 Aug 2015.

Beaty, L., Cousin, G., & Hodgson, V. (2010, May). Revisiting the e-quality in networked learning manifesto. In *Proceedings of the 7th International Conference on Networked Learning* (pp. 585–592).

Biggs, J., & Tang, C. (2007). *Teaching for quality learning at university* (3rd ed.). Society for Research into Higher Education. Maidenhead: Open University Press.

Brookfield, S. (1998). Critically reflective practice. *Journal of Continuing Education in the Health Professions, 18*(4), 197–205.

Brookfield, S. (2007). Diversifying curriculum as the practice of repressive tolerance. *Teaching in Higher Education, 12*(5–6), 557–568.

Brookfield, S. (2011). Discussion as a way of teaching: Workshop packet for teachers college. http://wp.stolaf.edu/asc/files/2015/09/BrookfieldDiscussionPresentation-1.pdf. Viewed 1 May 2016.

Brookfield, S., & Preskill, S. (1999). *Discussion as a way of teaching*. San Francisco: Jossey-Bass.

Burke, P. J., & Crozier, G. (2012). Teaching inclusively: changing pedagogical spaces. https://www.heacademy.ac.uk/sites/default/files/projects/teaching_inclusively_resource_pack_final_version_opt.pdf . Viewed 1 Feb 2016.

Chávez, A. F. (2007). Islands of empowerment: Facilitating multicultural learning communities in college. *International Journal of Teaching and Learning in Higher Education, 19*(3), 274–288.

Clark, S. (1964). Literacy and liberation. *Freedomways*, First Quarter, 113–124.

Clark, S. P., & Blythe, L. (1962). *Echo in my soul*. New York: Dutton.

Coffield, F., & Edward, S. (2009). Rolling out 'good','best'and 'excellent'practice. What next? Perfect practice? *British Educational Research Journal, 35*(3), 371–390.

Connolly, M. R., Savoy, J. N., Lee, Y.-G., & Hill, L. B. (2016). *Building a better future STEM faculty: How doctoral teaching programs can improve undergraduate education*. Madison, WI: Wisconsin Center for Education Research, University of Wisconsin-Madison.

Dennen, V. P. (2008). Looking for evidence of learning: Assessment and analysis methods for online discourse. *Computers in Human Behavior, 24*(2), 205–219.

Elbow, P. (1983). Embracing contraries in the teaching process. *College English, 45*(4), 327.

Elbow, P. (1987). Embracing contraries: Explorations in learning and teaching. New York: Oxford University Press.

Fink, L. D. (2004). A self-directed guide to designing courses for significant learning. http://cte.virginia.edu/wpcontent/uploads/2013/08/Fink_Designing_Courses_2004.pdf. Viewed 20 Nov 2016.

Gómez, D. S. (2008). Women's proper place and student-centered pedagogy. *Studies in Philosophy and Education, 27*(5), 313–333.

Horton, M. (2003). Decision-making processes. *The Myles Horton reader: Education for social change* (pp. 233–250). Knoxville: Univ. of Tennessee Press.

Horton, M., Freire, P., Bell, B., Gaventa, J., & Peters, J. (1990). *We make the road by walking: Conversations on education and social change*. Philadelphia: Temple University Press.

Kaplan, M., & Miller, A. T. (Eds.). (2007). *Scholarship of multicultural teaching and learning: New directions for teaching and learning, Number 111* (Vol. 98).

Kernohan, D. (2013). MOOCS and Open Courses – what's the difference? Jisc blog. https://www. jisc.ac.uk/blog/moocs-and-open-courses-whats-the-difference-13-mar-2013. Viewed 20 Nov 2016.

Lather, P. A. (1991). *Getting smart: Feminist research and pedagogy with/in the postmodern*. New York: Routledge.

Milligan, C., Littlejohn, A., & Margaryan, A. (2013). Patterns of engagement in connectivist MOOCs. *MERLOT Journal of Online Learning and Teaching, 9*(2), 149.

Pentland, A. (2014). *Social physics: How good ideas spread-the lessons from a new science*. New York: Penguin.

Ryberg, T., & Sinclair, C. (2016). The relationships between policy, boundaries and research in net-worked learning. In *Research, boundaries, and policy in networked learning*. Cham: Springer.

Sawyer, R. K. (2004). Creative teaching: Collaborative discussion as disciplined improvisation. *Educational Researcher, 33*(2), 12–20.

Shrewsbury, C. M. (1987). What is feminist pedagogy? *Women's Studies Quarterly, 21*, 8–16.

Steeples, C., Jones, C., & Goodyear, P. (2002). Beyond e-learning: A future for networked learn-ing. In C. Steeples & C. Jones (Eds.), *Networked learning: Perspectives and issues, Computer supported cooperative work*. London: Springer.

UDL on Campus: Universal Design for Learning in Higher Education (n.d.). Cast web page. http:// udloncampus.cast.org/home. Viewed on 20 Nov 2016.

Waite, M., Mackness, J., Roberts, G., & Lovegrove, E. (2013). Liminal participants and skilled orienteers: Learner participation in a MOOC for new lecturers. *MERLOT Journal of Online Learning and Teaching, 9*(2), 200–215.

Wallace, J. (2000). The problem of time: Enabling students to make long-term commitments to community-based learning. *Michigan Journal of Community Service Learning, 7*, 133–142.

Wallace, J. (2004; updated 2011). Notes on learning circles. Bonner Foundation Toolkit. [Personal correspondence].

Wiggins, G. P., & McTighe, J. (2005). *Understanding by design*. Alexandria: Ascd.

Chapter 9
Tools for Entertainment or Learning? Exploring Students' and Tutors' Domestication of Mobile Devices

Magdalena Bober and Deirdre Hynes

Abstract This paper presents findings from a research project at a school of humanities, languages and social science at a UK university that investigated attitudes towards and uses of mobile devices (smartphones, tablets and laptops) by students and tutors. It applied the domestication of technology approach (Silverstone and Hirsch, Consuming technologies: Media and information in domestic spaces. London: Routledge, 1992) to understand how mobile devices have been appropriated by users in their everyday lives, how they have become part of daily routines and spatial arrangements and what rules are being negotiated around their use. This approach can be enriching to research in networked learning but has so far not been applied in this area before. It focuses on the ICT aspect of networked learning and on the multiple contexts in which networked learning takes place. Data was collected via in-depth interviews with 18 teaching staff and 6 focus groups with a total of 19 students across different departments in the school. The research identified distinct uses of different devices in terms of university-related and personal uses but also areas of overlapping use. Students and tutors associated important symbolic meanings with their devices, had incorporated them into daily routines and spatial arrangements in new ways and attempted to self-regulate use in different situations. While tutors were starting to make use of mobile devices in their teaching practice in innovative and meaningful ways, students had a less well-defined understanding of the educational benefits of mobile devices.

M. Bober (✉)
Audiences North, BBC, Manchester, UK
e-mail: Magdalena.bober@bbc.co.uk

D. Hynes
Department of Languages, Information and Communications, Manchester Metropolitan University, Manchester, UK
e-mail: d.hynes@mmu.ac.uk

© Springer International Publishing AG, part of Springer Nature 2018
N. Bonderup Dohn et al. (eds.), *Networked Learning*, Research in Networked Learning, https://doi.org/10.1007/978-3-319-74857-3_9

Introduction

Mobile, hand-held devices, such as smartphones and tablets, are becoming increasingly important and more widely used in higher education – in the way students learn in and outside of the classroom and how tutors use them for teaching, research and administrative tasks. To understand the uses and meanings such devices have acquired in higher education, it is important to investigate how they fit into users' everyday lives, as they are also consumer devices. Their applications cross uses between public, i.e. work and study, and private spheres, i.e. entertainment and communication with friends and family. Smartphones, in addition to the traditional functions of a mobile phone, which are voice calls and text messages, usually have Internet access and features of other multimedia technologies, such as GPS, a media player and photo and video camera, all converging onto one device that is operated via a touchscreen. A tablet is usually larger than a mobile phone and can be described as a mobile computer with a touchscreen display that has many of the added functions of a smartphone. Ownership of smartphones among young people is relatively high, and there is a rise in tablet uptake among the general adult population: 90% of 16–24 year olds in the UK claim to have a smartphone compared to 66% of the adult population, and a tablet device can be found in 54% of UK households (Ofcom 2015). Traxler (2010) argues that with more students bringing their own mobile devices into universities, there is huge potential for enhancing learning as these devices allow students to 'create, access and publish' (p. 155) information quickly and easily. However, such devices also pose a threat to universities who cannot control access to and distribution of knowledge anymore. Mobile devices challenge traditional forms of delivery and acquisition of knowledge, as well as ways of working, in higher education. The increasingly widespread presence of mobile devices has the potential to influence networked learning and teaching – in the classroom, online and in the spaces in between.

This chapter adopts the enhanced definition of networked learning by Dohn (2014, p. 30): 'Networked learning is learning in which information and communications technology (ICT) is used to promote connections: between one learner and other learners; between learners and tutors; between a learning community and its learning resources; between the diverse context in which the learners participate'.

Dohn adds the last element 'between the diverse context in which the learners participate' to the widely used definition of networked learning by Goodyear et al. (2004). She argues that the context in which learning takes place is crucial but that often networked learning activities risk being 'detached from the "primary contexts" [...] of the participants' (Dohn 2014, p. 29) in which the learning takes place. The primary context of learners can be physical or virtual but refers to learners' everyday life – at home, at work and in education. This is precisely where mobile devices are domesticated. Thus, they may help traverse between primary and other contexts of networked learning.

This chapter therefore focuses on the ICT element of the definition of networked learning, notably mobile devices, and the 'diverse contexts' in which they are embedded for learners' and tutors' lives. The materiality of the devices is also important to consider in understanding how it impacts on networked learning and enabling connections.

This chapter illuminates the use of mobile devices in a higher education context and investigates how this is linked to the use of such devices in the home environment. The aim is to find out how these two spheres are inextricably linked. The research is based on a qualitative study in a school of humanities, languages and social science at a UK university, involving interviews with teaching staff and focus groups with students. The authors were both tutors at said school during the project. The study forms part of a wider research project on staff and students' use of and attitudes towards learning technologies at the school. Investigating the humanities and social sciences is important in this context because take-up of technology-enhanced learning is lower compared to other disciplines (UCISA 2014).

Theoretical Background

The study uses a domestication of technology approach to understand how mobile devices have been appropriated by users in their everyday lives and asks whether staff and students assign similar, or different, meanings to these technologies and whether devices have a distinct use or traverse seamlessly between public and private. The domestication of technology (Silverstone and Hirsch 1992) is a sociotechnical approach which falls under the social shaping of technology paradigm (MacKenzie and Wajcman 1999; Bijker 1995).

Creanor and Walker (2012) argue that sociotechnical approaches have been under-used in writing and research on networked learning. The authors provide a list of useful concepts that can enrich the networked learning literature and help avoid technologically determinist explanations of technology use that can be found in the learning technology literature, such as sociotechnical systems, soft systems, social informatics, social shaping of technology and social construction of technology, actor network theory and activity theory. While actor network theory (ANT) (Latour 2005) has recently started making a considerable contribution to studies in networked learning (e.g. Thompson 2012), the domestication of technology has not been used yet to the knowledge of the authors of this chapter.

Domestication of technology offers a useful framework for studying the reciprocal relationship between people and technology (Hartmann 2006) – how it affects us and how we adapt it to our needs. The domestication metaphor is used to depict 'the transformation of an object from something unknown, something "wild" and unstable, to become known, more stable, "tamed"' (Sørensen 2006, p. 46). Users of technology are seen as active agents who make the technology useful to them rather than using it in a prescribed way (Hynes 2009). In this respect, domestication of technology is similar to actor network theory. The domestication process is described as a four-phase process, comprising of appropriation (making sense of the technology prior to purchase, then acquiring the technology and bringing it home), objectification (how the technology is displayed in the home, on the body or in a public space), incorporation (how the technology becomes part of existing patterns and routines, how it changes these and creates new ones) and conversion (how the owner of the technology relates and presents themselves to the outside world and to other people via this technology) (Silverstone et al. 1992). In this process, technology moves from the public sphere into the private sphere as it enters the home and then back into the public sphere again in the conversion phase (ibid.; Haddon 2005). However, this process is not necessarily linear and never complete as technologies can also fall into disuse or renewed use. Non-use, rejection and transformation of use over time are an important focus of the domestication approach (Haddon 2011; Sørensen 2006). Thus, it goes beyond earlier diffusion of innovation models which stipulated that a technological innovation would spread through a social system until it reaches saturation (Rogers 2003), and it also challenges technologically deterministic thinking which assumes that the technology is the source of change.

Domestication theory developed in the 1990s, mainly in the UK and in Scandinavian countries. In the UK, domestication of technology was initially focused on households as units of study and on stand-alone technologies, such as the computer or video recorder. In the Scandinavian tradition, domestication was seen as a 'multi-sited process that transcends the household space' (Sørensen 2006, p. 47), examining how 'national institutions and collective discourses are involved together with the production of individual practices' (ibid.), such as in the domestication of the car in Norway. More recently, the approach has been applied to mobile technologies (e.g. Ling 2004; Hartmann 2013) and nondomestic settings, such as small businesses (Pierson 2006) or university campuses (e.g. Hynes et al. 2010; Shekar 2009). Nevertheless, domestication studies in higher education settings are rare; therefore this study aims to contribute to this area.

What can the domestication of technology approach add to the networked learning literature? Sørensen (2006) argues that

> the main advantage of the domestication perspective is that it is a conceptual device that sensitizes the analyst to the complexity of integrating artefacts into dynamic socio-technical settings, like the household, the workplace, or society. It is a reminder to be concerned with the practical, symbolic and cognitive aspects of the work needed to do this integration, at multiple sites (p. 56).

The multisited nature of domestication theory can be used to examine the 'diverse context in which the learners participate' which is highlighted in Dohn's definition above. These 'multiple sites' or 'diverse contexts' are located in public and private spheres, which are often blurred and which domestication theory is keen to explore, i.e. in this study the campus and the home and the various places in between, online and offline, where learning and technology use occur. Domestication of technology offers a framework for thinking about, understanding, exploring and articulating how users interact with ICTs, how patterns of use/non-use are being established, how users relate to ICTs and create meaning around devices and how this may in turn contribute to users' own identity construction. Examining the relationships between people and technology is important for networked learning as it is the ICTs and devices that enable the connections between learners, between learners and tutors and between learners and learning resources – across different contexts, public and private, formal and informal. Domestication focuses on meaning and practice. With its focus on practice, it has the potential to make another valuable contribution to networked learning, as 'the practice side' has been neglected in networked learning's use of social practice theories (such as activity theory or social learning theory), according to Dohn (2014).

The chapter will now provide a brief overview of the themes found in a number of empirical studies on the uses of mobile devices in higher education. Findings from these studies will be referred to in more detail throughout the chapter where relevant. Such studies make reference to everyday uses of mobile devices; however more in-depth explorations of the link between educational and personal use are limited in existing empirical studies. Hence, by filling this gap, this chapter also makes a contribution to the field of mobile learning in higher education. Existing studies that only focus on the educational context investigate gender differences in students' smartphone use (Park and Lee 2014), psychological factors impacting upon acceptance of mobile learning among students (e.g. Cheon et al. 2012; Mahat et al. 2012), the advantages and challenges of mobile-based approaches in learning and teaching (e.g. Gikas and Grant 2013), reasons for accessing content unrelated to learning in the classroom (Barry et al. 2015) or to what degree mobile devices transform academic practice (Aiyegbayo 2014). However, for mobile technologies to be appropriated successfully for educational purposes, they need to fit into teachers' and learner's everyday cultures. A specific technology may not be used as intended, as Caron and Caronia (2009) demonstrate in a study of learners' resistance to podcasting of lectures: an entertainment device, the iPod in this case, does not always fit neatly into an educational context. Students can also have certain perceptions about the affordances of devices, e.g. laptops being 'better' than smartphones and tablets for study-related tasks (Curtis and Cranmer 2014), which may be influenced by their levels of digital literacy in relation to newer devices.

Methodology

Data was collected involving semi-structured, in-depth one-to-one interviews with 18 teaching staff and 6 focus groups with a total of 19 students across different departments. The interviews covered respondents' use of ICTs in everyday life and in teaching and learning. The staff sample consisted of 9 female and 9 male tutors. Four were aged between 30–39 years, 9 were aged 40–49, 4 were aged 50–59 and 1 was aged 60–69. Of the tutors eight were employed at lecturer grade and ten at senior lecturer grade or above; however there were no professors in the sample.

The student sample consisted of 17 female and 2 male students. They were aged between 18 and 34 years. The majority were undergraduate students, with eight in Foundation Year or Year 1, five in Year 2 and three in Year 3. Three further students were enrolled on post-graduate Masters' programmes. Staff and student respondents were recruited from all teaching disciplines in the school of humanities, languages and social science: sociology, politics, public services, philosophy, history, English, languages and information and communications. The project purposely recruited a spread of tutors across different disciplines who had been using a variety of different digital tools in their teaching practice that went beyond the basic use of PowerPoint or standard use of the VLE (virtual learning environment) as a repository for lecture notes; hence staff participants can be counted as 'early adopters' of innovative learning tools. The students were recruited via online or in-class announcements across different departments in the school and were a self-selecting sample. The researchers had no prior knowledge of their experience of using mobile devices and their technological self-efficacy. Data collection took place between January and May 2015. The staff interviews were 2 h long on average and sometimes carried out over two sessions; the student focus groups lasted for 1 h on average. The staff interviews were all conducted by the first author. The student interviews were carried out by a graduate student intern to avoid an imbalance in the power relationship between the student participants and the interviewer which might have occurred had the authors, both tutors at the school, conducted the student interviews. All interview sessions were audio recorded, transcribed and analysed thematically (Gibbs 2007). The categories for analysis were derived from domestication theory, for example, device acquisition and ownership, location of use and integration into daily routines. Additional categories were developed bottom-up from the data, for example, those related to educational use, such as rules for in-class use, or specific technological applications, such as email or Kahoot (explained further below). These were used to code and categorise the data.

Findings

The findings will be presented using three themes which draw upon components of the domestication approach and its different phases: device acquisition and ownership; device usage, including types of use and associated meanings; and situating devices within daily routines and spaces. In each section, results from the staff and student data will be compared. The main interests of this paper are smartphones and tablets as these are newer devices, and meanings surrounding them are still being formed, uses defined and rules negotiated. However, respondents were also questioned about other devices they used for learning and teaching, namely, laptops and desktop computers. Where relevant, these findings will also be reported.

Device Acquisition and Ownership

The reasons for acquiring a technological device are a critical part of the domestication approach as they constitute the first phase of meaning-making even before the device is purchased, with future owners imagining how they could use a device and how it would enhance their lives.

All staff respondents owned at least a work laptop and their own smartphone. Over half of the staff respondents ($n = 10$) owned another laptop or desktop computer which they used at home; some of them also brought this additional device into the office, preferring it to the work laptop. Smartphones were, in all cases, an upgrade from a previous model; hence the technology and associated habits had established themselves in the lives of the respondents over a number of years. Some respondents recalled being 'urged' by friends or family to get their first mobile phone in order to be 'contactable'; others had acquired it for work purposes. The respondents used their phones to varying degrees for personal and work-related purposes. This is discussed further in the next section. Just over half of the staff respondents ($n = 10$) also owned a tablet; six had been provided with an iPad by the university. For example, the English department had purchased an iPad for all its staff for the marking of coursework; other departments had purchased iPads for staff where there was a specific need by that staff member for teaching-related purposes, e.g. for developing a distance learning course or for teaching on a media production unit. Therefore, the decision to obtain such devices was taken over by the institution. This was also the case regarding the work laptops which were upgraded to a newer model by the university every few years. Respondents who did not own an iPad were not always interested in obtaining one as they did not see any immediate uses for this technology in their lives.

In the student sample, all respondents owned a laptop and a smartphone, while ownership of tablet devices was lower, with only 6 of 19 students having acquired one. Especially the laptops and tablets had been purchased with educational motives in mind, i.e. to support studies at university or at college prior to that (see also Hynes and Rommes 2006). Some of these devices had been bought by parents. Owning a laptop was seen as a necessity for a university degree, even though the university had computer labs for students to work in outside of class, and the respondents reported that all students on their course had one. Ownership of tablet devices was less common, similar to the staff sample, as discussed above. Some student respondents also reported having bought a tablet due to their laptop being too heavy to take into university on a daily basis. Laptops were therefore seen as less mobile than smartphones and tablets. They also had a shorter battery life and required access to a power point more frequently than phones and tablets, which was not always possible on campus. Smartphones were often acquired as part of an upgrade from an older to a newer model. A similar result was found in the staff sample, as discussed above.

Device Usage: Types of Use and Associated Meanings

Once a device is purchased and brought home, certain uses start establishing themselves in their owners' lives. Uses are not fixed and can change over time or migrate over to other devices. Technological devices also acquire certain symbolic meanings for their owners (Silverstone and Haddon 1996; Bijker 1995; Berker et al. 2006).

Among the staff respondents, the use of mobile devices varied considerably, depending on how the devices fitted into the respondents' home and working lives. For some respondents, their smartphone or tablet played a central role in their technology use, e.g. the iPad for English tutors who had been given the devices for a specific purpose or the smartphone for some female respondents for whom it fulfilled social, communicative functions (see also Park and Lee 2014). For others, use was centred around their own laptop, rather than the one provided by the university, or their home computer. These tended to be more technologically confident tutors. Laptops and computers were clearly seen as the main work tools on which to carry out university-related administrative tasks, teaching preparation, assessment and research. However, mobile devices had also taken on work-like functions, including email which was a main use, organising and managing time via the calendar functions and, especially on the iPad, reading lecture notes and marking students' written coursework. Personal use varied depending on how embedded mobile devices were in tutors' lives. The most important ones which applied to all cases were 'being contactable' in case of a home emergency and being able to communicate with family and friends. These original uses of mobile phones when they first entered the market as consumer devices were still seen as their key ones, even though mobile devices have now acquired a variety of further features. In addition to these key functions, respondents also used their phones for checking information online, accessing social networking apps, reading books, watching videos, listening to music or the radio, playing games or taking photos and videos and, for one respondent, even self-tracking with the help of sleep and fitness apps.

The student participants saw their smartphone mainly as a personal device for entertainment, finding information, communication and social networking, whereas their laptop was considered as a study tool. In the focus groups, students would always mention personal uses first when talking about what they used their phone for most. Below are typical examples of common smartphone uses, here from Focus Group 1, which were mirrored by the other focus groups:

> Student 1: Snapchatting, using apps such as Facebook, Tinder, Messenger. And I use it for Google searches and calling and keeping in contact with people.
>   Student 2: Basically the same, internet, social networking, Skype to talk to my family in Ireland and stuff like that.

The above quotes demonstrate the importance of maintaining a connection with family and friends for students. They use mobile devices to maintain their personal social network, but they understand the value of a social learning network less. As can be seen in the following quotes from a range of different focus groups, educational uses seemed to be of secondary importance or were only mentioned when prompted by the interviewer. Such uses included recording lectures, quickly needing to check email or finding information:

Student 1: I use [my phone] for recording sometimes. If it's a good seminar I'll use my voice recorder so I can look back and make notes, or if it's a confusing seminar maybe.
Student 2: You can get apps for helping you reference as well, in your essays. (Focus Group 1)
Interviewer: Do you use your phone to support your studies outside class?
Student: Not really, only if I've found something really interesting and I fancied googling it on the bus... or if I needed to check an I email, I would use the [university's] app... otherwise I would use my laptop. (Focus Group 2)
Student: I would only use my phone to check emails that are important... and notes that I've taken or pictures that I've taken from my lecturer's notes. (Focus Group 4)

This is similar to the findings of Henderson et al.'s (2015) study of university students which found that digital technologies are used less frequently for purely learning-related activities but more for organising and managing studies. The students in Henderson et al.'s study reported learning activities such as 'viewing and listening of lecture recordings' or using 'digital technologies to "research information"'(ibid., p. 4). This is also mirrored in Jones' (2012) research. Jones conducted a longitudinal study of students' experience of networked learning in English universities and found that 'students are still using ICT in somewhat predictable ways, e.g. to communicate with their tutors and to access course materials' (p. 31).

Some students saw a clear divide between what different devices were used for, i.e. the phone for personal, entertainment and social use and the laptop for study, research and work. Others detected an overlap:

Student 1: I think I use my phone and my laptop for completely different things. My laptop really is just for uni work unless I'm emailing, but my phone is very much personal use and my iPad is just a mix of both, so – No, I think it depends more on what I'm doing, so like if I want to go on Facebook, I'll just do that on my phone, but if I want to write an essay, I can't do that on my phone, so I'll just use my laptop.
Student 2: Yeah, I think there is just like an overlap because they're basically like the same. Because you can start something on the phone, and then I can just press a button on my laptop and it brings up the exact thing what I had on my phone and I can continue it. Yeah, I wouldn't say essays, no, especially emails or any webpage I've got on my phone, I just press a button and it comes up on my laptop. They basically are the same but as long as it's not essays. (Focus Group 2)

Students who owned a tablet used it both for entertainment and for study, as in the first quote below, or they used it as an extension of their laptop, as in the second example:

I use it for listening to music, taking notes when I don't feel like lugging my laptop around because I do have a keyboard. I watch Netflix on it. I take pictures when I go on vacation... I sometimes, I'll write my story on there or I'll plot it out or I'll use my Kindle app to read books for the courses or books that I have to review for my blog and my YouTube channel. (Student, Focus Group 4)
I just switch between using my iPad and my laptop. If all I need to do is check my emails, I'll just do it on my iPad, like if I just need to quickly send my tutor an email, I'll do

it on my iPad. Or if I've been reading an article like online while I've been in uni and I haven't finished it, I'll just leave it open on the app so when I get home I can just quickly pick up where I left off. (Student, Focus Group 2)

For most of the student respondents, their smartphone turned out to be their most important device as could be seen from answers to the question about which of their devices they would miss most if they lost it. They associated meanings of convenience, ease of use, contact with family and friends and a feeling of safety in an emergency situation with their smartphone. One respondent also stressed how she found it easier to communicate with people via social media on her smartphone and saw it as an extension of her identity. While some students were also worried about losing their laptop if their university work was stored on it, emotional attachment to their laptop had decreased for those respondents whose content was stored remotely 'in the Cloud'. For them it mattered less if the device broke down, was lost or stolen, and university computers could also be used as a backup.

For tutors, their mobile devices had acquired meanings of being a constant companion or an assistant to help them micromanage their lives. Mobile devices were also seen as multifunctional tools, like a Swiss army knife, or even assigned magical properties by respondents awed by their technical capabilities. Some tutors had embedded their mobile devices into their lives to such a degree that they saw them as their 'everything' or a 'hub' for their whole life. It is important to explore this symbolic meaning and attachment as it affects how these devices will be used in networked learning.

Situating Devices Within Daily Routines and Spaces

Where do users keep their devices during the day and put them at night? How do they fit into and potentially rearrange daily routines? What rules and practices have established themselves around using devices in specific spaces or times of day? These are important questions from a domestication of technology perspective that help us understand how these technologies have become embedded into users' lives.

Similarities between the tutor and the student sample could be observed in relation to smartphones. The student respondents tended to always carry their smartphone with them, take it into class and have it on or under the table, ready to check if an important message appeared, i.e. to be constantly 'networked'.

[I keep it] as close as possible, so if I've got clothes with pockets in, it usually goes in my pocket. If not, it will be in my handbag. But whenever I'm sat down it's always in front of me. (Student, Focus Group 4)

Tutors for whom their smartphone played an important communicative function also carried it with them at most times. The trouser pocket, jacket pocket or a handbag was a typical place to keep it. It was also taken into the teaching room to check messages during breaks. Other respondents who were less 'attached' to their phone left it in their workbag during the day if not needed. At home, some respondents carried their phone with them at most times or left it in one specific place, such as the sofa or a shelf. During the night, many respondents put their phone on charge and had a dedicated space for this, e.g. in the kitchen or on their bedside table, the latter especially if the phone served as an alarm in the morning.

Keeping the phone on the bedside table overnight and using it as an alarm was also common among the student respondents. Furthermore, it was often the first thing they checked in the morning. It had become part of users' morning routine, like getting dressed and brushing one's teeth, but some respondents also expressed a reluctance to 'reconnect' straight away, as can be seen in the following quotes from Focus Group 1:

> Student 1: I use it for my alarm in the morning.
>   Student 2: Yeah, I use mine for my alarm.
>   Interviewer: So do you check other things out also?
>   Student 3: When I wake up, I'll check Facebook and Twitter.
>   Student 1: I'll see if there's anything on the phone screen when I've woken up, I'll obviously check them, but if there's nothing on it, I'll wake up and do what I'm going to do...
>   Student 3: I look at Twitter just to wake me up in the morning like... You know, if I have a message, I tend to ignore it in the morning. Just for a bit while I get ready. Cos I'm too tired to deal with it.

Many respondents, both staff and students, recognised that the amount of time they spent on their smartphones, willingly or unwillingly, was problematic and that this could have an impact on other parts of their life, e.g. university work or general well-being. Some students said their phone was like an 'addiction' and that they used it too much (see also Israelashvili et al. 2012). Interestingly, use of laptops or tablets was not seen as problematic. Some students tried to self-regulate their usage, e.g. trying not to use their phone in class, putting it in their bag and on silent, putting it away when studying at home or not using it at bedtime.

> Yeah, I use my phone entirely way too much. It is an addiction and I am tied to it... But when I am sitting down writing, I do turn my phone off and put it across the room. I put my headphones on so I won't hear it, so I can write. Otherwise it'll distract me. (Student, Focus Group 4)

For staff, self-regulating usage was mostly concerned with trying to maintain a healthy work-life balance, especially in relation to work email. Email formed a major, and often time-consuming, part of their device usage. Smartphones and tablets were used to keep on top of email at work when away from the office laptop, for 'getting through' emails during their commute or checking emails from home. The following quote highlights common tensions for staff:

> It's balancing pros and cons, it's great [for] picking things up straight away. So I'll respond to email and I respond at all times, and it's probably unhealthy and I should turn it off, but it's very hard when you hear the 'bing'. (Sociology tutor 1)

In this context, institutional policy also had an impact on individual use: a few months before the fieldwork was carried out, the university introduced an IT security policy that required staff to add a passcode to their personal mobile devices if they had linked their work email to the phone's email app. Some staff interviewed had decided to remove the work email from their devices; others reported that email access on their phones had 'stopped working', and they chose not to reinstall it. They could still use the Internet browser on their phone to access work email online, but this added an extra layer of access – which some respondents welcomed to help distance themselves from work communications while at home.

An area where rules around the use of mobile devices are in flux is use in class. Educational institutions are shifting from outright bans of mobile devices in the classroom to incorporating and encouraging their use in order to harness their potential educational benefits. Among the tutors interviewed, attitudes to use in class varied, an observation also noted by Barry et al. (2015). Some tutors had explicit rules for non-use, some 'tolerated' use in class, albeit reluctantly, whereas others had incorporated mobile devices into learning activities:

> I don't mind at all if my students have devices out in class... My observation... is that the youngsters these day can multitask and that's how they are learning... What they are doing is that they are going online to research and consulting with friends to work, collaborating. (Creative writing tutor)
>
> I do have a problem with it where they're trying to read [an 18th Century novel on their phones]... It's when they're squinting at those screens, scrolling [through a] 300 page novel... Or they're on Wikipedia desperately trying to analyse a poem. I say, 'Put the phones away, you're not going to have that in the exam'. (English tutor 1)

Students brought their smartphones into class and admitted checking personal messages but justified this by also checking class-related information. All focus groups reported that they had also observed their peers using phones in class which seemed to make it a more acceptable activity for everyone. Barry et al. (2015) found that students will often use mobile devices to relieve boredom in an uninspiring lecture. Some students in the present study felt distracted by peers who engaged in heavier, more frequent phone use in class. This mirrors findings by Sana et al. (2013) who identified that laptop use of unrelated content by students was also distracting to their peers seated nearby. Students in the present study also reported varying attitudes from their tutors towards device use in class, as described above, and had learned to manage different tutors' expectations and fit their own in-class use of mobile devices around this.

The tutors interviewed reported incorporating the following examples of innovative use of mobile devices in their teaching practice, listed here in order from simple to more complex tasks (for a discussion, see Bober 2016):

- Using a tutor tablet as a demo tool
- Using a tutor tablet for video conferencing with an external speaker
- Making podcasts of lectures available for download onto students' own mobile devices
- Getting students to use their own devices in class to research a topic
- Using classroom response systems via mobile devices (e.g. Kahoot, Socrative)
- Researching a mobile format, 'selfies', and getting students to take, share and critically analyse their own selfies

- Using student devices for accessing an electronic pinboard (Padlet) in and out of class
- Voice recording on mobile phones for pronunciation practice in language teaching
- Using smartphones to record video footage for video assessments, e.g. in a foreign language class or during a work placement
- Using university tablets for group communication (email, Facebook, Skype) in international student projects

Tutors often commented on the transformative effect the technology had on their teaching in the way that it managed to engage the students. The focus was not on using smartphones, but the transformative potential came from the services and functions that could be accessed and used by the students for the learning activity via these devices. Their educational benefits had clearly established themselves in many tutors' understanding of mobile devices.

> If you ask [students] a really sensitive question, putting your hands up reveals an awful lot about you so, in this case, Socrative or Kahoot, it allows privacy… I was allowing everyone from the shyest to the most… extrovert to engage and that was amazing. (Sociology tutor 2)
>
> Because they were contributing to this kind of – [it] seemed like a bit of magic really, they were contributing to something that everybody was going to see and that there could be a record of. They really engaged in a way that far exceeded what I'd hoped they would do, they really took to it. (English tutor 2, talking about her use of Padlet)

During the period the fieldwork was carried out, the school had a trolley of 20 tablets, specifically Apple iPads, that tutors could book for use in class, but its existence was less widely known, or staff did not know how to book the devices or felt the number was not sufficient for their class size. Only the last of the activities listed above employed these iPads. All other activities relied on students bringing their own devices into class. However, tutors did not specifically ask students to do so as they could usually rely to a sufficient number of mobile devices to be present in the classroom so that students could share these and do the activity in groups.

Feedback from student participants who had experienced mobile device-based activities in class was mixed. It has to be noted that the students were not all taught by the tutors interviewed for this study, so the following responses are not feedback on the activities listed above. Most participants in the focus groups had experienced the use of classroom response or poll systems, or being asked to search for information on their phones during class, so their responses are in relation to these tasks. Some students said they found it difficult to access the activities on their devices and to log in, they did not understand how the online tools worked or this had not been explained to them properly. Other respondents felt that their classmates did not 'really take it seriously' (Student, Focus Group 2), that they could not remember what they had learnt from the activity and that it was too quick to make notes of the correct answers. However, there was also positive feedback, with students saying it was fun and engaging, and a useful recap of a previous lecture. Furthermore, one student said that it was better getting students to research something themselves 'rather than being dictated to' (Student, Focus group 3).

Several respondents recognised that such activities would help engage students 'who don't like to speak aloud' (Student, Focus Group 2), and it was 'good to see other people's ideas' (Focus Group 6).

While there were no specific university-wide rules on the use of mobile devices in class and it was down to individual tutors to set the ground rules, the university had introduced two projects that encouraged smartphone use. These were the university smartphone app, which gave students access to the VLE, their timetable, university email and other resources, and a new self-registration pilot that required Foundation and Year 1 students to register their attendance electronically, either using their own mobile device, which could be done in class, or the computers in university labs. This is another interesting example of how institutional policy can impact on attitudes towards mobile devices. Many student participants reported accessing the university app on their devices and found it useful to check class resources; however several students complained about the self-registration system as it would frequently not work due to poor Wi-Fi access in certain teaching rooms. It is possible that perceptions around this system impacted negatively on attitudes towards mobile devices in learning more generally.

Discussion and Conclusion

This study has shown how mobile devices have established themselves as important technologies in the lives of university students and tutors. The findings suggest that there is a mutual, reciprocal relationship between the user and the technology, in that the users adopt those functions of the technology which fit into their lives and which serve their current needs rather than adopting the technology outright and fitting their lives around it.

While ownership of laptops and smartphones was universal in the sample, fewer participants owned tablet devices. Use of mobile devices varied, depending on how embedded they were in people's lives. There was a distinction between laptops as work and study tools and smartphones as personal devices. However, smartphones had also acquired work-like functions for staff and study-related uses for students. Tablet devices often bridged work and entertainment uses. Mobile devices played a variety of different roles in users' lives as could be detected from users' symbolic meaning-making around their devices. Some respondents saw their use as problematic and tried to self-impose rules, such as limiting especially their smartphone use when it had the potential to impact negatively on their study success or well-being.

Rules around use of mobile devices are still in flux in classroom settings. Attitudes towards using them in class varied among staff, from outright bans to innovative educational uses, and students had learnt to negotiate tutors' expectations. Students in this research had mixed views on educational uses of mobile devices in the classroom, shaped by institutional policy to some degree. Jisc (2015) also comments that students are less aware of the educational benefits of mobile technologies or digital technologies in general.

The findings of the present study have important implications for educational institutions planning to implement mobile device-based learning. Even though staff and students bring personal devices into university, this does not mean that use for educational purposes will follow as a matter of course. This process is in constant flux, meanings and uses need to be renegotiated, and it takes time for the devices and their uses to become successfully domesticated within students' and tutors' daily lives and routines.

To support this process of meaning-making, universities should promote a variety of innovative educational uses that offer clear benefits which learners and educators can easily recognise. At a pedagogical level, Barry et al. (2015) argue that more engaging classroom activities need to be built into lessons so that mobile device use is not misaligned with the learning outcomes and students do not engage in unrelated tasks on their mobile devices to relieve boredom. At a cultural level, institutions and educators wishing to implement mobile device-based learning need to be aware of the differences between efficient academic culture and learners' more diverse everyday culture and that therefore devices from one area may not so easily be transposed into the other (Caron and Caronia 2009). At a psychological level, attitudes towards mobile device-based learning activities are also important, such as perceived ease of use and usefulness of mobile learning tasks, self-efficacy, as well as peers' and tutors' views on mobile learning (Cheon et al. 2012). Furthermore, training and support for tutors is needed if they are to embed mobile devices in their practice effectively (Aiyegbayo 2014), as well as digital literacy training for students in relation to using mobile devices for educational purposes (Curtis and Cranmer 2014).

Although the findings are based on a case study of one particular school at a UK university, they can be seen as generalisable to a degree. They correspond with other studies on mobile and technology-enhanced learning in higher education as highlighted in several places in this chapter. This study forms part of a wider research project on staff and students' use of and attitudes towards learning technologies at the school. This chapter sets the groundwork for a more detailed investigation of specific mobile device-based learning activities and an exploration of how tutors enact their professional identity through the use of digital technology in their work and private lives – analysis of the data is underway.

To return to the theoretical approach of this chapter, this study has shown that domestication of technology can be applied meaningfully in a higher education context as it highlights the importance of the link between public and private, i.e. between the educational and the domestic sphere, which mobile devices easily cross. However, as an ideal model, the domestication approach can be problematic due to the increased functionality and utility of mobile devices. New applications can be added, and the devices rarely have only one dedicated function. Therefore, their uses are changing, fluid and dynamic, and meanings have to be renegotiated constantly in a process of renewed domestication (Haddon 2011).

The domestication of technology can make a valuable contribution to networked learning by focusing on the multiple contexts in which networked learning and associated use of ICTs takes place – in public or private, at home, at work, in formal and informal educational settings and in the various places in between. It also makes the researcher aware of, and sensitive towards, the complexity of how ICTs are appropriated into social environments. Domestication focuses on meaning-making and use – the practice aspect perhaps being an element that networked learning researchers should focus on more (Dohn 2014).

The focus of this chapter was mobile devices – so what implications does the ubiquity of mobile devices have for networked learning? It can be said that they have the potential to bridge the gap between educational and other contexts and make learning more integrated into, and relevant to, learners' 'primary contexts' or everyday lives. However, this is far from straightforward as was demonstrated by the variety and richness of uses and meanings that emerged from the data in this study. It is hoped that networked learning scholars will pursue this interesting and fast-changing area of meaning-making and practices surrounding mobile device use in learners' everyday lives further.

Acknowledgements This research was funded by a Scholarship of Teaching and Learning grant from the Centre for Excellence in Learning and Teaching at Manchester Metropolitan University. The authors would like to thank all staff and students who gave up their time to take part in and contribute to this project. Special thanks go to Anshul Lau for carrying out the student focus group interviews.

References

Aiyegbayo, O. (2014). How and why academics do and do not use iPads for academic teaching? *British Journal of Educational Technology.* https://doi.org/10.1111/bjet.12202.

Barry, S., Murphy, K., & Drew, S. (2015). From deconstructive misalignment to constructive alignment: Exploring student uses of mobile technologies in university classrooms. *Computers and Education, 81*, 202–210.

Berker, T., Hartmann, M., Punie, Y., & Ward, K. (2006). *Domestication of media and technology.* Maidenhead: Open University Press.

Bijker, W. (1995). *Of bicycles, bakelites, and bulbs: Toward a theory of sociotechnical change.* Cambridge, MA: MIT Press.

Bober, M. (2016). Beyond Moodle and Powerpoint: Mobile and technology-enhanced learning in the humanities, languages and social sciences. *Learning and Teaching in Action, 12*(1), 35–50, http://www.celt.mmu.ac.uk/ltia/Vol12Iss1/4_Bober_beyond_Moodle_and_Powerpoint.pdf. Viewed 27 Feb 2017.

Caron, L., & Caronia, A. H. (2009). Mobile learning in the digital age: A clash of cultures? In S. Kleinman (Ed.), *The culture of efficiency: Technology in everyday life* (pp. 190–212). New York: Peter Lang.

Cheon, J., Lee, S., Crooks, S. M., & Song, J. (2012). An investigation of mobile learning readiness in higher education based on the theory of planned behavior. *Computers & Education, 59*(3), 1054–1064.

Creanor, L., & Walker, S. (2012). Learning technology in context: A case for the sociotechnical interaction framework as an analytical lens for networked learning research. In L. Dirckinck

Holmfeld, V. Hodgson, & D. McConnell (Eds.), *Exploring the theory, pedagogy and practice of networked learning* (pp. 173–187). New York: Springer.

Curtis, F., & Cranmer, S. (2014). Laptops are better. Medical students' perceptions of laptops versus tablets and smartphones to support their learning. In *Proceedings of the 9th International Conference on Networked Learning* (pp. 67–75).

Dohn, N. (2014). Implications for networked learning of the 'practice' side of social practice theories: A tacit-knowledge perspective. In V. Hodgson, M. de Laat, D. McConnell, & T. Ryberg (Eds.), *The design, experience and practice of networked learning* (pp. 29–49). New York: Springer.

Gibbs, G. (2007). *Analysing qualitative data*. London: Sage.

Gikas, J., & Grant, M. M. (2013). Mobile computing devices in higher education: Student perspectives on learning with cellphones, smartphones and social media. *Internet and Higher Education, 19*, 18–26.

Goodyear, P., Banks, S., Hodgson, V., & McConnell, D. (Eds.). (2004). *Advances in research on networked learning*. Dordrecht: Kluwer.

Haddon, L. (2005). Empirical studies using the domestication framework. In T. Berker, M. Hartmann, Y. Punie, & K. Ward (Eds.), *Domestication of media and technology* (pp. 103–122). Maidenhead: Open University Press.

Haddon, L. (2011). Domestication analysis, objects of study, and the centrality of technologies in everyday life. *Canadian Journal of Communication, 36*(2), 311–323.

Hartmann, M. (2006). Triple articulation of ICTs: Media as technological objects, symbolic environments and individual texts. In T. Berker, M. Hartmann, Y. Punie, & K. Ward (Eds.), *Domestication of media and technology* (pp. 80–102). Maidenhead: Open University Press.

Hartmann, M. (2013). From domestication to mediated mobilism. *Mobile Media & Communication, 1*(1), 42–49.

Henderson, M., Selwyn, N., & Aston, R. (2015). What works and why? Student perceptions of "useful" digital technology in university teaching and learning. *Studies in Higher Education, 5079*(January), 1–13.

Hynes, D. (2009). [End] users as designers: The internet in everyday life in Irish households. *Anthropology in Action, 16*(1), 18–29.

Hynes, D., & Rommes, E. (2006). Fitting the internet into our lives: IT courses for disadvantaged users. In T. Berker, M. Hartmann, Y. Punie, & K. Ward (Eds.), *Domestication of media and technology* (pp. 125–144). Maidenhead: Open University Press.

Hynes, D., Vuojärvi, H., & Isomäki, H. (2010). Domestication of a laptop on a wireless campus. *Australasian Journal of Educational Technology, 26*(2), 250–267. http://www.ascilite.org.au/ajet/ajet26/vuojarvi.pdf. Viewed 9 Apr 2015.

Israelashvili, M., Kim, T., & Bukobza, G. (2012). Adolescents' over-use of the cyber world – Internet addiction or identity exploration? *Journal of Adolescence, 35*(2), 417–424.

JISC. (2015). Mobile learning: A practical guide for educational organisations planning to implement a mobile learning initiative. https://www.jisc.ac.uk/guides/mobile-learning. Viewed 27 Feb 2017.

Jones, C. (2012). Networked learning, stepping beyond the net generation and digital natives. In L. Dirckinck Holmfeld, V. Hodgson, & D. McConnell (Eds.), *Exploring the theory, pedagogy and practice of networked learning* (pp. 27–41). New York: Springer.

Latour, B. (2005). *Reassembling the social: An introduction to actor-network theory*. Oxford: Oxford University Press.

Ling, R. (2004). *The mobile connection: The cell phone's impact on society*. San Francisco: Morgan Kaufmann.

MacKenzie, D. A., & Wajcman, J. (1999). *The social shaping of technology* (2nd ed.). Milton Keynes: Open University Press.

Mahat, J., Ayub, A. F. M., & Luan, S. (2012). An assessment of students' mobile self-efficacy, readiness and personal innovativeness towards mobile learning in higher education in Malaysia. *Procedia – Social and Behavioral Sciences, 64*, 284–290.

Ofcom. (2015). The Communications market report. http://stakeholders.ofcom.org.uk/binaries/research/cmr/cmr15/CMR_UK_2015.pdf. Viewed 27 Feb 2017.

Park, N., & Lee, H. (2014). Gender difference in social networking on smartphones: A case study of Korean college student smartphone users. *International Telecommunications Policy Review, 21*(2), 1–18.

Pierson, J. (2006). Domestication at work in small businesses. In T. Berker, M. Hartmann, Y. Punie, & K. Ward (Eds.), *Domestication of media and technology* (pp. 205–226). Maidenhead: Open University Press.

Rogers, E. M. (2003). *Diffusion of innovations* (5th ed.). London: Simon & Schuster.

Sana, F., Weston, T., & Cepeda, N. J. (2013). Laptop multitasking hinders classroom learning for both users and nearby peers. *Computers & Education, 62*, 24–31.

Shekar, M. (2009). *Domestication of the cell phone on a college campus: A case study* (Masters dissertation). London School of Economics and Political Science. http://www.lse.ac.uk/media%40lse/research/mediaWorkingPapers/MScDissertationSeries/Past/Shekar_final.pdf. Viewed 9 Apr 2015.

Silverstone, R., & Haddon, L. (1996). Design and the domestication of information and communication technologies: Technical change and everyday life. In R. Silverstone & R. Mansell (Eds.), *Communication by design: The politics of information and communication technologies* (pp. 44–74). Oxford: Oxford University Press.

Silverstone, R., & Hirsch, E. (1992). *Consuming technologies: Media and information in domestic spaces*. London: Routledge.

Silverstone, R., Hirsch, E., & Moreley, D. (1992). Information and communication technologies and the moral economy of the household. In R. Silverstone & E. Hirsch (Eds.), *Consuming technologies: Media and information in domestic spaces* (pp. 15–31). London: Routledge.

Sørensen, K. (2006). Domestication: The enactment of technology. In T. Berker, M. Hartmann, Y. Punie, & K. Ward (Eds.), *Domestication of media and technology* (pp. 40–61). Maidenhead: Open University Press.

Thompson, T. (2012). Who's taming who? Tensions between people and technologies in cyberspace communities. In L. Dirckinck Holmfeld, V. Hodgson, & D. McConnell (Eds.), *Exploring the theory, pedagogy and practice of networked learning* (pp. 157–172). New York: Springer.

Traxler, J. (2010). Will student devices deliver innovation, inclusion, and transformation? *Journal of the Research Center for Educational Technology, 6*(1), 3–15.

UCISA. (2014). 2014 survey of technology enhanced learning for higher education in the UK. https://www.ucisa.ac.uk/bestpractice/surveys/tel/tel. Viewed 27 Feb 2017.

Chapter 10
CmyView: Learning by Walking and Sharing Social Values

Lucila Carvalho and Cristina Garduño Freeman

Abstract Networked learning practices are impacting the field of cultural heritage, both tangible and intangible, with implications for the way in which places of cultural significance are understood, managed, documented, engaged with and studied. Our research explores the intersection between walking, photography, technology and learning, investigating how mobile devices can be used to foster community participation and assess social value within a networked framework for digital heritage. The chapter introduces *CmyView*, a mobile phone application and social media platform in development, with a design concept grounded on both digital heritage and networked learning perspectives. *CmyView* encourages people to collect and share their views by making images and audio recordings of personally meaningful sites they see while walking outdoors in the natural or built environment. Each person's walking trajectory (along with their associated images and audio files) then becomes a traceable artefact, something potentially shareable with a community of fellow walkers. The aim of *CmyView* is to encourage networked heritage practices and community participation, as people learn by documenting their own and experiencing others' social values of the built environment. Drawing on a framework for the analysis and design of productive learning networks, we analyse the educational design of *CmyView* arguing that the platform offers a space for democratic heritage education and interpretation, where participatory urban curatorship practices are nurtured. *CmyView* reframes social value as dynamic, fluid and located within communities, rather than fixed in a place. The chapter presents preliminary findings of the activity of a group of four undergraduate students at an Australian university, who used *CmyView* to explore the immediate surroundings of their campus, in an activity outside of their formal curriculum. Participants interacted with the platform, mapping, capturing, audio recording their impressions and sites of interest in their walks. In so doing, they created shareable trajectories, which were subsequently experienced by the same group of participants on a second walk. The

L. Carvalho (✉)
Institute of Education, Massey University, Auckland, New Zealand
e-mail: l.carvalho@massey.ac.nz

C. G. Freeman
Australian Centre for Architectural History, Urban and Cultural Heritage,
The University of Melbourne, Parkville, VIC, Australia

chapter concludes with a discussion about the impact of our research for the design of mobile technologies that embrace participation and sharing, through a networked learning perspective. The chapter brings together concepts that sit at the intersection of previously separate fields, namely, digital heritage and networked learning, to find their synergies.

Introduction

Networked learning practices are impacting the field of cultural heritage, both tangible and intangible, with implications for the way in which places of cultural significance are understood, managed, documented, engaged with and studied. In this chapter we explore the intersection between walking, photography, technology and learning, investigating how mobile devices can be used to foster community participation and assess social value within a networked framework for digital heritage. The chapter introduces *CmyView*, a mobile phone application and social media platform in development, with a design concept grounded on both digital heritage and networked learning perspectives.

In 15 years of research and development in networked learning, we have seen a shift from its initial focus in higher education towards broader educational practices, including, for example, work-based scenarios, professional development, schools and even informal learning (Hodgson et al. 2014). During this time, technology has significantly evolved, transforming and extending the modalities and settings in which people learn. Ubiquitous and portable technologies nowadays enable people to connect to others and/or to learning resources anywhere, and as a result networked learning is no longer circumscribed to a specific physical space. Instead, it may take place while people are walking outdoors, traveling on public transport, eating in a café or sitting comfortably at home. Mobile computing is affecting and arguably augmenting (or at times curtailing) people's experiences of physical spaces. It not only allows for 'learning on the go' but adds to and modifies the structural composition of the physical spaces where such activities unfold, which in turn can affect the ways that people think and perceive their physical environment (Kirsh 2013). There are new complex configurations of tools, tasks and people emerging, and these are not yet fully understood (Goodyear et al. 2016). The *CmyView* project capitalizes on mobile computing, networked practices and physical environments and spaces, to offer a way to collect, document and assess social value through embodied social practices. *CmyView* makes an innovative contribution to the ongoing yet critical issue, within the field of heritage, of understanding and documenting social value.

Until the 1990s heritage significance was primarily understood through expert assessment of the historic, scientific or aesthetic value of a place. Since then, community values as indicators of cultural significance have increasingly been recognized (ICOMOS 1999). Values are important because they frame places' broader public meaning (Waterton 2010). The field of heritage sees the concepts of *social value* and *place* as intertwined where *social value* is a fluid and dynamic cultural process (Smith 2006) and *place* a geographical construct that incorporates people's sense of attachment to the built environment (Hayden 1997). However, even though social value is now more readily recognized, it continues to be complex to assess (Canning and Spenneman 2001). To date, assessment has tended to rely on social sciences methods such as surveys, workshops and interviews, forms of inquiry not usually carried out in situ (Johnston 2003). *CmyView* harnesses the opportunities afforded by mobile digital technologies to design new ways to assess social value.

CmyView encourages people to collect and share their views by making images and audio recordings of personally meaningful sites they see, while walking outdoors in the natural or built environment. Each person's walking trajectory (along with their associated images and audio files) then becomes a traceable artefact, something potentially shareable with a community. It brings together, ideas from existing mobile 'apps' that focus specifically on mapping walks (e.g. Map my Walk, Glympse or Trails) and posting/sharing photographs (e.g. Instagram, Flickr and Facebook) and extends these by adding the ability to make an audio recording that is linked to the GPS point and image taken. By facilitating the collection and sharing of information about the connections between people and places, *CmyView* also allows for a form of community curatorship of place. It engages people in observing and reflecting on their connections to the built environment by prompting them to create a GPS-enabled photograph and add commentary via an audio recording. Location, image and audio are then packaged up into a shareable traceable representation of a 'walk'. Others can select a previously created 'walk', search for the places photographed by someone else by looking for these images in situ and then listen to the significance of these for the walk's creator. In so doing, *CmyView* offers opportunities for asynchronous situated connections between people, as walks can be made visible and catalogued in an accessible and searchable format. Coupling embodied ubiquitous practices, such as walking, with questions of social value, brings a new spatial context through which to see and make decisions around what aspects of places are valuable. Using photography as a representational embodied and creative practice to document an element of interest, and distinguish it as significant, shifts the process of assessing social value from a one-way community consultation process into an informal learning network that emphasizes relationships between people and place. *CmyView* is both a 'tool' and 'a way' to explore places. It could be framed as digital heritage, intangible heritage, and as a form of citizen place interpretation. In thinking through the design of the system, its effect on the activity of users, its potential to contribute to the assessment of social value and its ability to develop communities around curatorial practices of place, it becomes clear that this project sits at the intersection of the fields of heritage and networked learning.

Networked learning has been described as involving learning situations in which collaboration and participation are mediated via technologies (Steeples and Jones 2002; Goodyear et al. 2004). Having in mind the softening of the boundaries between formal and non-formal learning and digital and physical spaces, the notion of place-based spaces for networked learning offers a suitable framing for the *CmyView* project (Carvalho et al. 2017). The networked learning perspective highlights the opportunities for connections between people, as they assess and create (learning) resources, while experiencing both the physical and ephemeral elements and aspects of the built environment in different ways. Facets of places may become more salient when people walk around imbued with the aim of capturing sites that are of interest to them. While photography on mobile devices has become ubiquitous, the conscious task of observing, making representations and articulating the motivations for the decisions offers an opportunity for developing visual and spatial knowledge, or even a 'good eye' (Rogoff 2002). Observation and reflections are established methods in the pedagogical approaches of creative education (Schön 1985). They are of particular importance for architecture students (within a formal learning context) but are also becoming pertinent for less formal learners as knowledge is increasingly dispersed across various visual, textual and spatial modalities (e.g. virtual reality). Observation and reflection is an open methodology for informal learners who have an interest in issues associated with the social value of heritage sites. This opportunity is extended through intentional sharing where multiple viewpoints can engender a form of socio-visual empathy. Connections between people may arise when one person decides to experience and see the sites of interest that the walking trajectory of another may bring. *CmyView* creates a network of participants, each contributing to the repository of potential walks and each exploring how individuals can have significantly different forms of attachment to the same places. In this way, the assessment of social value is enabled not only by collecting data to inform government and corporate decisions, but *CmyView* also helps to form and inform communities' ideas about social value itself.

In this chapter, we discuss the assemblage of tasks, tools and people involved in *CmyView* through the Activity-Centred Analysis and Design (ACAD) framework (Goodyear and Carvalho 2014). The ACAD framework suggests that designing for complex learning situations involves considerations about *structures of place* (or elements in set design), *task* (or elements in epistemic design) and *social organization* (or elements in social design) and how these, in turn, may influence activity. The framework also acknowledges that people exercise agency in reshaping or co-creating what has been designed. The chapter presents preliminary findings reporting the use of *CmyView* as a method for engaging with the urban environment. The next three sections present the background of our research, which includes (i) learning as social participation, bringing together the notions of situated learning, embodied cognition and networked learning, (ii) a discussion about the blurry boundaries between formal, non-formal and informal learning, and (iii) digital culture and heritage, and issues associated with the use of mobile technologies in heritage activities of collection, preservation and interpretation of digital artefacts. Then, we introduce concepts from the ACAD framework, situating the analysis of the educational design of *CmyView*. This is followed by a discussion of preliminary findings of participants' interactions with (and their impressions of) the platform/ methodology and the future directions of this research.

Networked Learning, Situated Learning and Embodied Cognition

In line with many contemporary theories, our research acknowledges both the physically and socially situated nature of learning (e.g. Illeris 2009). Our focus here is on learning as social participation, where people are seen as active participants in the practices of social communities and where their identities are shaped by, and connected to, the communities in which they participate (Wenger 2009). Drawing on the notion of situated learning we bring together activity, context and culture (Lave and Wenger 1991) in order to examine situations where knowledge is encountered in authentic contexts and within a community of practice (Sharples et al. 2007). A community of practice establishes a social space for participants to discover and engage in learning partnerships related to common interests (Wenger et al. 2011). This is particularly important for learning about the built environment where knowledge and skill is based on an iterative process of generation, reflection and observation. This social space is even more essential for learning about the social value of places, which may or may not be formally designated and recognized as sites of heritage.

In this chapter, our focus is on learning about the built environment that is mediated by mobile technologies. A networked learning perspective offers a collaborative and participatory conceptualization of learning, in which people and resources are connected via technology (Goodyear et al. 2004). However, as pointed out by Wenger et al. (2011):

> Participation in a network does not require a sustained learning partnership or a commitment to a shared domain. In this sense, learning in a network does not have to have an explicit collective dimension. The learning value of network derives from access to a rich web of information sources offering multiple perspectives and dialogues, responses to queries, and help from others—whether this access is initiated by the learner or by others. (Wenger et al. 2011, p. 12)

Both community and network are aspects of a social fabric, with different effects on learning in terms of value, risks and challenges (Wenger et al. 2011). Although it is possible for community and networks to not necessarily be combined, a community will often include a network of relationships, and likewise, networks will evolve and prosper because of participants' commitment to a shared interest, even if not explicitly expressed. This accords with definitions from media studies of participatory culture, which also recognizes that audiences (or networks) are not necessarily passive and can in fact operate more akin to communities in digitally mediated spaces (Jenkins 1988, 2006). We see both community and networks as part of the social fabric in *CmyView*. We are particularly interested in the analysis of the connections between the design of mobile technologies for learning and the emergent activity of networked users (Goodyear 2005). Sprake and Rogers (2014) speak of 'participatory sensing' as an emerging field of study, in which people are able to learn and teach each other about their own environments, facilitated by technology. Participatory sensing involves the ability to gather data related to personal or local enquiries, going beyond information that is provided by official sources. In this scenario, common people 'can learn about and understand the world around them better and can be a part of the decision-making in improving environments for all' (p. 753). *CmyView* focuses on connections encouraging people to engage in social practices, on the topic area of curatorship of *place*. The concept design in *CmyView* draws our attention to the role of the physical and the 'qualities of the material' in the built environment and their effects on people's activity.

CmyView foregrounds heritage places in a non-formal learning situation, in scenarios that could be characterized as place-based spaces for networked learning (Carvalho et al. 2017). Place-based networked learning still involves co-creation of knowledge (Goodyear et al. 2016) and paying attention to the movement of people, objects and texts (Goodyear and Carvalho 2014). Co-creation of knowledge is becoming central to definitions of heritage as the importance of social value increases and as digital media blurs the boundaries between assessment and interpretation.

The theory of embodied cognition (Clark 2008; Kirsh 2013) helps us further theorize the potential connections between bodies, minds and technologies. Kirsh (2013) asserts that 'the concepts and beliefs we have about the world are grounded in our perceptual-action experience with things, and the more we have tool mediated experiences the more our understanding of the world is situated in the way we interact through tools' (p.3:3). Cognition grounds our behaviour while underpinned by our perceptual system, as we align our actions to predictions that we make about the environment (Markauskaite and Goodyear 2016). Embodied cognition suggests that humans think also with their bodies, not exclusively with their brains, and so interactions with tools that prescribe particular goals are likely to change the way people think and perceive. In this way, walking with the intention of recording social value through GPS, photographs and audio is distinct from walking or taking photographs for pleasure or other purposes or simply walking for pleasure. Knowing by doing is considered more powerful than knowing by seeing (Kirsh 2013). As we analyse the educational design of *CmyView* and its influence on people's activity, we examine not only design elements that may encourage people's social engagement as part of an emerging community, but we are also interested in people's exchanges on a topic that relates to their embodied experiences of sites. The physical trajectory, finding the site located and hearing the audio recording in situ, overlays one's own experience over that of the original creator. *CmyView* assumes that a heterogeneous learning network is formed through participants' asynchronous interactions with others, with self-curated places (representing places of significance to them), with the physical surroundings and the 'quality of materials', which are all part of their networked interaction.

Formal, Non-formal and Informal Learning

Formal learning is usually associated with established educational institutions, involving activities that happen as part of courses at universities, vocational training centres and schools. Such activities are often characterized as being organized and structured and designed to meet certain learning objectives through specific experiences (OECD 2016). Those who engage in these activities will do so with an explicit intent to gain knowledge, skills or competences. Learners' achievements will also often be measured and/or assessed (quantitatively and/or qualitatively). Informal learning, on the other hand, is not specifically organized nor structured, and it is not often associated with formal education systems. The Internet has greatly facilitated this type of learning, which is also referred to as curiosity-based and self-directed (Johnson et al. 2016). Informal learning does not have a set of objectives, nor a clear set of learning outcomes to be achieved, measured or assessed. In between these two modes, authors sometimes also refer to a third one, characterized as non-formal learning. Non-formal learning can also be organized and structured and foregrounds learning 'as a by-product of more organized activities, whether or not the activities themselves have learning objectives' (OECD 2016, n.p.). Educational activities within a museum setting would usually fall under this category, as museum staff may devise tasks for visitor's learning, but these are not necessarily formally assessed or measured. Non-formal and informal are sometimes used interchangeably.

However, the boundaries between these descriptions are often blurry, particularly after the advent of the Internet and the emergence of mobile technologies. There has been little contention on the usefulness of such characterizations (Boys 2011). Yet, the terms imply a neat divide between formal, non-formal and informal learning which is often 'simplistically translated into spatial/representational design metaphors, rather than related through specific, situated learning and teaching practices' (Boys 2011, p. 3). The reality is more fluid and complex and importantly, the Higher Education Edition of the New Media Consortium Horizon Report states that 'many experts believe that a blending of formal and informal methods of learning can create an environment that fosters experimentation, curiosity, and above all, creativity' (Johnson et al. 2016, p. 22). The value of non-formal and informal learning in higher education is being addressed in the forthcoming policy of the European Commission who has recently issued a report describing a range of initiatives to identify ways by which informal learning activities could be evaluated and incorporated into institutions (Johnson et al. 2016). In essence, learning 'may be intentional or incidental – it is often both. Some learning outcomes are the intended result of participation in a study activity; some are incidental by-products of study activities; some are by-products of activities other than deliberate study' (Goodyear and Carvalho 2014, p. 5).

In this chapter, we discuss people's experiences with *CmyView*, through an example situated within a formal learning context, but as a form of non-formal or informal networked learning. The architecture students who are using the app were all part of the same design studio group undertaking the same unit as part of an undergraduate course in higher education. However, the activity of using the app was outside of the prescribed curriculum and undertaken on a voluntary basis for this research. The walking activity was undertaken within the scheduled studio time and began on the university campus but asked students to explore places beyond the university campus. While the activity did not comprise of an assessment task, the exercise would arguably contribute to students' development of important abilities, related to visual skills of observation, spatial knowledge and the significance of heritage sites that they were likely already familiar with. However, the design of *CmyView* goes beyond the specific example in this chapter, as the app is intended to be used outside by a lay person interested in the built environment, heritage interpretation and community engagement.

The aim of *CmyView* is to encourage networked heritage practices and community participation, as people learn by documenting their own and experiencing others' social values of the built environment. Design principles informing the concept design for the app are closely related to networked learning key ideas, such as ways of promoting collaboration, participation and connection amongst people, and encouraging people's involvement in knowledge creation and knowledge building activities. In this case, *CmyView* would entail an informal (or non-formal) version of networked learning, when used as a vehicle for expanding the process of assessing social value. As participants contribute with their shared views via their created artefacts, they are also contributing to moving from an expert-led community consultation process – where a specialist identifies and recommends a valuable site – into an informal learning network, built by a collection of contributions by networked participants, with their multiple perspectives, dialogues and shared understandings of the relationships between people and place.

Digital Culture and Heritage

Research in digital culture and heritage is mainly carried out in museum studies, usually concentrating on the digitization of objects and places of cultural significance, the conservation of digital artefacts and the relationship between the digital and material artefacts (Kalay et al. 2008; Cameron and Kenderdine 2007). Even though it has been over a decade since UNESCO (2003) promoted the international adoption of instruments for the preservation of digital heritage, this area of scholarship is still under researched, with little insight on the relations between social media and heritage, particularly in the topic area of participation and the contribution of information. Nevertheless, in recent years, there has been a growing movement acknowledging the significance of everyday activities as contributing to heritage (Smith 2006).

Giaccardi (2012) points to the opportunities and transformations afforded by social media, investigating the potential links between everyday practices and forms of heritage, as manifest through online participation. Participatory culture is about the use of social media in a way that enables a 'complex set of social practices that interweave memories, material traces and performative enactments to give meaning and significance in the present to the lived realities of our past' (Giaccardi 2012, p. 1). Importantly, the intersection between participatory culture and participatory media is pointing to new ways of describing the value of, and learning about, heritage. However, understanding emerging digital heritage practices may require analysis and the reframing of online representations (Garduño Freeman 2010, 2013). Garduño Freeman (2010, 2013) examined the significance of online representations of heritage sites, connecting numerous online representations of the Sydney Opera House (Australia) to practices of heritage and interpretation. She argues that connections between visual and material culture are evidence of the relationship people have with place and that these online instances of participatory culture do not diminish the significance of a heritage site. Instead they evidence social value. Garduño Freeman (2010, 2013) reframes the emotional attachment that people place on buildings, such as the Sydney Opera House, and their expressions of these attachments through their use of representations, as socio-visual value arguing that posting representations and textual contributions online are new audience engagements of digital heritage. They are examples of how participatory culture manifests in a networked society, where the emergence of dispersed communities and audiences at a global level come together to participate and enact online forms of public engagement.

Three thematic areas are of critical interest for digital heritage: *social practice*, *public formation* and *sense of place* (Giaccardi 2012). *Social practice* relates to how participatory media enables new kinds of social and visual practices, for example, offering opportunities for the collection of images and production of representations, which can be used to mediate online communication, and also as expressions of personal accounts, that are, then, legitimized within communities. *Public formation* highlights the ways social media allows for the blurring of boundaries between community and audiences, enabling that new types of group formations emerge in the public realm. A *sense of place* explores experiences of social media that go beyond the online 'realm', embracing it as a way to engender and extend 'real' experiences with places of heritage.

Drawing on the notion of a sense of place in the fields of architecture and cultural geography, Giaccardi's (2012) articulation seems to touch on aspects related to research in embodied cognition (Kirsh 2013). Social media can potentially augment the significance of traditional forms of heritage by 'bring[ing] to the fore the character of place as the very matrix out of which human significance and meaning arise' (Malpas 2008, p. 207). Conversely, social media can also augment nontraditional or everyday forms of heritage by starting with the aspects of place as touchpoints for cultural significance. Heritage scholars speak of 'community' as homogeneous collectives or groups of people with agreed viewpoints (Waterton and Smith 2010). 'Community' often refers to a geographically connected group of people as distinct from the term 'audiences' used to denote visitors who 'consume' but are not attached to places of heritage. In contrast to communities, 'audiences' need to be made aware of the significance of places for the local communities – they are outsiders, coming from other places, and do not have a prior connection with the site of heritage. This intellectual distinction is important because preservation is

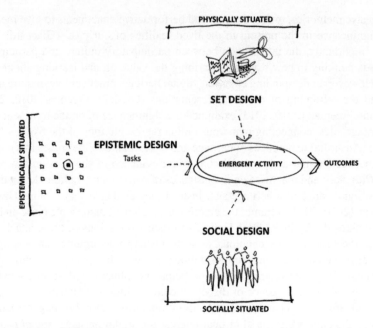

Fig. 10.1 Activity-Centred Analysis and Design (ACAD) framework. (Adapted from Goodyear and Carvalho 2014, p. 59)

dependent on people understanding why sites of heritage are valuable (Tilden 1977). Yet the advent of social media complicates assumptions about audiences, as people develop relationships with places via representations, both published in traditional means and those posted online, without having necessarily actually visited a site in person. In the *CmyView* project, we begin to explore participants' perspectives of a sense of place, as they visit physical sites with the intentional task of finding and registering places of personal interest. In the next section, we introduce the Activity-Centred Analysis and Design (ACAD) framework, discussing specific aspects in the educational design of *CmyView*.

Activity-Centred Analysis and Design Framework

Inspired by ideas from architecture and design thinking, the Activity-Centred Analysis and Design (ACAD) framework (Goodyear and Carvalho 2014) suggests that designing for complex learning situations is best approached when connections between four main structural elements are understood; three of these elements are 'designable' and one not (Fig. 10.1). ACAD has been used to frame the analysis and design of several different types of complex learning situations including, for example, professional networks (De Laat et al. 2014), networks in higher education (Westh Nicolajsen and Ryberg 2014), in schools (Yeoman 2017; Thibaut et al. 2015), libraries (Bitter-Rijpkema et al. 2014) and museums (Carvalho 2017) and design studio spaces involving multi-user and multi-surfaces (Martinez-Maldonado et al. 2017; Thompson et al. 2013).

Activity is what matters the most; it is about what people think, feel and do – an emergent process in which people exercise agency. While the framework acknowledges that design elements are likely to influence people's activity, activity cannot be entirely predicted. The four structural elements are:

(i) *Set design* – the material and/or digital elements that are brought together to compose a learning situation – the tools, resources, artefacts and affordances of place
(ii) *Epistemic design* – the 'plan' for what people will do including the proposed learning tasks, along with their structuring, sequencing and pacing of how information is to be communicated to learners
(iii) *Social design* – social arrangements and roles, divisions of labour and who is expected to do what
(iv) *Co-creation and co-configuration activity* – relates the above designable components to people's activity, acknowledging that they may rearrange and reconfigure the designed learning situation

The framework has been applied in the analysis of over 20 case studies, involving participation and collaborations mediated via technology in a range of complex learning situations. These include learning networks in graphic design, chemistry, teacher education and other disciplinary areas and within different educational contexts, such as courses in higher education, schools, continuing professional development and informal learning spaces, involving online as well as place-based scenarios (Carvalho and Goodyear 2014; Carvalho et al. 2017).

CmyView can be analysed through the ACAD framework (Fig. 10.2). Here, set design involves the app, deployed in a mobile technology, which users carry around. Even though the main tool participants interact with is the app, their experience will also be mediated by elements in the physical environment where the activity unfolds, as the spatial stage in which users undertake their actions. Thus, the technology is to be used in combination with elements in the physical surroundings. Similar to the blackboard, the chairs and tables in a classroom, 'built forms' were not specially 'brought' to the learning situation by the educational designer, albeit they are still part of the set design. In the case of *CmyView*, the affordances of place are very open and might include buildings, constructions and natural elements in the environment, encountered in the user's walk.

Epistemic design relates to the proposed tasks that suggest that participants walk, observe, make a representation and articulate why the representation was made (via recording). These are then repeated (via prompts) in the next iteration at the next point of interest. Participants not only collect but also share their views, and it is the purpose of the task and its intentionality that make this a learning task, even if, in this case, participants are not being formally assessed. Epistemic design involves two main proposed tasks: (i) *collecting* social value and (ii) *sharing* social value

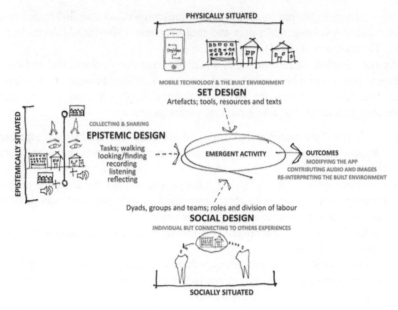

Fig. 10.2 *CmyView* in the (ACAD) framework

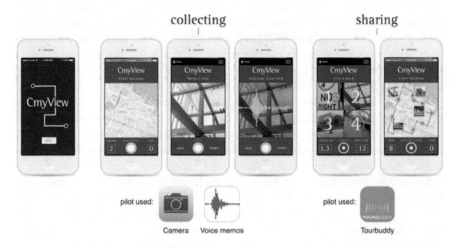

Fig. 10.3 Collecting and sharing social value

(see Fig. 10.3). The two tasks are structured through walking through the physical environment. In 'collecting' the task is structured through suggestions to look and record and in 'sharing' to find and listen at each 'view' in the created or followed trajectory. Both are followed by an implied opportunity for reflection on the social value of places, as the tasks invite participants to explore relationships between the built environment, personal values and ways by which their values about the built environment can be represented and communicated in mediation with *CmyView*.

In the 'collecting' mode, participants are asked to take a walk in their local environment and to make 'views' during this activity. A 'view' is created when a participant takes a photograph of something significant to him/her. The possible number of 'views' is dependent on the distance walked; in other words 'views' are not immediately available, but rather, as the participant walks, the opportunity for making 'views' increases, a design that purposefully encourages movement through the physical environment. The task also requests that participants reflect on their choices and audio record descriptions of why they chose to take that photograph. There are two main purposes for the use of audio to capture the specific meaning of the photograph. In contrast to text, audio can be recorded while the person continues to walk, thereby making the experience more fluid and less interrupted. Audio also enables emotion to be communicated and is a more intimate form of communication than text.

A group of 'views' made by a participant is packaged as a 'walk' that can be shared with others. In the 'sharing' mode, *CmyView* operates as a repository of image and audio representations of what people have found significant. In contrast to the 'collecting' mode, the epistemic design here enables an urban treasure hunt to take place. Once a 'walk' is selected, participants can follow that person's footsteps and use the GPS, visual and aural information to find or situate the photographic representation back in the physical environment. This enables digital representations to be resituated through embodied walking experiences, as the person is able to listen and learn about others memories and associations to places. Another feature in the epistemic design of *CmyView* relates to the collection of information for reuse. The data, both that which is gathered in the collecting mode, as well as any feedback received through the sharing mode, becomes a powerful tool to understand people's engagement with the urban environment. *CmyView* collects a rich layered dataset comprising three types: locational, visual and verbal that quantify intangible aspects about the built environment.

In the social design, participants are invited to asynchronously collaborate with others, while they complete their walks individually. However, other possibilities of group organization may, nevertheless, be possible with *CmyView*. Dyads or larger groups could work together to both identify places that are significant and together record their combined views on selected places. This aspect would be one of the ways in which participants could cocreate the experience within the overall design of *CmyView*.

Understanding elements in set, epistemic and social design as separate entities can at times be difficult, as they all come together as part of an assemblage. As relational elements, one enables and influences the other. The app deployed via a mobile technology (elements of set design) will tell the user what task she is to do (epistemic design), in this case collecting or sharing a view (epistemic design). As the user walks the trajectory of an invisible other (social design), again the app (set design) will alert the user to pay attention (epistemic design) to specific elements of the built environment (set design). As the user takes photographs and add their own views (cocreation and co-configuration activity), they modify the app by populating it with new elements (set design).

Overall, *CmyView* aims at reframing social value as dynamic, fluid and located within communities, rather than fixed in place, and shifts the role of documentation from a professional expert to participants, building upon existing social and cultural participatory practices, such as photography and walking. The focus on walking is intentional with a view of capturing its positive effect on creative thinking (Oppezzo and Schwartz 2014).

CmyView Prototype

In its current stage of development, *CmyView* was prototyped in two ways. The tasks associated with collecting mode were deployed via an iPhone app. The sharing mode was modelled through another self-curated walking app, Tour Buddy, which is available by subscription. The transfer of data from the collecting to the sharing mode was carried out manually by one of the researchers. The use of this approach allowed us to rapidly capture and model experiences of participants with *CmyView*, and in doing so, we were able to understand and refine aspects of set, social and epistemic design before further technological development was carried out.

In the prototype version, set design involved an iPhone, with its interactive screen interface inviting people to select which mode they wish to use either collecting or sharing 'views' (social design) (see Fig. 10.3). The iPhone was used in combination with elements in the built environment, as participants walked around the vicinity of the university campus.

The collecting mode begins with a standard map interface, which shows current location and maps the route walked as 'views' are made. There are 'touch-able' images that enable participants to 'make a view' and indicators on available 'views' (dependent on distance walked) and those already made. The iPhone's camera interface is used to produce a square format photograph. Once a photograph is submitted, the next screen prompts the participant to make an audio recording about the place depicted in the photograph selected. Both the audio and photographs can be deleted and replaced while making the 'view'. Once made, the 'view' is then plotted on the map in the original screen.

The app used for deploying the sharing mode currently adopts the interface of the Tour Buddy app on an iPhone and iPad. The interface offers categorization of 'views' into 'walks'. Once a 'walk' is selected, the first view is loaded onto the screen. Directions to the location can be sought via the native Apple Maps app, which loads the GPS information. The interface shows the photograph taken, the location on the map and the audio recording in one screen. Tour Buddy can be enabled to automatically play the audio within a 1–5 metre radius of the GPS location.

Data Collection and Analysis: Extracts from *CmyView* and Survey

The methodology and the prototype version of *CmyView* described above were tested by four university students, enrolled in an undergraduate architecture course, who volunteered to participate in a non-formal activity that was not part of their course work. Data collection involved a collecting mode and a sharing mode. In the collecting mode, participants were instructed to take a walk and make 'views' of things in the built environment, which were of significance to them, so that together they would be documenting social value. They were intentionally not directed to specific locations or asked to identify places of positive or negative personal value. The 'walks' were about 30 min long each and comprised between 6–12 'views'. We collected their photographs, audio recordings and the geolocation identifiers of each participant's walk, and afterwards, participants completed a short survey. In the sharing mode, participants were given an iPad with their four 'walks' loaded and were asked to select one of the 'walks' made by their peers. Each participant then went into the field, found the photographs of their peers while listening to their audio recordings and completed a second survey afterwards. The two data collection sessions were carried out in Geelong (Australia), in the immediate university surroundings, during the late afternoon 1 week apart. The two online surveys (5 min each) used open-ended questions to elicit participants' opinions on the methodology and prototype version of *CmyView*.

In the ACAD framing, the students' production of photographs and audio files is part of their *co-creation and co-configuration activity*. They modify *CmyView* by populating it with visual and audio artefacts as they interact with the environment through the app (*set design*), completing the proposed tasks – collecting and sharing views (*epistemic design*) – and are invited to asynchronously collaborate (*social design*). The audio files were transcribed and analysed together with the photographs and actual locations which were familiar to one of the researchers. The anonymous survey responses then offered insights into the experiences and reflections of the participants.

Our analysis of the audio files and photographs reveals how people ascribe different forms of attachment to places. For example, the first passage below describes historical connections between old and new aspects of a building (first passage), while the second passage highlights fluidity and contrast as facets of interest.

> I chose this second view because I feel though it incorporates sort of the new and old of what Geelong was, I suppose in the wool store days, and what has become now, in front of sort of Victoria's biggest educational institutions here, and sort of incorporating the old and new style architecture. (Walk 3 View 2) – Fig. 10.4A

> This view I was attracted to I think largely because of the straight lines that the trees have been planted in, which sort of seems to me contradicts the very sort of fluid and also maybe sharped angled nature of the branches and the leaves that are partially alive but mainly dead and crumbling. (Walk 2 View 2) – Fig. 10.4B

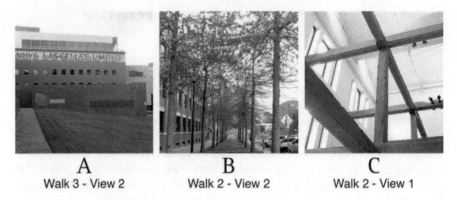

A   B   C
Walk 3 - View 2   Walk 2 - View 2   Walk 2 - View 1

Fig. 10.4 Images collected on walks

Three themes emerged in relation to participants' experiences with *CmyView*: (i) changing perceptions and thinking, (ii) connections to others and (iii) extending understandings of design and architecture. In the passage below, the participant acknowledges how the exercise enabled a new perspective about a familiar space.

> I found interesting (…) in that it is a space that I would walk through probably everyday but it is not until you have an exercise like this where, (…) you have to stop and think about… that I really appreciate the old and new, I suppose, and you see through the old bends and then the… this clean sort of light plaster board and then also in the right hand corner the light which back lit up the bean, I thought it was really interesting. (Walk 2 View 1) – Fig. 10.4C

Survey responses gathered several similar impressions by all four participants, where engagement in the collecting mode's proposed learning task (*epistemic design*) mediated by the tool (*set design*) seems to encourage noticing subtleties in the environment and thinking 'more critically':

> I think the idea of having to explain why something stood out to you is a good one because it makes you actually stop and realise all of the beautiful things around you (Participant 1 - Survey 1)

> It (…) allowed me to look at certain views at a different angle, and analyse why I was attracted to these particular angles rather than others. (Participants 3 - Survey 1)

> The action of taking the photograph made me consider the idea of a view more critically. Whilst when you observe with your eyes you take in the area around the view, the photo makes you be more concise with what you would like to show. Recording a memo reinforces this point of why the photo came about. (Participant 2 - Survey 1)

The second theme reflected participants' interest in connecting to others, where they welcomed the opportunity of engaging in the learning task in the sharing mode, where they indicated their experiences led to them learning about the built environment and what is valuable to others:

> I am more interested in viewing other people's walks and the idea of sharing the experience and explore areas I haven't seen or thought about. (Participant 4 - Survey 1)

Quite often we get tied up in our own constrained view of the world and by opening it up to that of [other] people is something valuable to be able to learn and understand from. (Participant 1 - Survey 2)

Seeing someone else's views (or journey) was almost an intimate experience. These journeys are personal and walking on someone else's journey is just a glimpse [of] their personal take on things. It allowed me to enter into someone else's headspace and see things the way they do. (Participant 2 - Survey 2)

The third theme, focused on the participant's ability to connect their experiences of the environment gained through *CmyView* to other learning areas, with a particular focus on their understandings of design and architecture:

It challenged my thought process as to what was and was not worth documenting. Something that was interesting with the other person's walk that I completed was that a lot of what was captured was not specifically buildings. It broadened my understanding of built environment towards how we shape our natural environment also. (Participant 3 - Survey 2)

The way that different people see different views, helped me understand that the experiences you hope to make of your architecture may not always be successful in that respect. Your architecture will provoke a variety of experiences as different people, will experience different things driven by their different personalities. (Participant 2 - Survey 2)

Participants also reported that the overall experience elicited conversations outside the app – which is in line with the thought that in already established communities, the act of sharing experiences becomes a talking point for other types of discussions about the built environment.

Conclusion and Future Directions

This chapter brings together concepts that often sit at the intersection of separate fields, namely, digital heritage and networked learning, to find their synergies. The chapter argues that *CmyView* supports the reframing of social value as dynamic, fluid and located within communities, rather than fixed in a place, reflecting networked practices and contributing to more egalitarian heritage practices. People's interaction with the app allowed them to connect to others and have an impact on how they experience their physical surroundings, through the sharing of their social values about sites of interest. The chapter argues that these activities reflect networked learning practices that cross boundaries of time and space, formal and informal learning, with people walking together while being apart, and learning by sharing.

Drawing on a framework for the analysis and design of productive learning networks, we analysed the educational design of *CmyView* arguing that the platform offers a space for democratic heritage education and interpretation, where participatory urban curatorship practices are nurtured, and in alignment with networked learning practices. The educational design of *CmyView* aims at enabling people to collaborate and participate in an ongoing dynamic activity of curating places.

The ACAD framing helped us analyse ways of designing for community participation and assessment of social value. It allowed us to account for and consider the levels of complexity that are inherent in such augmented experiences. We were able to bring together, loosely coupled components in set, social and epistemic design, to analyse how they constrained and enabled the activities of participants. Part of set design (i.e. the app) could be altered and controlled, and others could not; the built environment is already in existence yet needs to be taken into account as part of the complex learning situation. Social design in this case prompted indirect collaboration between students and made us think about future possible social arrangements, potential hierarchical structure between participants, their connections, and who was viewing whose 'walks'. In epistemic design, the proposed tasks in both modes were about observation. In the collecting mode, it involved careful observation of one's own experience of the built environment. In the sharing mode the task is also about observation, but in contrast it involves understanding someone else's experiences. Locating the original places photographed in an embodied task enables a kind of embodied cognition – putting the image back in context or recontextualizing these places. *CmyView* enters a new phase of development as we fine-tune the app and explore new configurations for part of its designable elements.

References

Bitter-Rijpkema, M., Verjans, S., Didderen, W., & Sloep, P. (2014). Biebkracht: Library professionals empowered though an inter-organisational learning network – design principles and evolution. In L. Carvalho & P. Goodyear (Eds.), *The architecture of productive learning networks* (pp. 152–167). New York: Routledge.

Boys, J. (2011). *Towards creative learning spaces*. Oxford: Routledge.

Cameron, F., & Kenderdine, S. (2007). *Theorizing digital cultural heritage*. Cambridge: The MIT Press.

Canning, S., & Spenneman, D. (2001). Contested space: Social value and the assessment of cultural significance in New South Wales, Australia. In M. Cotter, B. Boyd, & J. Gardiner (Eds.), *Heritage landscapes; understanding place and communities* (pp. 457–468). Lismore: Southern Cross University Press.

Carvalho, L. (2017). The O in MONA: Reshaping museum spaces. In L. Carvalho, P. Goodyear, & M. de Laat (Eds.), *Place-based spaces for networked learning* (pp. 144–159). New York: Routledge.

Carvalho, L., & Goodyear, P. (Eds.). (2014). *The architecture of productive learning networks*. New York: Routledge.

Carvalho, L., Goodyear, P., & de Laat, M. (Eds.). (2017). *Place-based spaces for networked learning*. New York: Routledge.

Clark, A. (2008). *Supersizing the mind: Embodiment, action, and cognitive extension*. Oxford: Oxford University Press.

De Laat, M., Schreurs, B., & Sie, R. (2014). Utilizing informal teacher professional development networks using the network awareness tool. In L. Carvalho & P. Goodyear (Eds.), *The architecture of productive learning networks* (pp. 239–256). New York: Routledge.

Garduño Freeman, C. (2013). Participatory culture as a site for the reception of architecture: Making a giant Sydney Opera House cake. *Architecture Theory Review, 18*(3), 325–339.

Garduño Freeman, C. (2010). Photosharing on Flickr: Intangible heritage and emergent publics. *International Journal of Heritage Studies, 16*(4), 352–368.

Giaccardi, E. (Ed.). (2012). *Heritage and social media*. New York: Routledge.

Goodyear, P. (2005). Educational design and networked learning: Patterns, pattern languages and design practice. *Australasian Journal of Educational Technology (Online), 21*(1), 82–101.

Goodyear, P., & Carvalho, L. (2014). Framing the analysis of learning network architectures. In L. Carvalho & P. Goodyear (Eds.), *The architecture of productive learning networks* (pp. 48–70). New York: Routledge.

Goodyear, P., Carvalho, L., & Dohn, N. (2016). Artefacts and activities in the analysis of learning networks. In S. Bayne, M. de Laat, T. Ryberg, & C. Sinclair (Eds.), *Research, boundaries and policy in networked learning*. New York: Springer.

Goodyear, P., Banks, S., Hodgson, V., & McConell, D. (Eds.). (2004). *Advances in research in networked learning*. Dordrecht: Kluwer Academic Publishers.

Hayden, D. (1997). *The power of place: Urban landscapes as public history*. London: The MIT Press.

Hodgson, V., de Laat, M., McConnell, D., & Ryberg, T. (Eds.). (2014). *The design, experience and practice of networked learning*. New York: Springer.

ICOMOS Australia. (1999). The Burra Charter: The Australia ICOMOS Charter for Places of Cultural Significance 1999.

Illeris, K. (Ed.). (2009). *Contemporary theories of learning: Learning theorists – In their own words*. New York: Routledge.

Jenkins, H. (2006). *Convergence culture: Where old and new media collide*. New York: New York University Press.

Jenkins, H. (1988). Star Trek reread, rerun, rewritten: Fan writing as textual poaching. *Critical Studies in Mass Communications, 5*(2), 85–107.

Johnston, C., Riches, L., McGregor, A., & Buckley, K. (2003). *Inspirational landscapes*. Canberra: Australian Heritage Commission.

Johnson, L., Adams Becker, S., Cummins, M., Estrada, V., Freeman, A., & Hall, C. (2016). *NMC Horizon Report: 2016 Higher Education Edition*. Austin: The New Media Consortium.

Kalay, Y., Kvan, T., & Affleck, J. (2008). *New heritage: New media and cultural heritage*. New York: Routledge.

Kirsh, D. (2013). Embodied cognition and the magical future of interaction design. *ACM Transactions on Computer-Human Interaction, 20*(1), 3. 1–3:20.

Lave, J., & Wenger, E. (1991). *Situated learning: Legitimate peripheral participation*. Cambridge: Cambridge University Press.

Markauskaite, L., & Goodyear, P. (2016). *Epistemic fluency and professional education: Innovation, knowledgeable action and actionable knowledge*. Dordrecht: Springer.

Martinez-Maldonado, R., Goodyear, P., Carvalho, L., Thompson, K., Hernandez-Leo, D., Dimitriadis, Y., Prieto, L. P., & Wardak, D. (2017). Supporting collaborative design activity in a multi-user digital design ecology. *Computers in Human Behavior, 71*, 327–342.

Rogoff, I. (2002). Studying visual culture. In N. Mirzoeff (Ed.), *The visual culture reader* (2nd ed., pp. 24–36). London: Routledge.

Malpas, J. (2008). New media, cultural heritage and the sense of place: Mapping the conceptual ground. *International Journal of Heritage Studies, 14*(3), 207.

OECD. (2016). Recognition of non-formal and informal learning (Online). Available at: http://www.oecd.org/edu/skills-beyond-school/recognitionofnon-formalandinformallearning-home.htm. Accessed 24 Nov 2016.

Oppezzo, M., & Schwartz, D. (2014). Give your ideas some legs: The positive effect of walking on creative thinking. *Journal of Experimental Psychology: Learning, Memory, and Cognition, 40*(4), 1142–1152.

Schön, D. (1985). *The design studio: An exploration of its traditions and potentials*. London: RIBA Publications for RIBA Building Industry Trust.

Sharples, M., Taylor, J., & Vavoula, G. (2007). A theory of learning for the mobile age. In R. Andrews & C. Haythornthwaite (Eds.), *The sage handbook of e-learning research* (pp. 221–247). London: Sage.

Smith, L. (2006). *Uses of heritage*. London: Routledge.

Sprake, J., & Rogers, P. (2014). Crowds, citizens and sensors: Process and practice for mobilising learning. *Personal Ubiquitous Computing, 18*(1), 753–764.

Steeples, C., & Jones, C. (Eds.). (2002). *Networked learning; perspectives and issues*. London: Springer.

Thibaut, P., Curwood, J. S., Carvalho, L., & Simpson, A. (2015). Moving across physical and online spaces: A case study in a blended primary classroom. *Learning, Media & Technology, 40*(4), 458–479.

Thompson, K., Ashe, D., Carvalho, L., Goodyear, P., Kelly, N., & Parisio, M. (2013). Processing and visualizing data in complex learning environments. *American Behavioral Scientist, 57*(10), 1401–1420.

Tilden, F. (1977). *Interpreting our heritage*. Chapel Hill: University of North Carolina Press.

UNESCO. (2003). Charter on the preservation of the digital heritage.

Waterton, E. (2010). The advent of digital technologies and the idea of community. *Museum Management and Curatorship, 25*(1), 5–11.

Waterton, E., & Smith, L. (2010). The recognition and misrecognition of community heritage. *International Journal of Heritage Studies, 16*(1–2), 4–15.

Wenger, E. (2009). A social theory of learning. In K. Illeris (Ed.), *Contemporary theories of learning: Learning theorists – In their own words* (pp. 209–217). New York: Routledge.

Wenger, E., Trayner, B., & de Laat, M. (2011). *Promoting and assessing value creation in communities and networks: A conceptual framework* (Vol. 18). Heerlen: Open Universiteit.

Westh Nicolajsen, H., & Ryberg, T. (2014). Creating a peer-driven learning network in higher education: Using web 2.0 tools to facilitate online dialogue and collaboration. In L. Carvalho & P. Goodyear (Eds.), *The architecture of productive learning networks* (pp. 94–108). New York: Routledge.

Yeoman, P. (2017). A study of correspondence, dissonance and improvisation in the design and use of a school-based networked learning environment. In L. Carvalho, P. Goodyear, & M. de Laat (Eds.), *Place-based spaces for networked learning* (pp. 41–58). New York: Routledge.

Chapter 11
Reflections and Challenges in Networked Learning

Nina Bonderup Dohn, Julie-Ann Sime, Sue Cranmer, Thomas Ryberg, and Maarten de Laat

Abstract In this last chapter, we reflect on the issues taken up in the nine chapters forming the body of the book and how they relate to the trends identified in the introductory chapter as well as how they combine to characterize the field of Networked Learning today and on from here. We start with a short presentation of each of the chapters. This leads us to identify broader themes which point out significant perspectives and challenges for future research and practice. Among these are social justice, criticality, mobility, new forms of openness and learning in the public arena (all leading themes at the next Networked Learning Conference in 2018), differences between participants and in participant experiences, learning analytics and different understandings of Networked Learning.

In our introductory chapter, we identified some general trends in Networked Learning research as they have emerged and faded over the years since the first Networked Learning Conference in 1998. This acknowledges the 10th biennial conference in 2016 and the development of research within the field to which the conference series bears witness. It serves also to provide a backdrop for the nine chapters providing the body of this book, based as they are on selected papers from the 10th biennial conference, and speaking as they do to this developing field. In this final chapter, we look back on the issues taken up in the nine chapters and reflect on how they combine to characterize the field of Networked Learning today – with a

N. Bonderup Dohn (✉)
Department of Design and Communication, University of Southern Denmark, Kolding, Denmark
e-mail: nina@sdu.dk

J. -A. Sime · S. Cranmer
Educational Research, Lancaster University, Lancaster, UK

T. Ryberg
Department of Communication and Psychology, Aalborg University, Aalborg, Denmark

M. de Laat
Learning, Teaching & Curriculum, University of Wollongong, Wollongong, NSW, Australia

view to the identified trends of the past and a look to emerging issues for the future. We start with a short recapitulation of the focus of the book's parts and the individual chapters, thereby also providing the reader with an overview of the content of the book. This leads on to the second section of this chapter where we identify broader themes which point out significant perspectives and challenges for future research and practice within Networked Learning.

Summary of Issues and Perspectives in the Chapters

The book is structured into two main thematic sections, Parts 1 and 2, comprising five and four chapters, respectively, and further includes the Introduction and this concluding chapter. Part 1, entitled *Situating Networked Learning: Looking Back, Moving Forward*, picks up on the Introduction's identification of trends in the field of Networked Learning, by providing an expanded characterization of foci within this field in relation to current debates. From different theoretical perspectives, the three chapters by Parchoma, Jones and Lee do this by reflecting upon the past, depicting the present and looking to the future. The next two chapters by Cutajar and Czerniewicz supplement these perspectives on developing views by positioning Networked Learning clearly within prominent contemporary discussions. Together, the chapters display Networked Learning as a distinct field within educational research, simultaneously aligned with broader discussions and taking more particular stances on them.

More specifically, the first chapter in Part 2, *Traces of cognition as a distributed phenomenon in networked learning* by Gale Parchoma, explores the notion of 'cognition as a distributed phenomenon'. Parchoma initially argues that in Networked Learning connectivity and dialogue are central pedagogical and philosophical principles, and rather than viewing knowledge as a transmissible property, it is seen as emergent and the outcome of relational dialogue and collaborative interactions embedded in sociocultural contexts. She continues to trace the history of distributed cognition across a number of differing perspectives within Networked Learning. In the section 'De-coding Cognition through Varied Conceptualizations of the Human Mind', Parchoma thus presents five different conceptualizations of the human mind: a neuropsychological, an environmentalist, a phenomenological, a situated sociocultural account and finally a mentalist perspective. She argues that if one takes a relational view of learning as an interaction between mind and world, then they can all 'accommodate the proposition of cognition as a distributed phenomenon without becoming caught in the dualism of abstract mind and concrete material social practice' (Parchoma, Chap. 2 this volume). She then explores how ideas of distributed cognition can be traced in the varying views of 'networked learning design and facilitation' and highlights differences between Ingold's (2011) (individualistic) notion of wayfaring and Goodyear et al.'s (2014) conceptualization of distributed agency as a collaborative endeavour. These social and collaborative aspects are further discussed in relation to how communities are understood within Networked

Learning. In conclusion, Parchoma points out that 'democratic values and sociomaterial, relational views of learning experiences' (Parchoma, Chap. 2 this volume) are
key characteristics of Networked Learning. She suggests that the idea of cognition
as distributed can bridge different perspectives and serve as a unifying theoretical
concept underpinning the political, ontological and epistemological aspects of networked learning.

Parchoma's chapter is a theoretically very interesting disassembling and reassembling of differing theoretical ideas and perspectives within Networked Learning
(and beyond). In the chapter, she zooms to the finer details of differences in theoretical approaches to learning, dissects and distinguishes them from each other but also
reassembles the parts – though not as a unity or common mass. Rather, she argues
that the approaches are all underpinned by ideas of cognition as distributed and that
this understanding can serve as an underlying and unifying perspective. Further, by
relating this view to the way design, facilitation and community are conceptualized
within Networked Learning, she contributes a more nuanced understanding of these
phenomena. She thus manages to look back into a complex theoretical and conceptual history of both Networked Learning and educational theory while also contributing a refreshed view of how we can theoretically conceptualize commonalities
within Networked Learning in the years to come.

The next chapter, *Experience and Networked Learning* by Chris Jones, is also
firmly influenced by recent attempts to articulate and theorize a sociomaterial
understanding of Networked Learning. The chapter focuses on post-human and
actor-network theory approaches which decentre the subject, situating it in a hybrid
networked constellation of actors (including humans and machines). Jones embraces
and criticizes these approaches by actively researching the place of the human subject and how it informs the development of research agendas within Networked
Learning. The main question addressed by Jones in this chapter is therefore: 'In
what ways can Networked Learning think about and incorporate the idea of experience with regard to de-centred persons in the entanglements forming assemblages?'
According to Jones 'Experience can be thought of as either the essential distinguishing component of the individual human subject, or experience can be understood as the subjective component of one kind of element in a wider assemblage of
humans and machines. In the latter understanding of experience in assemblages
human experience does not separate the human actor from other actors in a network
and they are understood symmetrically' (Jones, Chap. 3 this volume). Here, Jones
clearly uses a sociomaterialist perspective conceptualizing 'knowledge and capacities as being emergent from the webs of interconnections between heterogeneous
entities, both human and non-human' (Jones, Chap. 3 this volume). However, Jones
defends that human actors have a special place, even if they may be decentred, one
that is not symmetrical with non-human actors. Human actor accounts of networked
learning are relevant as they 'provide an insight into how human actors respond in
and to the interactions they encounter in educational assemblages and the world
more generally' (Jones, Chap. 3 this volume). They may thus inform both design
and understanding of networked learning.

Traditionally, the Networked Learning research community has always taken a great interest in qualitative accounts of learning in networked settings, and Jones continues this rich tradition and further fuels the discussion by concluding that Networked Learning research 'needs to retain a focus on human experience and to develop an empirical and theoretical understanding of how the de-centred human experience in human-machine assemblages can help in the design and development of successful learning networks' (Jones, Chap. 3 this volume).

The third chapter in this Part, *Discursive effects of a paradigm shift rhetoric in online higher education: Implications on Networked Learning research and practice* by Kyungmee Lee, takes a critical look at the discursive effects of the 'paradigm shift' rhetoric that is commonly used in the advocacy of online higher education. The paradigm shift involves rhetorical moves that position distance education (DE) pedagogies as 'old' and bounded within a behaviourist-cognitivist paradigm and instead suggests an intentional, normative move towards progressive, 'modern' modes of learning often associated with 'constructivist' and 'collaborative learning' as articulated within the field of online higher education (HE). Lee argues that this rhetorical move for one thing diminishes the insights and practices developed within DE but also, more importantly, that it ignores the historical and context-specific reasons for why those practices initially developed. Thus, calls for collaboration and constructivist pedagogies overlook the fact that DE has been committed to providing affordable, accessible learning to a large number of people many of whom might not have the time and resources to engage in 'collaborative learning' and would prefer individual, self-paced, flexible modes of learning. Lee traces the development of the paradigm shift rhetoric by critically analysing the paper 'Shift happens: Online education as a new paradigm in learning' by Harasim (2000). From a Foucauldian perspective, she argues that the discourse of a 'new paradigm' has come to permeate thinking within online higher education, but not necessarily practice, and that it is also dominant within fields such as CSCL (computer-supported collaborative learning) and Networked Learning, despite the latter's self-understanding of critical scholarship. She concludes that we need to overcome simplistic dichotomies between 'the old DE' and the 'new online HE' to create a more politically, historically and appreciative understanding of practices that might – at a first glance – sit uncomfortably within the Networked Learning community.

Lee's chapter stands as an interesting challenge to reflect on both the theory and practice of Networked Learning. She illustrates, in her chapter, how there is often a problematic, and somewhat lazy, tendency to latch onto a discourse of 'new' vs 'old' and rhetorically locate certain pedagogies as rooted in an 'old', instructivist paradigm associated with behaviourist/cognitivist theories of learning. In her chapter she challenges the Networked Learning community not to fall prey to such simple dichotomies and instead appreciate that there might be historical, contextual and practical reasons for distance education (DE) pedagogies, reasons associated with access, in terms of affordability but also in terms of the individual's time, resources and capacities to engage with demanding forms of collaborative, dialogical pedagogies. As democratic access, equity and opportunity are key principles of education from a Networked Learning perspective, Lee's chapter is a welcome contribution to help us reflect on whether Networked Learning pedagogies may at times be at odds with these principles.

In line with Lee's general points about the gap between rhetoric and practice, the next chapter, *Variation in students' perceptions of others for learning* by Maria Cutajar, examines the difference between theory and practice in collaborative learning. Through a phenomenographic study, Cutajar questions the assumptions in Networked Learning literature: that active student participation is prevalent in learning networks, that students appreciate the value of learning from others in their network and that they work together towards a shared goal of improving everyone's understanding. Her study explores the perspectives of young adults, aged 16–18 years, as they engage in Networked Learning in a formal education context to qualify for university entry. It shows how the use of Networked Learning technologies for teaching and learning is a challenge that is not embraced uniformly by learners. In particular, Cutajar's study points to three broad, hierarchically inclusive categories of student perceptions of the student-teacher relationship: teacher as director and students as independently learning, teacher as organizer and students as contributors and teacher as convenor and students as cocreators of learning. These variations in perception of responsibility for learning in teachers and students are positioned as different positions on a continuum. Responsibility for learning and teaching is assumed to be shared in Networked Learning literature, but these findings suggest that the reality is not as clear. Cutajar concludes that there must be support for the transition into networked learning with reconceptualization of the relationship between teachers and learners and broadening awareness of the value of others in learning.

Cutajar's contribution to the field is a qualitative account of learning within a networked setting which continues a long-established approach of examining the individual experience within Networked Learning. As argued in Jones' chapter, there is still a need to provide insight into how individuals respond to interactions within a networked learning setting to develop empirical and theoretical knowledge and also assist in refining design and develop activities. Cutajar's chapter provides empirical evidence of the different conceptions of the student-teacher relationship amongst her learners and in so doing reminds us of the potential diversity within student groups engaged in networked learning. She calls upon the Networked Learning community to take active steps towards accommodating this diversity in student perception and actively encourage students to embrace different perceptions of others and explore different student roles within Networked Learning.

The final chapter in Part 1, *Inequality as Higher Education goes online* by Laura Czerniewicz, situates Networked Learning within current discourses of inequality. Within this general setting, the chapter argues for values-based pedagogically shaped online learning to circumvent what the author characterizes as an increasingly austere higher education environment. Here, Czerniewicz builds on the initial conceptualization of Networked Learning as critical and political, therefore having the facility to support and encourage democracy, diversity and inclusion. She problematizes emerging global market-dominated models of online higher education which have profound, potentially negative implications, for the diversity of learners, digital literacy, cultural capital and language. Thus, she argues that the European and UK drive towards 'open educational resources' and 'open access' could make it more difficult for developing countries 'as it means that online content from the global south cannot be found amidst the large volumes of content flowing from the north' (Czerniewicz, Chap. 6 this volume). Likewise, ideal models of the capacities of 'networked learners' as digital natives can gloss over that the realities are: 'of very differentiated learner engagement with the digital world; digital skills which are shallower than previously thought; [...] the minority of active knowledge creation and sharing; activities typically introduced by educators; consumer practices and populist values dominating the digital space, with many feeling excluded or worse (Beetham 2015)' (Czerniewicz, Chap. 6 this volume). These issues, she points out, are seldom recognized, let alone confronted. The chapter draws on Therborn's equality/inequality framework through interrogation of three types of inequality: vital inequality, resource inequality and existential inequality. Given this framework, Czerniewicz explores the ways inclusion and exclusion are expressed and experienced. In conclusion, she emphasizes the urgent need for critical research, inequality-framed intervention, policy and advocacy to bring forth new and more socially just global business models.

The chapter by Czerniewicz is a useful and important contribution to the field of Networked Learning, given its emphasis on the need for further critical, politically motivated studies and initiatives. It takes an explicit social justice lens to the field and challenges current and emerging inequalities. It helps identify blind spots within the community such as a tendency for overly positive evaluation of increasing openness of resources and institutions. It thus also inspires an increased focus on social justice issues in the future.

Taken together, the chapters in Part 1 situate and exemplify Networked Learning as a field within the broader landscape of educational research. Though perspectives of course differ, so that chapter authors may not necessarily agree to all points made by other chapter authors – nor, indeed, would all authors within the wider Networked Learning community agree to all points – an outline of the current status of the field is suggested by the critiques of sociomaterial renderings of human agency and cognition provided by Jones (this volume) and Parchoma (this volume), respectively, and the challenges to rethink collaboration (Cutajar, this volume), collaborative pedagogies (Lee, this volume) and equality (Czerniewicz, this volume) from the perspective of actual educational practice. A focus on individual learners (networked to others) and their experiences remains important (Jones, this volume), though their agency may be decentred and their cognition best conceptualized as distributed (Parchoma, this volume). Learner experiences may challenge theoretical expectations that idealize, e.g. student collaboration, overlooking tensions between student perspectives (Cutajar, this volume) and neglecting the practical circumstances out of which online learning – and networked learning with it – spring (Lee, this volume). These considerations exemplify the more general need to critically reflect on assumptions and blind spots in the prevalent rhetoric. The rhetoric, as shown in Czerniewicz (this volume), may hide new inequalities on a global scale emerging out of idealized understandings of, e.g. openness. Thus, the chapters in

Part 1 between them depict Networked Learning as a field characterized by a strong interest in theory development, an emphasis on human agency and cognition understood as integral parts of their sociomaterial contexts and a recurring focus on critical assessment of (one's own and others') presuppositions in theory and practice.

Given this situating in Part 1 of Networked Learning within the general educational research landscape, the chapters in Part 2 have been chosen for their more specific common focus on the current tendency, hinted at in Part 1, to broaden the scope of education beyond clearly demarcated and bounded courses or programs. Part 2 is entitled *New challenges: Designs for Networked Learning in the public arena*. Its chapters explore the use of technology in different ways to cross boundaries and to create learning spaces in the open, public arena as well as between open arenas and the bounded settings of home or school. More specifically, the chapters by Koutropoulos and Koseoglu (this volume) and Alexander and Fink (this volume) both deal with designs for Networked Learning in massive open online courses (MOOCs) which – being 'massively open' – are themselves forms of (near)-public networked learning spaces. In contrast, the chapters by Bober & Hynes (this volume) and Carvalho & Freeman (this volume) investigate different ways in which Networked Learning through mobile devices can be used in physical, public arenas and to cross boundaries between public, school and private spaces.

The first chapter in Part 2, *Hybrid presence in networked learning: A shifting and evolving construct* by Apostolos Koutropoulos and Suzan Koseoglu, thus explores the potential for Networked Learning theory and practice to influence the design and delivery of MOOCs. MOOCs are often heralded as innovative, disruptive and revolutionary technology that can address issues of equality by opening up access for all. However, there are significant differences in how MOOCs are designed and delivered and in the underlying vision for education. Koutropoulos and Koseoglu (this volume) argue that the power of a MOOC is not in the delivery mechanism or in its accessibility but in the literacy of the participants and in the pedagogy and learning design. Taking the notion of learners as teachers, the authors reframe the notion of learner presence and teacher presence proposing a new hybrid presence that includes elements of both teaching presence and learning presence but also has its own additional elements. From this new hybrid presence, they propose four learning design principles according to which teachers need to (1) 'prepare to cede authority' and see themselves as convenors of co-learners, (2) 'embrace plasticity' to be responsive to learner voice, (3) 'be present with fellow learners' to build relationships with others in the learning network and (4) 'leave assessments at the door' (Koutropoulos and Koseoglu, Chap. 7 this volume), providing badges for participation in learning activities such as reflection, artefact creation or project work, rather than traditional summative evaluation. While Koutropoulos and Koseoglu (this volume) acknowledge that it is not possible to know every learner within a MOOC, they emphasize the quality of relationship between teacher and learner and the role of the teacher as crucial. The learning design principles are therefore offered as a means of improving the quality of pedagogy by promoting hybrid presence within an open networked learning environment.

Koutropoulos and Koseoglu's contribution is to theory and practice in the learning design of MOOCs through their proposal for a new hybrid presence and learning design principles for practitioners. As with the chapter by Cutajar (this volume), this chapter examines the relationship between the teacher and learner acknowledging a range of different roles. While Cutajar examines the student perspective on the relationship as it happens in practice, Koutropoulos and Koseoglu examine the teacher role. Their design principles provide support for the teacher to make the transition along the relationship described by Cutajar and transition from director of individual students to organizer of student contributors and to tutor as convenor and students as cocreators of learning.

The next chapter, *Designing an inclusive intercultural online participatory seminar for higher education teachers and professionals* by Ilene Dawn Alexander & Alexander Fink, further investigates the potential of utilizing open access ideas from MOOCs within Networked Learning, in the context of an inclusive, intercultural online participatory seminar for higher education teachers and professionals. Drawing upon critical pedagogies and with a commitment to social justice, Alexander and Fink's design for the seminar combines the open access approach of MOOCs with a Networked Learning perspective emphasizing community and the fostering of supportive relationships through collaboration, co-construction and discussion that is critical and reflective. In the chapter, the authors provide an insider account of the process of codesigning, developing and evaluating outcomes, exploring a range of issues in design, particularly how to counter repressive tolerance so that all voices are heard even when they may raise uncomfortable narratives, e.g. on racism or sexism, and how to include 'lurking learners' ('lurners') and support the wider range of ways of participating online. To address repressive tolerance, Alexander and Fink propose learning circles where facilitators assist in three cycles of a structured discussion with additional responsibility to attend to instances of repressive tolerance and ensure democratic participation. Further, an inclusive design, based on Chavez's six elements of an empowering multicultural learning environment, enables an exploration of the experiences of learners including 'lurners' who did not fully participate in assessment (badge) activities, in order for their feedback to influence the second delivery of the open online participatory seminar. Analysis of survey data found that open participation and open access to resources resulted in 'lurners' using resources and organizing learning experiences in a variety of ways within their local settings that were not reflected in the online space.

Alexander and Fink's contribution is to provide a rich example of how practitioners can design, develop and evaluate a MOOC that is inclusive, democratic and appropriate for a multi-cultural cohort of learners. While they do address issues of inequality in MOOCs as discussed in Czerniewicz (this volume), they adopt a learning design perspective and focus on how to support a multi-cultural learning community. They also provide valuable empirical evidence, like Cutajar (this volume), on the experience of learners as they interact with resources. They call for increasing tolerance of difference between learners and how they engage with resources and appeal to educators to provide support for a wider range of online participants. This resonates with Cutajar's call for tolerance of differing perceptions of the student-teacher relationship and aligns with the argument in Jones (this volume) to retain a focus on human experience.

The issue of resource use not being fully transparent to educators is picked up from a different angle in the third chapter of Part 2, *Tools for entertainment or learning? Exploring students' and tutors' domestication of mobile devices* by Magdalena Bober and Deirdre Hynes. The chapter focuses on the use of mobile devices (smartphones, tablets and laptops) across educational and noneducational settings. The authors draw on Dohn's (2014) concept of 'primary contexts' and apply a domestication of technology approach to understand how mobile devices are used (or not) to help learners connect between their 'primary contexts'. Bober and Hynes report a study of staff and student approaches to mobile devices which investigated how mobile devices have been appropriated by users in their everyday lives, how they have become part of daily routines and spatial arrangements and what rules are being negotiated around their use. Distinct uses of different devices (in terms of university-related and personal uses) were identified, but also areas of overlapping use. The study showed that students and tutors associate important symbolic meanings with their devices, have incorporated them into daily routines and spatial arrangements in new ways and attempt to self-regulate use in different situations. The authors compare results from staff and student data, finding both similarities and differences. In conclusion, they state that mobile devices have the potential to bridge between learners' different contexts and to make learning more integrated with their primary contexts. However, realizing this potential, they argue, is far from straightforward because of the variety of uses and meanings ascribed to the devices by staff and students alike.

Bober and Hynes contribute with a nuancing of our understanding of the resources used by learners across different contexts. In particular, they provide an explication of the symbolic barriers that both learners and educators may experience to engaging their mobile devices in broadening the scope of education into private spheres. Their study is thus a timely sobering of overly optimistic characterizations of the potentials of the 'mobile revolution' for rendering the 'networked individualists' of today always accessible, with their homes just 'bases for networking with the outside world', (Rainie and Wellman 2014, p. 12), and of corresponding hopes from educators of seamlessly integrating learners' educational and noneducational contexts.

The last chapter, *CmyView: Learning by walking and sharing social values* by Lucila Carvalho and Cristina Freeman, focuses on the use of mobile devices to foster community participation in open, public spaces. The chapter introduces CmyView, a mobile phone application and social media platform, which has a design concept grounded in both digital heritage and Networked Learning perspectives. With it, users make personal trajectories with images and audio recordings as they go for walks in the natural or built environment. These trajectories can then be shared with others, enabling the collection, documentation and assessment of the social value ascribed by participants to the encountered sites. Carvalho and Freeman report their research on the use of CmyView within the field of cultural heritage. Their empirical study of architecture students' use of the app supports their claims that CmyView has the potential both for supporting community curatorship of place and for facilitating informal learning about design and architecture through experiencing the walking trajectory of others. The authors utilize the Activity-Centred Analysis and Design framework, developed by Carvalho and Goodyear (2014), for analysing the educational design of the app and how it constrained and enabled the activities of the students. The core elements of this framework are structures of place (or elements in set design), task (or elements in epistemic design) and social organization (or elements in social design). In conclusion, Carvalho and Freeman argue that the app offers a space for democratic heritage education and interpretation.

Carvalho and Freeman contribute with a detail-rich example of a successful use of mobile devices to broaden the scope of education into informal, public learning spaces, as well as to create informal user-driven learning opportunities and democratic negotiation of cultural heritage. Their chapter complements the chapter by Bober and Hynes (this volume) by illustrating that mobile-mediated activities can be experienced as meaningful and engaging by a network of learners when the mobile functionality is utilized for establishing and re-walking specific trajectories. The example is thus an indication that learners' potential symbolic barriers to mobile use across contexts can sometimes be circumvented in practice. One might speculate that the circumvention was due in no small degree to precisely the democratic user involvement and participants' freedom to negotiate meaningful cultural sites.

Between them, the chapters in Part 2 give detailed examples of the challenges involved in utilizing technologies to broaden the scope of education beyond demarcated physical and institutional educational spaces into the public arena. The chapters illustrate a number of potentials, too, however, as well as provide guidelines and design principles for overcoming some of the challenges. Thus, an initial challenge may be the symbolic meanings attached by participants to the technologies themselves, when they have been 'domesticated' to familiar, personal use. This was shown by Bober and Hynes (this volume) to be a problem for engaging mobile devices across educational and noneducational settings. It may equally apply to other technologies, platforms and sites when used in non-familiar ways or contexts. Similarly, as the scope of education is broadened into the public arena, in terms of participant numbers and/or location of participation, it becomes increasingly hard for educators to monitor the resources learners engage with and the ways in which they do so. This challenge implicitly follows from Bober and Hynes' study (this volume) and is discussed by Alexander and Fink (this volume), who argue for a more tolerant attitude towards 'lurners', allowing them to utilize resources for their own local purposes even if they do not participate much in course activities. Alexander and Fink identify yet another challenge in the form of addressing repressive tolerance in open, multi-cultural course settings such as their MOOC and suggest learning cycles of structured discussion to meet this challenge. The design principles developed by Koutropoulos and Koseoglu (this volume) here supply further guidance for addressing divergent student and teacher perspectives in MOOCs through fostering forms of hybrid teacher-learner presence. Finally, Carvalho and Freeman (this volume) show how the public arena can be engaged in user-driven ways through mobile technologies. They thus provide further illustration that bringing education into the public arena not only poses challenges but holds potentials, too, in particular, as concerns enabling new forms of democratic education.

Emerging Issues in the Field of Networked Learning

In the first section of our Conclusion chapter, we have identified and discussed the contributions which each of the book's chapters make, individually and together, to the field of Networked Learning. In this second section, we take a look at broader issues emerging out of the book's chapters as significant perspectives and challenges for future research and practice within Networked Learning. Many of these issues were touched upon also in other papers presented at the Networked Learning Conference 2016, apart from the ones that form the basis for this book – along with, of course, a number of other questions. We draw on these further papers in our account too, as well as on other literature, to enable a more elaborate identification of key issues for our community, today and in the years to come. The conference papers are openly available at http://www.networkedlearningconference.org.uk/past/nlc2016/index.htm.

Learning Spaces

As indicated, the Networked Learning Conference 2016 sparked a lot of interest and debate in other areas in addition to the ones represented in this book, suggesting further current and emerging trends within the field. One area of interest in particular needs to be mentioned here, as it was addressed in both keynotes (and in several other papers) and actually plays an important, if largely implicit, role for the issues discussed in the chapters presented here, too. This is the focus area of *diverse dimensions of learning spaces*. This area was discussed at the conference in relation to different educational settings, such as higher education, and mobile or online networked spaces, such as MOOCs, all of which are well-represented in this book. Interestingly, the area was also discussed in relation to the fluidity of learning in 'diffused and re-infused [spaces] through open, online information sharing and knowledge construction' (Haythornthwaite 2016). Moreover, it was argued that Networked Learning facilitates the production of 'newly' produced space enabled through the 'complex choreography of on-campus and off-campus practices' (Bayne 2016). Other selective examples included Bell's (2016) exploration of 'heterotopias', 'unsettling fragmentary places' and specifically how learners need to practice 'disconnection' as a digital literacy or capability in order to negotiate learning in spaces such as social networking sites (SNS) that are also sites for advertising. Koseoglu (2016) brought attention to 'third spaces', spaces which are 'neither formal nor informal' and able to support situated learning. These examples and others at the conference point to the current and emergent importance of research around the many dimensions of learning spaces that need to be explored.

Mobility, New Forms of Openness and Learning in the Public Arena

The focus on learning spaces further reflects at least two trends in the Networked Learning community and the field of learning and education in general. The first of these trends is the growing awareness of the significance of the sociomaterial *place* of learning in determining activities, interactions and learning outcomes (Carvalho et al. 2017). The second trend concerns what might be viewed as the dialectical opposite of this focus, i.e. the significance of *boundary crossing* (Akkerman and Bakker 2011; Wenger 1998) for initiating and inspiring new cognitions and practices. These trends combine also in the first theme which we see emerging from the chapters of this book as an area of focus deserving further investigation in the future: *mobility, new forms of openness and learning in the public arena.*

Networked Learning has concerned itself with the theory and practice of establishing connections between people, ideas and resources from the very inception of it as a research field (E-Quality Network 2002) (Goodyear et al. 2004). Very often this has been done from the (implicitly presumed or explicitly articulated) perspective that such connections would empower learners (cf. Parchoma, this volume) both *as* learners within the formal education courses they were taking (Cutajar, this volume, McConnell et al. 2012) and as practitioners in whatever life contexts these courses were supposed to qualify them for (e.g. Pilkington and Guldberg 2009). In its origin, however, the space focus for Networked Learning research would primarily be that of an online forum, conference or LMS course 'hosting' or facilitating the connections between people, resources and ideas (as witnessed in the graphs presented in the introductory chapter of this anthology). The empowerment of connections was thought to happen within the bounded space of such online settings. This has been changing over the last few years. Empowerment through Networked Learning is still an important issue – coming to the fore explicitly in this anthology, e.g. in the chapters by Parchoma (this volume), Czerniewicz (this volume), Alexander and Fink (this volume) and Carvalho and Freeman (this volume) – but it is increasingly seen as taking place in the complex interplay between, on the one hand, what goes on at the specific sociomaterial sites of hybrid physical-virtual learning activities and, on the other hand, learners' boundary crossing between such sites (Ryberg et al. 2016a). In other words, *mobility* across contexts, as well as *increased openness* towards contexts outside of education, to the point of *taking learning into the public arena*, are all seen as adding new dimensions to Networked Learning. They add new dimensions by supplying content otherwise unavailable (e.g. the onsite viewing of buildings recommended by other learners through the CmyView app, reported in the chapter by Carvalho & Freeman) and by enabling the articulation of learning objectives not pursuable solely within the space of an online course (e.g. learning academic citizenship, Aaen and Nørgaard 2015). More broadly, they foster connections and increased interaction between people inside and outside of formal education settings (Dalsgaard and Thestrup 2015), thus diminishing the requirement for actual formal affiliation and taking instead 'relevance of contribution' as the pragmatic criterion for participation. The aim here is to further learning, empowerment and a sense of community belonging for both those that participate in the formal education and those that do not. In many ways, this was the original idea behind MOOCs (McAuley et al. 2010; Mackness et al. 2010), here represented in the chapter by Alexander and Fink, though MOOCs, of course, are still confined to a limited number of online sites. The opening up of learning contexts – both physical and virtual – for participation on the basis of relevance of contribution, rather than formal affiliation, would be an area for further theoretical, practical and empirical exploration within Networked Learning, in line with the European policy initiative of opening up education and to move towards learning in an open, public arena. The significant challenges which this move implies for higher education policy and pedagogical design should, however, not be overlooked (Jansen 2015). Among these challenges are *the difference between participants* and *social justice*, which are discussed in the next two subsections, respectively, as well as the potential symbolic barriers involved for participants in transgressing familiar contexts of learning and usages of technology (cf. Bober & Hynes, this volume).

Differences Between Participants and in Participant Experiences: Implications for the Practice of Online Educators

A further theme well-represented in the conference and in the selected papers for this edited book is understanding the learners' and tutors' experiences of networked learning. This theme is recurrent, rather than emerging, within Networked Learning research, a well-established and overarching theme since the 2002 manifesto (E-quality Network 2002). And rightly so, research that focuses on the practice of Networked Learning is of perpetual interest, providing valuable insight and, as technologies and practices develop, enabling us to examine the implications for the changing role of the tutor, assess the gap between theory and pedagogical practice and suggest strategies for tutors and designers to use to support learning communities. Jones' argument (this volume) for the need to retain a focus on human agents and their first-person perspective even within contemporary sociomaterial accounts of Networked Learning reflects and underpins this theme theoretically.

At the 2016 conference, a central focus within this theme was *differences*, both *differences between participants* and *differences in participant experiences*. Concerning the former, Söderback et al. (2016) discuss a study of the experiences of learners involved in Networked Learning, reporting that some groups of learners experience problems with collaboration while working in small groups due to 'large differences in motivation, commitment, prior knowledge and different working schedules' (p. 401). In addition to reminding educators of the differences between learners, this type of research into pedagogical practice emphasizes the need for an improved understanding of how to support and encourage collaboration in small group work. Hanif and Hammond (2016) examine the (differing) experiences of learners in online communities looking at how and why they help others within their online community. Results suggest that helpers are aware of the need to sustain the community and to engage in both receiving and giving help. The paper highlights strategies used for giving help and explains the circumstances surrounding when help is more likely to be given. Finally, it emphasizes that helpfulness needs to be grown and nurtured within an online community. While the implications of the findings are not straightforward, it is clearly an issue of which educators should be made aware. Cutajar's chapter (this volume), as discussed above, similarly explores learners' differing perceptions of 'others' within their networked learning environment and the corresponding differences in their expectations towards tutor and co-learners. This leads her to recommend that the difference be recognized and to suggest strategies for supporting different student approaches within Networked Learning pedagogical practice. These three examples serve to highlight the differences that can exist between learners, expand our understanding of that difference and remind educators and designers of the need to take these differences into account in their practice. While research like this, that focuses on the detail of pedagogical practice, may not always provide enough evidence to suggest a change to practice, it can provide food for critical reflection by raising awareness of these issues and in some cases may conclude with principles that can inform the professional development of online tutors.

Within MOOCs and other open arenas (cf. above and the chapters in Part 2), the difference in participants is likely to be much greater than in a closed higher education setting where entry requirements exist. This difference within the learner population is both a strength and a challenge for educators and designers. The rich experiences of a diverse learner group can provide added value to networked learning when participants share their unique experiences; difference can be seen as an opportunity for learning rather than a challenge (Reynolds et al. 2004). However, the varied past experiences of learning online and differing perceptions of Networked Learning may inhibit and affect ability to access and participate in learning. As indicated, the design of MOOCs to accommodate and benefit from differences between participants is a focal point of the chapters by Koutropoulos and Koseoglu (this volume) and Alexander and Fink (this volume), as well as of further papers in the conference, for example, Czerniewicz et al. (2016) who study the practices and perceptions of educators as they create a MOOC, in particular examining the educators' understanding of 'openness'. This supplements the discussion by Koutropoulos and Koseoglu (this volume) of learning design principles for MOOCs that support the relationship between teacher and learner based on a characterization of modes of teacher and learner presence. As for the participatory seminar approach of Alexander and Fink (this volume), their framework of learning circles to structure collaborative discussion amongst participants has been designed explicitly to build positively on differences between participants. This approach is innovative and at the forefront of social justice and democratic participation within the MOOC structure, in contrast to many MOOCs that are based on more instructivist pedagogies.

However, it is also clear from the chapters and papers discussed in this section that reconfiguring the relations between learners and teachers is not an easy, unproblematic enterprise. Rather, it is a process involving the renegotiation of expectations and identities of both teachers and learners. This, along with the more specific issue of learners' different perceptions of the usefulness of collaboration (Cutajar, this volume), points us to Hodgson and Reynolds (2005) and Ozturk and Hodgson (2017) critique of notions of community and its potential association with consensus and pressure to conform. As both texts stress, it is important that we maintain the value of 'difference'. '[T]raditional views of democratic communities are often tainted by unrealistic assumptions about consensus and relationships' Ozturk and Hodgson (2017, p. 24). The theme of understanding the learners' and tutors' experiences in networked learning therefore, finally, also contributes to wider discussion of the gap between learning theory and pedagogical practice. We return to this below.

Social Justice

The theme of 'social justice', forefronted in the MOOC design of Alexander and Fink (this volume, cf. above), and present in other contributions within the book and the conference, represents an emergent focus area within the general emphasis on design for democracy and empowerment often found within Networked Learning research. Returning to the writings of John Rawls (Rawls and Kelly 2001), an influential political theorist of the last century, he recommends that two principles concerning social justice should be kept in mind.

- Each person has the same indefeasible claim to a fully adequate scheme of equal basic liberties, which scheme is compatible with the same scheme of liberties for all.
- Social and economic inequalities are to satisfy two conditions: first, they are to be attached to offices and positions open to all under conditions of fair equality of opportunity; and second, they are to be to the greatest benefit of the least advantaged members of society (Rawls and Kelly 2001, pp. 42–3).

Yet as Hytten and Bettez (2011) have noted, social justice within education is often poorly defined and demonstrates 'confusion and conceptual looseness'. This is not surprising given that as McArthur states, social justice is complex without 'easy or simple definitions'. In her book, *Rethinking Knowledge within Higher Education* (2013), she adopts four key aspects to underpin an understanding of social justice: 'that it is multifaceted and which defies easy or simple definitions, a belief in the dual importance of process and outcomes to social justice; an emphasis on social justice grounded in the relationships between people, and achieved through those relationships; and finally, an imperfect understanding of social justice, such that our goal is to aspire to more justice and less injustice rather than some perfect state of "social justice"' (McArthur 2013, p. 24).

These ideas align with the arguments at the 2016 conference and within this book that issues of social justice should be emphasized more in relation to education generally and within Networked Learning specifically. As discussed, Czerniewicz's chapter (this volume) made a robust argument that a more critical and political stance needs to be taken in order to challenge the emerging and predominant global market-led model of online higher education and in particular to better promote and support equality and fairness. Other presentations at the conference focused on other aspects of social justice, through articulating roles of Networked Learning in relation to disabilities such as autism or Asperger's syndrome (Davis 2016), rehabilitation of people with a brain injury (Konnerup et al. 2016) collective well-being (Beetham et al. 2016), digital capabilities and how work and people are valued in employability (Beetham 2016), happiness (Zander et al. 2016), inclusive education (Tarek 2016), intercultural competence (Duin 2016), multiculturalism (Raistrick 2016) and social capital in online environments (Brett et al. 2016; Jordan 2016). The general tendency, however, is for social justice aspects of educational research to remain in the background without being made fully explicit, examined and understood. We need to consider, therefore, how bringing a more discernible social justice lens to other areas within Networked Learning research might act to achieve greater social justice more generally. Could examining Networked Learning through a more nuanced, granular account of how social justice issues play out in interactions in Networked Learning environments, for example, offer new insights and enable Networked Learning to achieve greater 'equality of opportunity' (Rawls and Kelly 2001)? Given the potentially transformative benefits of such approaches, it would seem to be worth focusing research more explicitly on issues and theories of social justice in order to understand and seek to promote greater social justice in networked learning environments.

Critical Look at the Criticality of Networked Learning

In the wider Networked Learning literature and in the books in the 'Networked Learning Research' series, a recurrent theme is critical pedagogy and the promotion of a critical stance towards technology and learning (Dirckinck-Holmfeld et al. 2012; Hodgson et al. 2014a; Jandric and Boras 2015; Jones 2015; Ryberg et al. 2016). These positions are often highlighted as emblematic of the Networked Learning community and were therefore, unsurprisingly, also present at the 2016 conference and are likewise represented in the chapters of the present book. For example, the practices of critical pedagogy are particularly well exemplified in Alexander and Fink's chapter (this volume) in their design of the inclusive intercultural online participatory seminar (cf. above). In general, courses rooted in critical pedagogies often seek to establish other relations between learners and teachers, such as more participatory, inclusive relations aimed at co-production of knowledge and mutual exploration of resources in smaller self-organized learning networks and groups, illustrated here in the chapters by Alexander and Fink (this volume), Koutropoulos and Koseoglu (this volume) and Cutajar (this volume).

As has been reiterated in different writings on Networked Learning, and in this volume by Parchoma, Networked Learning is not underpinned by one particular theory of learning or pedagogy, but rather embraces a number of theoretical perspectives (Jones et al. 2015). But more often than not, these are in line with what we could broadly call constructivist, collaborative or critical perspectives. It was therefore particularly interesting and challenging to read Lee's call to turn the critical gaze of Networked Learning onto some of the assumptions underlying the field itself (Lee, this volume). As discussed, Lee argued that calls for constructivist or collaborative learning are often couched as hegemonic discourses that position some forms of distance education as 'old', 'traditional' and as grounded in behaviourist or cognitivist theories, in contrast to what is promoted as progressive ideas of education. This led her to identify a clear gap between (idealizing) pedagogical theory and the 'mundane pedagogical practices' of actual online higher education, including networked learning. Following Lee's suggestion of turning the critical gaze upon Networked Learning's own presuppositions, we agree, firstly, that the alleged gap does seem to exist, as also emphasized by, for example, Selwyn (2014) and Jones (2015), cf. also Bober & Hynes (this volume). Secondly, recalling the graphs in Chap. 1 and the prominence of, e.g. 'constructivism', in the field of Networked Learning, it does seem important not to fall prey to simplified 'old' vs 'new' conceptualizations of designs for learning. As argued by Lee, there are historical reasons for particular ways of designing for distance education, for example, to cater to learners who might not otherwise have access but also learners that might find it difficult to learn in sync with other learners and prefer a more personalized pace in a course. Such challenges with multiple learners with varying conceptions and preferences are, as noted, magnified considerably by the surge of interest in MOOCs.

A further point for critical self-reflection for Networked Learning follows from Czerniewicz's (this volume) argument that the trend of global marketization of online education witnessed, e.g. in relation to MOOCs, may potentially lead to new kinds of inequality: Online higher education, and networked learning with it, runs the risk of becoming an even further global North-driven capitalization of new and emerging markets for education – even if well-meant.

The fast-changing landscape of higher education provision therefore warrants further debate within the Networked Learning community in terms of how we can work for democratized and equal access for education, and not only for students but equally how we ensure a wider global participation of researchers in the development of the global online learning landscape. It poses questions of how we maintain the underpinning values of Networked Learning in a globalized online learning landscape of much richer and varied participation where students enter with different experiences of and expectations for learning. In this endeavour we need to maintain the critical and reflexive roots and also turn this critical gaze onto Networked Learning itself and ask whether certain ideas, principles, designs, expectations or assumptions about students might be alienating or exclusive and whether such understanding might be so deeply rooted within Networked Learning that they can be difficult to see for us.

Different Understandings of Networked Learning

Across and behind the different themes identified as recurrent, contemporary or emerging within the field of Networked Learning, we also see new ways of understanding the field itself emerging. More specifically, we see a development of different understandings of:

A. What 'network' is a network *of*
B. How the network is viewed as supportive of learning
C. What it means for learning to be 'networked'

The often-cited early definition by Goodyear et al. (2004) states that networked learning is '…learning in which information and communications technology (ICT) is used to promote connections: between one learner and other learners; between learners and tutors; between a learning community and its learning resources (p. 1)'.

Here, the term 'network' refers *both* to the ICT infrastructure *and* to the social structure of relationships between people (issue A). This original ambiguity underlined the significance of both technology and people – and not least of their interplay – for providing access to resources and to ways of interpreting the ideas present in them (issue B). Learning was understood as networked in precisely this double sense of coming into being through the *ICT-mediated* connection with other *people* and their views (issue C).

This early definition lends itself very well to research within higher education or continuing professional development programs where students interact with each other, their tutors and their learning resources in designated online spaces. This was and still is one very important understanding of Networked Learning, represented in this book, e.g. by the chapters by Cutajar and by Jones. But other understandings have emerged, reflecting some of the changes already mentioned in this Conclusion chapter, i.e. the opening up of the spaces of learning, the increasing mobility of technology and people, the interplay of formal and informal education and the diversity of people involved in learning activities across the formal-informal boundary. The initial focus on connections between people remains an underlying tenet, though with some differences in the role played by other people, along with a basic socioculturally inspired view of what learning is. The following understandings can be identified.

The 'network' is a network of people (issue A). This view is represented in De Laat (2012) who states that networked learning 'aims to understand social learning processes by asking how people develop and maintain a 'web' of social relations used for their learning and development' (p. 26). It is also present in the emphasis which Carvalho and Goodyear (2014) place on *learning networks* in their characterization of Networked Learning (cf. also Carvalho and Freeman, this volume). On this understanding, and in contrast to the early definition by Goodyear et al., 'networked learning' does not necessarily involve ICT, though in specific cases it may of course make use of technology. What makes learning 'networked' is the connection to and engagement with other people across different social positions inside and outside of a given institution (issue C). The network is supportive of a person's learning through the access it provides to other people's ideas and ways of participating in practice as well as of course through the opportunity to discuss these ideas and ways of participating and to potentially develop nuanced, common perspectives (issue B). This understanding of 'network' is particularly relevant for research into professional development in or involving workplace practice as well as for educational programs/courses designed to breach the formal educational learning space by drawing substantially on learners' connections to people outside of the program/ course. Examples of the former are found in De Laat (2012). An example which combines both the former and the latter is reported in Van den Beemt and Vrieling (2016). Here, networked learning groups of student teachers, in-service teachers and teacher training educators worked together to improve language learning and teaching in the classrooms of the in-service teachers. For the student teachers, participation was part of their teacher training program; for the in-service teachers, it served as a practice-based professional development project.

The 'network' is a network of situations or contexts (issue A). This view is indicated in the addition to the early definition by Goodyear et al. suggested by Dohn (2014) in an earlier book in this Networked Learning series. Dohn emphasized the connections 'between the diverse contexts in which the learners participate' (Dohn 2014, p. 30) as significant for understanding learning beyond designated online learning spaces and, indeed, within them as well. In the cited chapter, Dohn follows Goodyear et al. in positing ICT as the mediator of such connections between the learners' contexts. However, given the focus of her arguments, the ICT mediation does not actually seem necessary. Her arguments centre on the way tacit, practical knowledge from one context can be drawn upon in new learning situations to provide propositional knowledge presented in the latter with depth of understanding by letting it resonate with tacit semantic content from the former. This is the sense in which the network, understood as a network of situations, supports learning: by offering tacit knowledge, perspectives and ways of acting from known situations for resituated use in new ones (issue B). 'Networked learning' on this understanding is the learning arising from the connections drawn between situations and from the resituated use in new situations of knowledge, perspectives and ways of acting from known ones (issue C). Utilizing ICT is one approach to supporting this process, but it might be supported by other means such as physical artefacts or artistic stimulation of senses and feelings. Connections may also be drawn spontaneously by the learners themselves. In the present book, this understanding of Networked Learning is represented in the chapter by Bober and Hynes (this volume), who discuss how mobile devices link (or not) the spheres of education and home environment.

The 'network' is one of ICT infrastructure, enabling connections across space and time (issue A). Given this minimal statement, there would not seem to be much to differentiate the approach of Networked Learning from other perspectives on the ICT mediation of learning. The support for learning provided by the network is one of infrastructure, i.e. the ease of saving, transporting and retrieving content for future use (issue B). Learning, it would seem, will be 'networked' whenever it is ICT-mediated, by that very fact (issue C), perhaps with the proviso that the situations of learning should indeed be separated in space and/or time so that the infrastructure (the 'network') is actually brought into play. This proviso would differentiate the field of networked learning somewhat from the field of computer-supported collaborative learning (CSCL), where many studies concern ICT-facilitated group work between physically co-located students. At its most basic, this is the understanding of 'network' present in the chapters by, e.g. Czerniewicz and Lee, in this book. It is also, at heart, the understanding of network underlying research focusing on establishing mobile and boundary-crossing connections between places of learning (cf. above). However, as emphasized in the chapters by Czerniewicz and Lee, and as also pointed out several times in this section on emerging themes, *the research field* of Networked Learning is characterized, not only by focusing on 'networks' but also by taking a certain *approach* to learning, focusing critically on aspects of democratization and empowerment. That is, studies adopting this understanding of 'networks' as ICT infrastructure will only belong to the category of Networked Learning if they address questions such as inequality, democracy, inclusiveness, empowerment or similar social justice issues.

The 'network' is one of the actants, consisting of both human and non-human agents in symmetrical relationship to each other (issue A). This is the view of actor-network theory (ANT) (Latour 1993, 1997) which has been quite popular within the Networked Learning community, as witnessed in the graph of theoretical perspectives presented in the Introduction chapter (cf. also Fenwick and Edwards 2010; Fox 2002, 2005). It is a systemic approach to learning, where individual learners' interaction and learning may be analysed as a result of sociomaterial entanglement with objects and other people, as in Wright and Parchoma (2014), cf. also Jones (this volume). Alternatively, the system itself may be analysed, for instance, to critique simple notions of community and to point at the implicit standardization of learning in an educational world aligning itself to American-English language and culture (Fox 2005). The network supports learning in the sense that any learning is in fact the result of concrete sociomaterial entanglement of physical, virtual and human actants (issue B). And because such sociomaterial entanglement is the reality of any learning situations on this understanding, all learning is actually networked learning (issue C).

Similar to the way Parchoma's chapter helps us to understand subtle differences in the theoretical underpinnings of Networked Learning, the approaches presented in this section enable us to grasp variations in understandings of ideas of 'networks' in Networked Learning. While some would argue that ICT mediation is a necessary component in Networked Learning, others emphasize that a network can be understood as a relation between learners even when these relations are not mediated by technology. Clarifying different approaches helps readers pinpoint the precise claims made by a given text as well as discern actual agreements or divergences between texts which may underlie immediate appearances. Moreover, in terms of future studies, the characterization provided of Networked Learning approaches will support researchers in identifying and demarcating the types of network and Networked Learning that they focus on, thereby aiding their adequate conceptualization of issues to investigate.

Learning Analytics

Finally, we wish to point to a theme which is rapidly emerging and is starting to become widely adopted by higher education institutes in one way or another but, as yet, has had relatively little exposure within the Networked Learning community: learning analytics. Browsing research from higher education institutes on this topic shows that it is rather technology-centred; however within the learning analytics community, there is a strong debate on putting more emphasis on pedagogies and building an evidence base for learning analytics to fulfil its potential. Tsai and Gasevic (2017) thus identify some of the key challenges of learning analytics as shortage of pedagogy-based approaches, limited evidence base to validate impact of learning analytics and insufficient training opportunities for end users to make effective use of learning analytics. This is not surprising in a new domain of research where various stakeholders and disciplines are still trying to come together and develop a shared language. A further focus is the area of policy and ethics where ethics, privacy and data protection are in general taken very seriously by all countries, though the approach and implementation varies and great cultural differences exist (Hoel et al. 2017). However, Hoel et al. (2017) conclude that even in cultures that give more value to organizational interests, as opposed to an individual focus, learning analytics system designers realize that without the confidence and trust of end users, new tools will be repurposed or circumvented if the end user only sees them as part of a surveillance apparatus. The big brother suggestion is still easily made by critics of learning analytics, and unless the domain is able to develop shared ethical standards (Hoel et al. 2017), clearly articulated information policies (Haythornthwaite 2017) and student engagement (Arnold and Sclater 2017) around use of data as well as evidence of learning analytics in improving the practice of learning (Ferguson and Clow 2017), the field may continue to suffer from this critique.

Given the significance of these issues, it is surprising to note that learning analytics in general has not been widely adopted as a research theme in the area of Networked Learning. This was already evident in Fig. 1.2 in the Introduction chapter, but it remains an interesting question why this is the case. Perhaps it is due to the strong interest in teaching and learning pedagogy in Networked Learning and its association with practice-based research, often at the expense of recognizing technology-driven innovation and its potential to drive the research agenda. Another reason can be the emphasis within Networked Learning on social learning, participation-based perspectives, criticality and the exploration of sociomaterial relationships that co-create learning environments. Although there is some interest within learning analytics in what is termed social learning analytics (Shum and Ferguson 2012), most of the attention goes to data analysis and mining in order to understand (and even predict) learning behaviour from a more individual perspective. One example is the design of visualization dashboards aimed at giving teachers better access to information about what is happening in their courses, to understand student attention and retention and to identify at-risk students early. Perhaps due to a more technology-driven agenda, this approach tends to facilitate the management of learning more than improving learning practices. Several papers at the Networked Learning Conference 2016 attempted to align with what is happening in the learning analytics domain, discussing ethical issues related to data protection and privacy as well as research methods for analysing data and providing feedback to teachers and learners (Bayne and Ross 2016; Perrotta 2016; Savin-Baden and Tombs 2016; Sclater and Lally 2016; Zander et al. 2016). It is, however, an area where much work still needs to be done and where there is great need for the critical perspectives associated with Networked Learning approaches.

Concluding Remarks

The purpose of this chapter has been to reflect on how the book's chapters combine to characterize the field of Networked Learning today and how they draw out significant perspectives and challenges for future research and practice. We have pointed out that the chapters in Part 1 situate Networked Learning within the general education research landscape as a field with a strong interest in theory development and critical assessment of (one's own and others') presuppositions and some preference for sociomaterial approaches to human agency and cognition. In the context of this general positioning of Networked Learning, the chapters in Part 2 offer different perspectives on a more specific common theme, namely, the current tendency to broaden the scope of education into the public arena. In the second section of the Conclusion, we have then identified a set of themes whose significance is emerging: learning spaces, mobility, new forms of openness and learning in the public arena, differences between participants and in participants' experiences, social justice, critical look at the criticality of Networked Learning, different understandings of Networked Learning and learning analytics.

Looking to the next conference in the Networked Learning Conference series, taking place in Zagreb in May 2018, we see several of these themes suggested or explicitly stated in the Call for Papers (cf. http://www.networkedlearningconference.org.uk/call/themes.htm). *Critical pedagogy and networked learning praxis* is thus a focus area, as are *Networked learning in the public arena, learning on the move* and *learning at scale and across boundaries. Learning analytics* and *big data* are specifically mentioned as examples of methodological approaches to be investigated. This speaks again to the prevalence of these themes within the Networked Learning community today. It also gives reason for optimism regarding the development of nuanced empirical and theoretical perspectives on them in the nearest future. Assuming that the themes will indeed be taken up in papers submitted for the conference, its proceedings and the following book of selected papers in this Networked Learning series may well be the future places to search for answers to the questions raised in this chapter.

References

Aaen, J. H., & Nørgård, R. T. (2015). Participatory academic communities: A transdisciplinary perspective on participation in education beyond the institution. Conjunctions. *Transdisciplinary Journal of Cultural Participation, 2*(2), 67–98.

Akkerman, S. F., & Bakker, A. (2011). Boundary crossing and boundary objects. *Review of Educational Research, 81*(2), 132–169.

Arnold, K. E., & Sclater, N. (2017). Student perceptions of their privacy in leaning analytics applications. In *Proceedings of the seventh international learning analytics & knowledge conference* (pp. 66–69). ACM.

Bayne, S. (2016). Campus codespaces for networked learners. *Keynote given at the 10th international conference on networked learning 2016.*

Bayne, S., & Ross, J. (2016). Manifesto Redux: Making a teaching philosophy from networked learning research. In S. Cranmer, N. B. Dohn, M. de Laat, T. Ryberg, & J. A. Sime (Eds.), *Proceedings of the 10th international conference on networked learning 2016* (pp. 120–128). Lancaster: Lancaster University.

Beetham, H. (2015, April). What is blended learning? Seminar presentation, Bristol UK. BIS. (2013). *Literature Review of Massive Open Online Courses and Other Forms of Online Distance Learning.*

Beetham, H. (2016). Employability and the digital future of work. In S. Cranmer, N. B. Dohn, M. de Laat, T. Ryberg, & J. A. Sime (Eds.), *Proceedings of the 10th international conference on networked learning 2016* (pp. 47–55). Lancaster: Lancaster University.

Beetham, H., Czerniewicz, L., Jones, C., Lally, V., Perrotta, C., & Sclater, M. (2016). Challenges to social justice and collective wellbeing in a globalised education system. *Symposium at the International Conference on Networked Learning 2016.*

Bell, F. (2016). (Dis)connective practice in heterotopic spaces for networked and connected learning. In S. Cranmer, N. B. Dohn, M. de Laat, T. Ryberg, & J. A. Sime (Eds.), *Proceedings of the 10th international conference on networked learning 2016* (pp. 67–75). Lancaster: Lancaster University.

Brett, C., Lee, K., & Öztok, M. (2016). Socialization and social capital in online doctoral programs. In S. Cranmer, N. B. Dohn, M. de Laat, T. Ryberg, & J. A. Sime (Eds.), *Proceedings of the 10th international conference on networked learning 2016* (pp. 264–268). Lancaster: Lancaster University.

Carvalho, L., & Goodyear, P. (Eds.). (2014). *The architecture of productive learning networks.* New York: Routledge.

Carvalho, L., Goodyear, P., & De Laat, M. (Eds.). (2017). *Place-based spaces for networked learning.* New York: Routledge.

Czerniewicz, L., Glover, M., Deacon, A., & Walji, S. (2016). MOOCs, openness and changing educator practices: An activity theory case study. In S. Cranmer, N. B. Dohn, M. de Laat, T. Ryberg, & J. A. Sime (Eds.), *Proceedings of the 10th international conference on networked learning 2016* (pp. 287–294). Lancaster: Lancaster University.

Dalsgaard, C., & Thestrup, K. (2015). Dimensions of openness: Beyond the course as an open format in online education. *The International Review of Research in Open and Distributed Learning, 16*(6), 78–97. Retrieved from http://www.irrodl.org/index.php/irrodl/article/view/2146

Davis, J. (2016). Networked learning: An opportunity to enhance the learning opportunities for students with high functioning autism or Asperger's syndrome? In S. Cranmer, N. B. Dohn, M. de Laat, T. Ryberg, & J. A. Sime (Eds.), *Proceedings of the 10th international conference on networked learning 2016* (pp. 507–515). Lancaster: Lancaster University.

De Laat, M. (2012). *Enabling professional development networks: How connected are you?* Heerlen: LOOK, Open Universteit of the Netherlands.

Dirckinck-Holmfeld, L., Hodgson, V., & McConnell, D. (Eds.). (2012). *Exploring the theory, pedagogy and practice of networked learning.* New York: Springer.

Dohn, N. B. (2014). Implications for networked learning of the 'practice' side of social prac-
tice theories – A tacit-knowledge perspective. In V. Hodgson, M. de Laat, D. McConnell, &
T. Ryberg (Eds.), *The design, experience and practice of networked learning* (pp. 29–49).
Dordrecht: Springer.

Duin, A. H. (2016). Designs for networked learning: Using personal learning networks to
build intercultural competence. In S. Cranmer, N. B. Dohn, M. de Laat, T. Ryberg, & J. A.
Sime (Eds.), *Proceedings of the 10th international conference on networked learning 2016*.
Lancaster: Lancaster University.

E-Quality Network (2002). *E-quality in e-learning Manifesto*. Paper presented at the Networked
Learning Conference, Sheffield, UK. Retrieved from http://csalt.lancs.ac.uk/esrc/

Fenwick, T., & Edwards, R. (2010). *Actor-network theory in education*. London: Routledge.

Ferguson, R., & Clow, D. (2017). Where is the evidence? A call to action for learning analytics. In *Proceedings of the seventh international learning analytics & knowledge conference*
(pp. 56–65). ACM.

Fox, S. (2002). Studying networked learning: Some implications from socially situated learning theory and actor network theory. In C. Steeples & C. Jones (Eds.), *Networked learning:
Perspectives and issues* (pp. 77–91). London: Springer.

Fox, S. (2005). An actor-network critique of community in higher education: Implications for
networked learning. *Studies in Higher Education, 30*(1), 95–110.

Goodyear, P., Banks, S., Hodgson, V., & McConnell, D. (Eds.). (2004). *Advances in research on
networked learning*. Dordrecht: Kluwer Academic.

Goodyear, P., Carvalho, L., & Dohn, N. B. (2014). Design for networked learning: Framing relations between participants' activities and the physical setting. In S. Bayne, C. Jones, M. de
Laat, T. Ryberg, & C. Sinclair (Eds.), *Proceedings of the 9th international conference on networked learning 2014* (pp. 137–144). Edinburgh University.

Hanif, H., & Hammond, M. (2016). Why and how do members provide help for others within
online communities? In S. Cranmer, N. B. Dohn, M. de Laat, T. Ryberg, & J. A. Sime (Eds.),
Proceedings of the 10th international conference on networked learning 2016 (pp. 385–389).
Lancaster: Lancaster University.

Harasim, L. (2000). Shift happens: Online education as a new paradigm in learning. *Internet and
Higher Education, 3*(1), 41–61.

Haythornthwaite, C. (2016). New metaphors for networked learning. *Keynote given at the 10th
International Conference on Networked Learning 2016*.

Haythornthwaite, C. (2017). An information policy perspective on learning analytics. In
Proceedings of the seventh international learning analytics & knowledge conference (pp. 253–
256). ACM.

Hodgson, V., & Reynolds, M. (2005). Consensus, difference and "multiple communities" in networked learning. *Studies in Higher Education, 30*(1), 11–24.

Hodgson, V., De Laat, M., McConnell, D., & Ryberg, T. (2014a). Researching design, experience
and practice of networked learning: An overview. In V. Hodgson, M. de Laat, D. McConnell,
& T. Ryberg (Eds.), *The design, experience and practice of networked learning* (pp. 1–26).
New York: Springer.

Hodgson, V., De Laat, M., McConnell, D., & Ryberg, T. (Eds.). (2014b). *The design, experience
and practice of networked learning*. New York: Springer.

Hoel, T., Griffiths, D., & Chen, W. (2017). The influence of data protection and privacy frameworks on the design of learning analytics systems. In *Proceedings of the seventh international
learning analytics & knowledge conference* (pp. 243–252). ACM.

Hytten, K., & Bettez, S. C. (2011). Understanding education for social justice. *Educational
Foundations, 25*(1–2), 7–24.

Ingold, T. (2011). Prologue: Anthropology comes to life. In *Being alive: Essays on movement,
knowledge and description* (pp. 3–14). Abington: Routledge.

Jandric, P., & Boras, D. (Eds.). (2015). *Critical learning in digital networks*. New York: Springer
Science+Business Media.

Jansen, F. (2015). MOOCs for opening up education and the OpenupEd initiative. In C. J. Bonk, M. M. Lee, T. C. Reeves, & T. H. Reynolds (Eds.), *MOOCs and open education around the world*. New York: Routledge Taylor & Francis Group. Retrieved from https://eadtu.eu/docu-ments/Publications/OEenM/OpenupEd_-_MOOCs_for_opening_up_education.pdf.

Jones, C. (2015). *Networked learning – an educational paradigm for the age of digital networks*. Cham: Springer.

Jones, C., Ryberg, T., & De Laat, M. (2015). Networked learning. In M. Peters (Ed.), *Encyclopedia of educational philosophy and theory* (pp. 1–6). Singapore: Springer.

Jordan, K. (2016). Academics' online connections: Characterising the structure of personal networks on academic social networking sites and Twitter. In S. Cranmer, N. B. Dohn, M. de Laat, T. Ryberg, & J. A. Sime (Eds.), *Proceedings of the 10th international conference on networked learning 2016* (pp. 414–421). Lancaster: Lancaster University.

Konnerup, U., Castro, M. D., & Bygholm, A. (2016). Rehabilitation of people with a brain injury through the lens of networked learning. Identity formation in distributed virtual environments. In S. Cranmer, N. B. Dohn, M. de Laat, T. Ryberg, & J. A. Sime (Eds.), *Proceedings of the 10th international conference on networked learning 2016* (pp. 532–539). Lancaster: Lancaster University.

Koseoglu, S. (2016). Third spaces of learning in open courses: Findings from an interpretive case study. In S. Cranmer, N. B. Dohn, M. de Laat, T. Ryberg, & J. A. Sime (Eds.), *Proceedings of the 10th international conference on networked learning 2016* (pp. 299–303). Lancaster: Lancaster University.

Latour, B. (1993). *We have never been modern*. Hemel Hempstead: Harvester Wheatsheaf.

Latour, B. (1997). *Science in action: How to follow scientists and engineers through society* (7. Print. ed.). Cambridge, MA: Harvard University Press.

Mackness, J., Mak, S., & Williams, R. (2010). The ideals and reality of participating in a MOOC. In L. Dirckinck-Holmfeld, V. Hodgson, C. Jones, M. De Laat, D. McConnell, & T. Ryberg (Eds.), *Proceedings of the 7th international conference on networked learning 2010* (pp. 266–274). Aalborg: Aalborg University.

McArthur, J. (2013). *Rethinking knowledge within higher education: Adorno and social justice*. London: Bloomsbury Academic.

McAuley, A., Stewart, B., Siemens, G., & Cormier, D. (2010). *The MOOC model for digital practice*. Retrieved from https://oerknowledgecloud.org/sites/oerknowledgecloud.org/files/MOOC_Final.pdf

McConnell, D., Hodgson, V., & Dirckinck-Holmfeld, L. (2012). Networked learning: A brief history and new trends. In L. Dirckinck-Holmfeld, V. Hodgson, & D. McConnell (Eds.), *Exploring the theory, pedagogy and practice of networked learning* (pp. 3–24). New York, NY: Springer.

Ozturk, T. H., & Hodgson, V. (2017). Developing a model of conflict in virtual learning communities in the context of a democratic pedagogy. *British Journal of Educational Technology, 48*(1), 23–42.

Perotta, C. (2016). The social life of data clusters: The potential of sociomaterial analysis in the critical study of educational technology. In S. Cranmer, N. B. Dohn, M. de Laat, T. Ryberg, & J. A. Sime (Eds.), *Proceedings of the 10th international conference on networked learning 2016* (pp. 32–37). Lancaster: Lancaster University.

Pilkington, R. M., & Guldberg, K. (2009). Conditions for productive networked learning among professionals and carers: The WebAutism case study. In L. Dirckinck-Holmfeld, C. Jones, & B. Lindström (Eds.), *Analysing networked learning practices in higher education and continuing professional development* (pp. 63–83). Rotterdam: Sense Publishers.

Rainie, L., & Wellman, B. (2014). *Networked. The new social operating system*. Cambridge, Mass: MIT Press. Paperback Ed.

Raistrick, C. (2016). Discursive psychology as a methodology to explore how multiculturalism affects use of learning technologies. In S. Cranmer, N. B. Dohn, M. de Laat, T. Ryberg, & J. A. Sime (Eds.), *Proceedings of the 10th international conference on networked learning 2016* (pp. 499–506). Lancaster: Lancaster University.

Rawls, J., & Kelly, E. (2001). *Justice as fairness: A restatement.* Cambridge, Mass: Harvard University Press.

Reynolds, M, Sclater, M., & Tickner, S. (2004). A critique of participative discourses adopted in networked learning. *Symposium at the International Conference on Networked Learning 2004.* Retrieved from http://www.networkedlearningconference.org.uk/past/nlc2004/proceedings/symposia/symposium10/reynolds_et_al.htm

Ryberg, T., Sinclair, C., Bayne, S., & De Laat, M. (2016). *Research, boundaries, and policy in networked learning.* Cham: Springer International Publishing.

Ryberg, T., Davidsen, J., & Hodgson, V. (2016a). Problem and project based learning in hybrid spaces: Nomads and artisans. In S. Cranmer, N. Bonderup-Dohn, M. de Laat, T. Ryberg, & J. A. Sime (Eds.), *Proceedings of the 10th international conference on networked learning 2016* (pp. 200–209). Lancaster: Lancaster University.

Savin-Baden, M., & Tombs, G. (2016). The glow of unwork= issues of portrayal in networked learning research. In S. Cranmer, N. B. Dohn, M. de Laat, T. Ryberg, & J. A. Sime (Eds.), *Proceedings of the 10th international conference on networked learning 2016* (pp. 449–455). Lancaster: Lancaster University.

Sclater, M., & Lally, V. (2016). Critical TEL: The importance of theory and theorisation. In S. Cranmer, N. B. Dohn, M. de Laat, T. Ryberg, & J. A. Sime (Eds.), *Proceedings of the 10th international conference on networked learning 2016* (pp. 56–64). Lancaster University.

Selwyn, N. (2014). *Distrusting educational technology: Critical questions for changing times.* New York/London: Routledge, Taylor & Francis Group.

Shum, S. B., & Ferguson, R. (2012). Social learning analytics. *Journal of Educational Technology and Society, 15*(3), 3.

Söderback, J., Hrastinski, S., & Öberg, L. M. (2016). Using distributed scrum for supporting an online community - a qualitative descriptive study of students' perceptions. In S. Cranmer, N. B. Dohn, M. de Laat, T. Ryberg, & J. A. Sime (Eds.), *Proceedings of the 10th international conference on networked learning 2016* (pp. 397–404). Lancaster: Lancaster University.

Tarek, S. A. (2016). Why 'one size fits all' concept and policies of inclusive education is insufficient to achieve 'true' inclusivity in a national context. Insight from a tablet based disaster preparedness training programme administered in Bangladesh. In S. Cranmer, N. B. Dohn, M. de Laat, T. Ryberg, & J. A. Sime (Eds.), *Proceedings of the 10th international conference on networked learning 2016* (pp. 134–141). Lancaster: Lancaster University.

Tsai, Y. S., & Gasevic, D. (2017). Learning analytics in higher education – challenges and policies: A review of eight learning analytics policies. In *Proceedings of the seventh international learning analytics & knowledge conference* (pp. 233–242). ACM.

Van den Beemt, A., & Vrieling, E. (2016). Dimensions of social learning in teacher education: An exemplary case study. In S. Cranmer, N. B. Dohn, M. de Laat, T. Ryberg, & J. A. Sime (Eds.), *Proceedings of the 10th international conference on networked learning 2016* (pp. 376–384). Lancaster: Lancaster University.

Wenger, E. (1998). *Communities of practice.* New York: Cambridge University Press.

Wright, S., & Parchoma, G. (2014). Mobile learning and immutable mobiles: Using iPhones to support informal learning in craft brewing. In V. Hodgson, M. de Laat, D. McConnell, & T. Ryberg (Eds.), *The design, experience and practice of networked learning* (pp. 241–261). Cham: Springer International Publishing.

Zander, P., Choeda, C., Penjor, T., & Kinley, K. (2016). Gross national happiness in the context of networked learning. In S. Cranmer, N. B. Dohn, M. de Laat, T. Ryberg, & J. A. Sime (Eds.), *Proceedings of the 10th international conference on networked learning 2016* (pp. 159–166). Lancaster: Lancaster University.

Endorsements

This book will stand as a major milestone in the movement toward creating a well-founded discipline of networked learning research. Celebrating the tenth biennial conference in networked learning covering a period of almost 20 years of research in the area is a great opportunity to reflect, to look back, and to address some of the new topics and challenges in networked learning research. As the editors, Dohn, Cranmer, Sime, Ryberg, and De Laat point out, networked learning continues to position itself within current discussions and debates, and is now seen to be a distinct and important area of higher education research.

This book presents a variety of articles, which bring forward important conceptualizations and re-conceptualizations of under-researched issues from the perspective of networked learning research. It is exciting to see that the field has reached a state of maturity in which it can draw on a shared body of experience and theoretical positions to deepen our intellectual roots and create new understandings of core concepts of relevance to networked learning. I highly recommend this book to everyone concerned with networked learning research, for newcomers to get an overview of emerging platforms as well as experienced researchers to revisit fundamental concepts and issues in educational research from a networked learning perspective.

Lone Dirckinck-Holmfeld
Aalborg University

Over the last 20 years, a growing community of researcher-practitioners has been studying the complex entanglements of people, technologies, ideas, emotions, and know-how that constitute networked learning. This book celebrates their achievements and provides a timely overview of work in the field.

A distinguishing feature of research and practice in networked learning is a shared commitment to critical and emancipatory forms of scholarship and education. This is educational technology with a strong moral purpose.

© Springer International Publishing AG, part of Springer Nature 2018
N. Bonderup Dohn et al. (eds.), *Networked Learning*, Research in Networked
Learning, https://doi.org/10.1007/978-3-319-74857-3

Contributions brought together in this book offer the new reader with an accessible introduction and the experienced researcher with an update on recent developments.

Peter Goodyear
The University of Sydney

Networked Learning: Reflections and Challenges is a milestone book that examines both the historical richness of the Networked Learning tradition and the cutting-edge developments in the field. Situated at the forefront of research in diverse, interconnected fields such as learning theory, environments, technology, and methodology, this book is the key resource for understanding and development of Networked Learning praxis in the present and future.

Petar Jandrić
Zagreb University of Applied Sciences, Croatia

Index

© Springer International Publishing AG, part of Springer Nature 2018
N. Bonderup Dohn et al. (eds.), *Networked Learning*, Research in Networked
Learning, https://doi.org/10.1007/978-3-319-74857-3

CPI Antony Rowe
Chippenham, UK
2018-06-11 22:39